The Moral and the Story

The Moral and the Story

✭

IAN GREGOR
&
BRIAN NICHOLAS

✭

FABER AND FABER
24 Russell Square
London

*First published in mcmlxii
by Faber and Faber Limited
24 Russell Square London W.C.1
Printed in Great Britain by
Latimer Trend & Co Ltd Plymouth
All rights reserved*

© *Ian Gregor and Brian Nicholas 1962*

Authors' Note

The book which follows is the result of continuous collaboration, especially as regards its outline and the linking of the various chapters. But though we have tried to profit from one another's ideas we have sometimes found ourselves growing jealous of our own idiosyncrasies; and these will probably reveal that the individual studies are by separate hands—chapters 2, 3 and 4 by Brian Nicholas, and the remainder by Ian Gregor. Many friends have helped us with their criticisms and suggestions, and it gives us great pleasure to thank them all; our particular gratitude must go to Mark Kinkead-Weekes and Frank McCombie for their constant help and encouragement.

We should like to thank Messrs. Eyre and Spottiswoode for permission to use quotations from Gerard Hopkins' translation of Mauriac's *Thérèse Desqueyroux*. The argument of this chapter did not seem to require the retention of the original French; on the other hand, in the case of *Madame Bovary* and *L'Assommoir*, where the writers' aims are more closely bound up with their style, it was thought best to print the original, followed where necessary by a translation. Zola's language presents the particular difficulty of containing a good deal of slang, which can hardly be translated satisfactorily into contemporary English idiom. We therefore took as a basis Arthur Symons' translation, which is nearer to the period, changing it only in the interests of greater accuracy.

Contents

AUTHORS' NOTE	page 7
PREFACE	11
1. THE TWO WORLDS OF 'ADAM BEDE'	13
2. THE NOVEL AS WORK OF ART: 'MADAME BOVARY'	33
3. THE NOVEL AS SOCIAL DOCUMENT: 'L'ASSOMMOIR'	63
4. THE CASE OF 'ESTHER WATERS'	98
5. THE NOVEL AS MORAL PROTEST: 'TESS OF THE D'URBERVILLES'	123
6. THE NOVEL OF MORAL CONSCIOUSNESS: 'THE AWKWARD AGE'	151
7. GRACE AND MORALITY: 'THÉRÈSE DESQUEYROUX'; 'THE END OF THE AFFAIR'	185
8. THE NOVEL AS PROPHECY: 'LADY CHATTERLEY'S LOVER'	217
9. THE MORAL AND THE STORY	249
INDEX	273

Preface

In the discussion of the novel few questions are more frequently raised than questions of morality; so much so that when we hear mention of an 'immoral book' we almost automatically assume that a novel is being referred to. But while the literary value of a novel is generally recognized to be dependent on an interplay of aesthetic and moral factors, it is often difficult, in practice, to define their relationship, or to avoid a distorting emphasis. At the worst we risk falling into two sorts of extremism: rejection of moral issues as irrelevant, a distraction from the critic's proper concern with the artist's technique; and the assumption that every novel holds, for good or ill, a literal moral message, which examination of the plot and characters will disclose. To reject these extremes is not to be doctrinaire, but simply realistic: it is true that the reading of a novel involves us in moral judgments which are very close to those we make in our daily affairs, and yet we also feel that the context in which these judgments are made is unique, and quite separable from those affairs. The novel has neither the moral explicitness of the sermon, nor the lack of moral reference of the abstract painting. The present book is an attempt to plot a course between these extremes, to see how, in the novel, art shapes morality and is in turn shaped by it.

Since our interest was primarily critical, rather than theoretical or historical, we chose for individual study a number of novels written during the last hundred years and dealing with a common theme—that of the innocent or guilty woman in society. This theme, a constantly recurring one in all forms of literature,

Preface

seemed to reveal in an especially clear way the nature and role of moral judgment in fiction. The theme has been given a fairly wide interpretation, so that we have been able to examine within the common framework novels as different as *Adam Bede*, *The Awkward Age* and *The End of the Affair*.

Although we have concentrated on the English novel of the period, three French novels have been included. The reasons for this have varied. In the case of *Madame Bovary* and *L'Assommoir* the attitude of the writer to his story is in such striking contrast to that of English novelists of the period that to describe and assess it helps to bring out further the range and complexity of the problem. In *Thérèse Desqueyroux*, on the other hand, the assumptions were so close to those of Greene's *The End of the Affair* that its inclusion allowed the issues raised by that novel to be explored with greater completeness than would otherwise have been possible.

It is hoped that the study of one novel will illuminate another —and the arrangement has been made with that in view; but it is only in the last chapter that all the works have been brought together. Here, however, the purpose was not so much to disclose an underlying pattern, as to obtain a perspective; and the conclusions of this final chapter take what force they have only from the critical analyses which lead up to them. Shelley wrote that 'the great instrument of the moral good is the imagination', and this book may be regarded as a number of inquiries into the various implications which that phrase has had for the writing and reading of fiction.

1

The Two Worlds of 'Adam Bede' (1859)

> One begins to suspect at length that there is no direct connection between eyelashes and morals. . . .
>
> ADAM BEDE (Ch. XV)

'My new story haunts me a good deal', George Eliot wrote to her publisher in October, 1857, 'and I shall start it without delay. It will be a country story—full of the breath of cows and the scent of hay.' This is the first description we have of *Adam Bede,* and in the century that divides us from the publication of that novel it has been echoed, in different tones of voice, many times. In the 1870's we find Henry James remarking that 'in *Adam Bede* the quality seems gilded by a sort of autumn haze, an afternoon light, of meditation', and recently Dr. Leavis observed that its success is conditioned by its 'charm'. If, however, there have been many voices to repeat that *Adam Bede* is a 'country story' there have been others, hardly less numerous, to remind us that it is very much a novel by the author of *Middlemarch,* a novel animated by a serious moral purpose. In recent years a number of critics, anxious to rescue *Adam Bede* from what they feel to be patronizing acclaim, have sought to stress this aspect of the novel, either by relating it to the whole convention of serious pastoral, or by seeing it as a direct exploration of the basis of right conduct.[1] These descriptions of *Adam Bede* are, in

[1] See note at the end of the chapter.

The Two Worlds of 'Adam Bede' (1859)

their various ways, extremely interesting, not simply because they help us to see this particular novel, but because they show that this novel records an important 'moment' in the development of English fiction, a moment when the relationship between 'the moral' and 'the story' is brought vividly into the foreground of our attention.

In her letters and journals George Eliot provides us with a detailed account of the genesis and development of *Adam Bede*. She says that the 'germ' of the novel was an anecdote told her many years previously by her aunt, a Methodist preacher, who related 'how she had visited a condemned criminal, a very ignorant girl who had murdered her child and refused to confess—how she had stayed with her praying and how the poor creature at last broke into tears and confessed her crime. My aunt afterwards went with her in the cart to the place of execution and she described to me the great respect with which this ministry of hers was regarded by the official people about the gaol'. It is not difficult to see what attracted the novelist in this anecdote—the saintliness of her aunt, the pitiful sinner, the dramatic confession, the relentless punishment. Guilt dramatically confronted by Innocence, this was the picture, like some Victorian narrative painting, that for nearly ten years 'haunted' George Eliot's imagination. At one time she thought it might become one of the 'Scenes from Clerical Life', but then, encouraged by Lewes, she decided she required 'the larger canvas' of the novel for its treatment. But if she was moved by a poignantly moral scene it was also a scene which belonged irretrievably to the 'past', which haunted simply by being over. The picture itself might have been a grim one, but when she came to dramatize and elaborate it she found herself drawing on personal reminiscence, portraits of her family and early friends, and setting the whole tale in a halcyon countryside of her childhood and youth. Just after completing the novel she wrote to a correspondent: 'At present my mind works with the most freedom and the keenest sense of poetry in my remotest past, and there are many strata to be worked through before I can begin *artistically* any material I may gather in the present.' Clearly this

The Two Worlds of 'Adam Bede' (1859)

is very much the mood of *Adam Bede*, and in creative impulse it is akin to Wordsworth's:

> ... *I would give*
> *While yet I may, as far as words can give,*
> *A substance and a life to what I feel;*
> *I would enshrine the spirit of the past*
> *For future restoration.*

With no less justice than Wordsworth, however, George Eliot could claim 'the mind of man' as the 'haunt and the main region of my song', and in *Adam Bede* we see her trying to make that 'song' harmonize with her impulse to 'enshrine the spirit of the past'. Wordsworth had his own way of dealing with this, but in *Adam Bede*, I suggest, we find that the descriptions 'a pastoral tale' and 'a moral study' remain stubbornly unreconciled alternatives; and the analysis of this particular dissociation opens up the general subject with which this book is concerned.

The afternoon sun was warm on the back of the five workmen there, busy upon doors and window frames and wainscotting. A scent of pine wood from a tent-like pile of planks outside the open door mingled itself with the scent of the elder-bushes which were spreading their summer snow close to the open window opposite; the slanting sunbeams shone through the transparent shavings that flew before the steady plane and lit up the fine grain of the oak panelling which stood propped against the wall.

Here, in virtually the opening paragraph of the novel, we feel the power of pastoral charm—the warm sunshine, the scent of the elder-bushes and pine woods pervade the atmosphere so that 'work' becomes simply a notation, expressive of the serious purpose of man. And this pattern, established so early, runs throughout the novel. A little later, Adam, rather too self-satisfied with his work, receives this rebuke from Wiry Ben: 'Ye may like work better nor play, but I like play better nor work. . . .' While this obviously tells us something about Adam, there is a sense in which the whole world of this novel, Adam's as well as Wiry Ben's, is a world of 'play'. If there is toil here, it is the idealized toil of Goldsmith's *Deserted Village* or Gray's *Elegy*.

The Two Worlds of 'Adam Bede' (1859)

We accept it as a natural colouring for this kind of scene. There is much talk of buying and selling, of the duties of landlord and tenant, but Mrs. Poyser's threatened expulsion has no relation to the expulsions described in, say, the Hammonds' *Village Labourer,* nor to those of the collapsing migratory rural community, which Hardy was later to describe, blocking the roads of Wessex. When Mrs. Poyser 'has her say' this is simply a variant expression of the conventional uneasiness that always exists between the honest, forthright tenant and the wily, unscrupulous landlord.

Though Arthur Donnithorne lives in a large house and has horses and servants at his disposal, we never think of him as being rich; similarly, we never think of the Bedes as being poor, though clearly their income is small. We do not think of work in economic terms at all; rather we see Adam with the sun on his back in the workshop; Mrs. Poyser just finishing her kitchen table, '. . . nowhere else could an oak table have got to such polish by the hand: genuine "elbow polish" as Mrs. Poyser called it . . . the oak table was usually turned up like a screen and was more for ornament than use'; Hetty in the dairy amidst 'the fresh fragrance of new-pressed cheese, of firm butter, of wooden vessels perpetually bathed in pure water'. The sun shines, however, not only into the workshop, the kitchen and the dairy, but across the ripening fields and the village green and into the neighbouring woods which were 'haunted by the nymphs. You see their white sunlit limbs gleaming athwart the boughs, or peeping from behind the smooth-sweeping outline of a tall lime; you hear their soft, liquid laughter—but if you look with a too curious, sacrilegious eye, they will vanish behind the silvery beeches.' If this is Arcadia, there are feelings to match. When Hetty thinks of Arthur 'it was as if she was being wooed by a river-god, who might at any time take her to his wondrous halls below a watery heaven.' When Arthur sees Hetty 'he may be a shepherd in Arcadia for aught he knows, he may be the first youth kissing the first maiden, he may be Eros himself, sipping the lips of Psyche.' If these are the mutual lovers, the sentiments of the hopeful lover are pitched in the same key. For Adam, to

The Two Worlds of 'Adam Bede' (1859)

marry Hetty, would, he thinks, be 'a marriage such as they made in the golden age, when the men were all wise and majestic and the women all lovely and loving'. This exalted, idealizing emotion belongs very much to the world of *Midsummer Night's Dream*, which weaves its spell regardless of the fact that the magic night will end and day will break.

And Time for all its meticulous appearance in this novel is not 'our' time. In spite of the repeated references to days, and dates, and months, the page of this calendar never really turns. The time may be 1799, but George Eliot is writing *Adam Bede* from a memory of a memory, and 1799 is 'a point in the past', near enough to avoid the remoteness of 'history', far enough away to escape 'the present'. It is historically dated in much the same way as western films are dated '1870', and traditional public school stories '1910'. We hear of the Napoleonic wars, but the rumble is a distant one, and 'the turn of the century' in *Adam Bede* is an archetypal 'turn'. The seasons mirror the narrative. In high summer we have Arthur's Coming-of-Age party and the climax of his passion for Hetty. As the year moves towards autumn and winter we have their exposure by Adam, Arthur's departure, and, in November, Adam's betrothal to Hetty:

> It was nothing to her—putting her arm through Adam's; but she knew he cared a good deal about her arm through his and she wished to care. Her heart beat no faster and she looked at the half-bare hedgerows and the ploughed field with the same sense of oppressive dullness as before.

The hedgerows finally become bare, Hetty's misery deepens and in February, to conceal her shame, she leaves Hayslope to search for Arthur. And we have the miserable journeys, through the bleak and cold countryside, under leaden skies which become dark in the late afternoon. March comes and the very day that Hetty and Adam were to have been married is the date fixed for her execution. But better times return. Adam and Dinah are married after the harvest festival and Mr. Irwine makes the conjunction explicit, 'what better harvest from that painful seed-time could there be than this?'[1]

[1] The function of time in *Adam Bede* has frequently been noted by critics of

The Two Worlds of 'Adam Bede' (1859)

The communal gathering is used here partly to endorse the personal values and partly because it is the most explicit way of emphasizing the values and traditions of the community itself. Throughout the novel we have a number of meetings, all of which express in a slightly different manner the essential nature of Hayslope life. We have Dinah's preaching on the Green, the funeral of Thias Bede, the Coming-of-Age of Arthur, and finally, the Harvest Supper. Man and God, Man and his master, Man and his fellow-man, all these relationships are caught up and revealed in these gatherings and over them all broods the Spirit of the Time, characteristically personified as Leisure: 'He was a contemplative, rather stout gentleman of excellent digestion—of quiet perceptions, undiseased by hypothesis; happy in his inability to know the causes of things, preferring the things themselves. He lived chiefly in the country among pleasant seats and homesteads, and was fond of sauntering by the fruit tree wall, and scenting the apricots where they were warmed by the morning sunshine, or of sheltering himself under the orchard boughs at noon, when the summer pears were falling.' He preferred the afternoon-church, which could be prefaced by a sunny walk through the fields. When the congregation finally assemble, the Rector, looking down from the pulpit, can see the Hayslope community—'hardy old men with bent knees and shoulders . . . roughly-cut bronzed faces . . . half a dozen well-to-do farmers with apple-cheeked wives . . . the clean old women . . . with their bit of snow-white cap border under their black bonnets, and with their withered arms, bare from the elbow, folded passively over their chests.' And as the congregation look at their minister, then in Mrs. Poyser's words, 'it's like looking at a full crop o' wheat, or a pasture with fine dairy cows in it; it makes you think the world's comfortable-like.' But it is precisely that thought which *Adam Bede*, if we look at it from another point of view, is anxious to dispel.

the novel, particularly Dorothy Van Ghent and Maurice Hussey. To see, however, the full complexities of this, it is worth looking at W. J. Harvey, 'The Treatment of Time in Adam Bede', *Anglia*, Autumn 1957. That the time scheme is sometimes inaccurate is indicated by Daniel P. Deneau, 'Inconsistencies and Inaccuracies in Adam Bede', *Nineteenth Century Fiction*, June 1959.

The Two Worlds of 'Adam Bede' (1859)

Three hours' ride from Hayslope the wind blows across the bleak tree-less region of Stonyshire. This is the country that Dinah Morris sees with affection: 'I love the Stonyshire side. . . . I shouldn't like to turn my face towards the countries where they're rich in corn and cattle, and the ground so level and easy to tread; and to turn my back on the hills where the poor people have to live such a hard life and the men spend their days in the mines away from the sunlight.' The Arcadian world of Loamshire falls into shadow and it is this new landscape that Adam comes to contemplate in his tragedy: '. . . the country grew barer and barer: no more rolling woods, no more wide branching trees near frequent homesteads, no more busy hedgerows; but grey stone walls intersecting the meagre pastures, and dismal wide-scattered grey stone houses on broken lands where mines had been and were no longer.' The broken land is, however, now seen through eyes which have come to know something of the meaning of human suffering. And in this way, the novel discloses an entirely different perspective from the pastoral world which has been described. Attention turns away from the community to the individual, from visual contemplation to imaginative participation.

'A story of the country, with the breath of cows and the scent of hay . . .'; George Eliot might describe *Adam Bede* in this way, but it is also a novel which leads towards a statement about the function of tragedy in classical terms: '. . . It is not ignoble to feel that the fuller life which a sad experience has brought is worth our own personal share of pain. . . . The growth of higher feeling within us is like the growth of a faculty, bringing with it a sense of added strength; we can no more wish to return to a narrower sympathy, than a painter or musician can wish to return to his cruder manner, or a philosopher to his less complete formula.' In this passage we come close not only to a central statement about the moral tragedy of this particular novel, but to a statement of George Eliot's attitude to fiction in general. How close can be judged by comparing it with this extract from one of her reviews:

The greatest benefit we owe to the artist, whether painter, poet or

The Two Worlds of 'Adam Bede' (1859)

novelist, is the extension of our sympathies. Appeals founded on generalisations and statistics require a sympathy ready-made, a moral sentiment already in activity; but a picture of human life, such as a great artist can give, surprises even the trivial and the selfish into that attention to what is apart from themselves, which may be called the raw material of moral sentiment.[1]

What the reader has to learn from fiction generally has, in *Adam Bede*, to be learnt by the characters themselves. In various ways, and with varying degrees of emphasis, four characters gradually come to learn the truth about themselves, to learn their essential vanity, and in consequence to give 'attention to what is apart from themselves'.

Adam's sin is spiritual pride; he is the good man, confident and proud of his goodness. He has to learn, through suffering, the narrowness of his outlook and the arrogance its restrictions imply. He sees life too exclusively in terms of his work—'I've seen life pretty clear, ever since I could cast up a sum'—and anything that cannot be fitted into this framework is brushed aside. The sensitivity of his conscience has become blunted with too much self-righteous display. As Mr. Irwine remarks, 'He has independence of spirit for two men—rather an excess of pride if anything.' With the death of his father, Adam takes the first step in his lesson towards an extension of sympathy: 'Ah, I was always too hard. . . . It's a sore fault in me as I'm so hot and out of patience with people when they do wrong, and my heart gets shut up against 'em, so I can't bring myself to forgive 'em.' It is a sentiment which is to be picked up later and tested more fiercely. What he lacks is 'fellow-feeling with the weakness that errs in spite of foreseen consequences'. Deceived by his best friend, betrayed by the girl he is going to marry, Adam's capacity for 'fellow-feeling' is rigorously put to the test. For a while the lesson is too bitter to be assimilated, he cannot forgive and he is tempted to abandon Hetty to her fate. From his rector and his schoolteacher he learns to modify his attitude, to see the futility of personal condemnation of Arthur. 'No man is an

---

[1] See J. D. Rust, 'The Art of Fiction in George Eliot's Review', *Review of English Studies*, April 1956.

The Two Worlds of 'Adam Bede' (1859)

island' is the drift of their lesson—and Irwine says 'there is no sort of wrong deed of which a man can bear the punishment alone; you can't isolate yourself, and say that the evil which is in you shall not spread. Men's lives are as thoroughly blended with each other as the air they breathe; evil spreads as necessarily as disease.' Nerved by this sense of common responsibility and quickened by the sight of Hetty's suffering, Adam resolves to stand by her 'for all she's been deceitful. They oughtn't to cast her off—her own flesh and blood. We hand folks over to God's mercy and show none ourselves. I used to be hard sometimes: I'll never be hard again.' He stands by Hetty, he forgives Arthur, he has seen through the inadequacies of his former moral calculus, '. . . I know there's a deal in a man's inward life you can't measure by the square.' This is the development of Adam which the novel traces, a development of moral sensibility, a new insight into the complexity of good and evil, and the realization that problems of the spirit are more subtle than 'casting up a sum'.

But if Adam's moral categories are prematurely hardened, Arthur Donnithorne's are dangerously fluid. If Adam minimizes the world of feeling, Arthur seeks to evade the responsibilities it entails. In Arthur candour is inextricably bound up with egotism: 'No young man could confess his faults more candidly; candour was one of his favourite virtues; and how can a man's candour be seen in all its lustre unless he has a few failings to talk of? But he had an agreeable confidence that his faults were all of a generous kind—impetuous, warm-blooded, leonine; never crawling, crafty, reptilian. It was not possible for Arthur Donnithorne to do anything mean, dastardly, cruel.' The passage is an interesting one as it blends judgment with description. Arthur values virtue in proportion to the opportunity it receives for public display, and it is this lack of grasp of the intrinsic nature of virtue that allows him to drift into a moral whirlpool, where all direction is lost. Faced with a problem the only direction he can see is a physical one, so he saddles his horse or joins the militia. Like Adam, he forgets, disastrously, that no one is completely alone. 'I'm a devil of a fellow for getting myself into a hobble, but I always take care the load shall fall on my own shoulders.' Here candour and the desire for approbation turn into pride, and it is this necessity to be publicly respected that constitutes Arthur's fatal weakness and his nemesis. He tries to seek the advice of Irwine but, feeling at the last moment that a confessed relationship with Hetty would darken his image in the rector's sight, evades the issue; the secret remains concealed. 'Our friend Arthur liked to do everything that was handsome and to have his handsome deeds recognized.' It is a keenly judged comment and suggests the horror of his doom—complete public humiliation and disgrace. He manages to save Hetty from the scaffold, but there is no longer a place for him within the community, and he must follow her into exile. Arthur's dream, proposed over the wine at his birthday feast, 'to be looked on by all my deserving tenants as their best friend', is remorselessly destroyed. 'I'm going away for years . . . it cuts off every plan of happiness I've ever formed . . . I make no schemes now.' But out of this wreck Arthur wins through to a certain measure of disinterestedness, seen chiefly in his respect for Dinah and her ministry to Hetty. If Adam's egoism had masked itself as scrupulous honesty, Arthur's is masked by benevolent public interest. The vanity in both men is a by-product of their virtue. The moral action of the story reveals both to them, and to us, that they are not what they seem, and through suffering they learn to make the appearance and the reality one.

With Hetty too, we have the deception of appearances and the underlying vanity. But here the vanity is not overweening self-esteem or self-respect, but more simply the vanity of the looking-glass. While Dinah is looking out of the window at the darkening world, Hetty is gazing at her looking-glass, fascinated by the image of herself, 'the delicate dark rings of hair lie so charmingly about her ears and neck; her great dark eyes with their long eyelashes touch one so strangely. . . . The dear, young, round, soft flexible thing! Her heart must be just as soft. . . .' But the image deceives; Hetty, is essentially 'hard', she seeks her own gratification. Like Arthur 'she would have borne anything rather than be laughed at, or pointed at with any other feeling than

The Two Worlds of 'Adam Bede' (1859)

admiration.' Like his, her humiliation too is a public one, and the poignancy of this lies behind her exclamation to Dinah, 'I daren't go back home again—I couldn't bear it. I couldn't have bore to look at anybody, for they'd have scorned me.' If Adam and Arthur learn through their suffering, Hetty seems unable to encompass the tragedy that overwhelms her—'there's nothing seems to give her a turn i' th' side'. She learns only 'the horror of this cold, and darkness, and solitude—out of all human reach . . .' and our last vision is of that 'wondrous Medusa-face, with passionate, passionless lips', gazing into the pool. In this no reflection meets her as the water lies 'black under the darkening sky'. Her image has been completely effaced.

With Dinah Morris George Eliot's moral purpose is considerably more complex. This is chiefly because she serves as a moral norm to define the weaknesses of the other three. She exposes the limitations of Adam's 'we must have something beside Gospel i' the world. Look at the canals, an' th' aqueducs, an' the coal-pit engines . . .'; she wins from Arthur a disinterested admiration and from Hetty a final confession. But when this has been recognized there is clearly a sense in which Dinah also is too complacent; she has to learn a subtler feeling for the community than her ministry allows. She must submit herself to the claims of the healthy as well as the needy, and Mrs. Poyser's thrust is a telling one, 'she'll never marry anybody, if he isn't a Methodist and a cripple.' There is, in Dinah, a tendency to indulge in suffering which is as intemperate as Hetty's in pleasure. And indeed it is from Hetty that Dinah learns: 'It is our habit to say that while the lower nature can never understand the higher, the higher nature commands a complete view of the lower. But I think the higher nature has to learn this comprehension, as we learn the art of vision, by a good deal of hard experience, often with bruises and gashes incurred in taking things up by the wrong end, and fancying our space wider than it is.' It is indirectly, through learning the restrictions of Hetty's consciousness and conscience, that Dinah grows and gradually learns that her spiritual place may indeed be to lead 'a quiet life among the green pastures and the still waters' of Hayslope, rather than in the

The Two Worlds of 'Adam Bede' (1859)

bleak land of Stonyshire, where the will of God can be more clearly apprehended. Dinah's spiritual exaltation has to be tempered in 'the land of Goshen'.

In Adam, Arthur, Hetty and Dinah, George Eliot is presenting us in varyingly direct ways with a critique of egotism and exploring it by revealing an enlargement of moral sympathy on the part of the characters involved. In Hetty's case vanity is the most openly declared and the most tragically fated; in Arthur it is bound up with indulgence and turns him into an exile, but he also learns a sharper recognition of the basis of human interdependence; in Adam and Dinah, righteousness and spiritual zeal have to be more subtly understood, and, when this is done, the way is prepared for an ideal marriage. This is the pattern which *Adam Bede* reveals when looked at in moral perspective. The question now arises as to how this perspective will fit into the one described earlier. Can the tree of good and evil grow in Arcadia?

From this description of the two worlds of the novel we might infer that the novelist's purpose was precisely to examine their relationship. The account might suggest that the Arcadian values of the Hayslope world were to be revealed as inadequate, by being silhouetted against a profound moral tragedy—the disgrace of the squire, the infanticide and exile of a milkmaid. People like the Poysers—the account might run—are caught up in a disaster they don't really understand, and the drama is grimly illustrative of the fact that 'men's lives are as thoroughly blended with each other as the air they breathe; evils spread as necessarily as disease.' The force of 'necessarily' would need no underlining. If this account is a true one, then *Adam Bede* presents a world of profound disharmony, where the beauty of nature mocks at human suffering. Can a novel which deals with murder, disgrace and exile end on a note of serenity, as *Adam Bede* does, without being simply meretricious?

A comparison with *Tess of the D'Urbervilles* will help to bring out the point more clearly. In Hardy's novel we have scenes of great pastoral beauty and the harmony of a rural community, so

The Two Worlds of 'Adam Bede' (1859)

that Tess is moved to a morning hymn, 'O ye Sun and Moon ... O ye stars ... ye Green things upon the earth ... ye fowls of the air. ... Beasts and Cattle. ... Children of Men ... bless ye the Lord, praise Him and magnify Him for ever.' But she stops suddenly and reflects, '... perhaps I don't quite know the Lord as yet.' And there, caught between the hymn and reflection, is the grim irony which the book relates. We come to see the lush landscape of the Var Vale give way to the starve-acre farm of Flintcomb Ash, illusions harden into reality. The joyful birds that wake Tess in the dawn at the dairy are cruelly deceptive, making way for the nameless birds that wake her at Flintcomb Ash, 'gaunt spectral creatures with tragical eyes ... which had beheld the crash of ice-bergs and the slide of snow hills. ...' Is this the kind of contrast we have present in *Adam Bede* between Loamshire and Stonyshire, between Hetty patting the butter in the dairy and blushing at the entry of Captain Donnithorne and Hetty 'toiling along on her weary feet, or seated in a cart, with her eyes fixed vacantly on the road before her, never thinking or caring whither it tends'? When Angel meets Tess at dawn, 'she was no longer the milkmaid. ... He called her Artemis, Demeter and other names ...', and when Arthur meets his milkmaid, 'he may be a shepherd in Arcadia for aught he knows ... he may be Eros himself sipping the lips of Psyche.' Are we meant to feel the same kind of tragic sense here, the loftiness of aspiration, the cruelty of realization? These questions force themselves upon us, because Tess and Hetty are required to face a common destiny of uncompromising tragedy.

When, however, we turn with these insistent questions in mind to look at the novel from the point of view of 'the community', the tragic outcome appears to have vanished. The whole perspective has shifted. Tracks that we have been following to discover the centre of the novel—the enlargement of moral sympathy in the central characters—seem to peter out and we are asked to review the scene not as a gradually unfolding destiny but as an omnipresent picture. *Adam Bede* becomes a moral triptych. In the first panel we have ease and hope, in the second disenchantment, in the third comfort and serenity. The pattern

The Two Worlds of 'Adam Bede' (1859)

is all, the individual figuration nothing. Tragedy cannot be examined here, though it may well take place. Hetty's fall becomes a graphic detail like Brueghel's Icarus:

> ... everything turns away
> Quite leisurely from the disaster; the ploughman may
> Have heard the splash, the forsaken cry,
> But for him it was not an important failure; the sun shone
> As it had to on the white legs disappearing into the green
> Water....[1]

'The sun shone as it *had* to'—this is the point; the necessity invoked here is not a philosophical one, but an artistic one, a fidelity to convention. If Adam and Dinah achieve serenity and joy and Hetty's ending is neglected, this is not in order to show that life is arbitrary and cruel; for tragic colours are not employed in this kind of picture. So we are driven in reading *Adam Bede* into understanding it *either* in terms of tragic irony in the Hardy manner, *or* in terms of pastoral convention in the *Winter's Tale* manner, in order to make it an effective whole. Unfortunately, for the sake of artistic coherence, neither appeal can be consistently made.

'In *Adam Bede*', Mr. V. S. Pritchett writes, 'we are shocked by two things: the treatment of Hetty Sorrel and the marriage of Dinah and Adam at the end.'[2] He elaborates this by saying that, in the case of Hetty, George Eliot was working out a personal fantasy, and that, in the case of Dinah and Adam, she refused to face the nature of sexual passion. In isolating these faults I suggest that Mr. Pritchett is pin-pointing exactly the places where the two worlds of the novel touch, but fail to intersect.

We do not need to indulge in psychological speculation to discover why the final treatment of Hetty is unsatisfying. She is an inhabitant of the pastoral world who has strayed into the world of moral enquiry and tragic destiny. Hetty lives simply by the coercive morality of the community and, when this is broken, she is destroyed; she has no life apart from this. When

---
[1] W. H. Auden, *Musée des Beaux Arts*.
[2] *The Living Novel*, pp. 83-4.

The Two Worlds of 'Adam Bede' (1859)

Hetty feels the impossibility of returning to Hayslope this is not simply shame, rather it is the feeling that she has broken a social bond which cannot be retied. George Moore wrote that 'a true moulding' of *Adam Bede* would show Hetty living in order to save her child, but this kind of moral decision and stamina is quite beyond Hetty. It is quite impossible for her to deal competently with the problem, not because she is morally callow, but because her artistic creation precludes it. Choice is incompatible not simply with Hetty's idea of her existence, but with George Eliot's too. When the order of life has been broken for this kind of character, she can only die. For all her vanity Hetty really belongs with the wronged women of folk tale who pine away for their lost lovers. This is not to say that Hetty is not vividly present to the reader *as a character*, but simply that she belongs to a play where the surface is all—it is the drama of the eyelashes. When Hetty contemplates 'the dark pool' this is a conventional gesture, the last steps in a tragic ballet. This is how Hetty is intended to fit into the world, but of course we experience her presence somewhat differently. We think of Hetty's agony in prison, we wonder at the cruelty of her transportation —however historically probable it may have been. Hetty's tragedy has been developed to a point which disturbs her role in the novel. *This* 'forsaken cry' is such that we cannot forget it when we are told 'the sun is shining as it has to', and we feel that forgetfulness is simply an evasion of the issue that has been raised.

How George Eliot has got herself into this position is not difficult to see. In addition to writing a novel of pastoral reminiscence she is also writing a novel of moral growth. While this centres most completely in Adam, it also concerns other characters. Because Hetty is involved in this pattern George Eliot is presented with the problem of giving her, too, a 'moral' character. But she is not interested in Hetty *in this kind of way* at all; Hetty is simply a fatally attractive focal point for the emotions of Arthur and Adam, someone for Dinah to 'rescue' dramatically. Quickly, she sketches in a 'depth' for Hetty— 'people who love downy peaches are apt not to think of the stone, and sometimes jar their teeth terribly against it.' But she is not happy with this presentation and a strained, embarrassed note is frequently struck. For instance in this passage where Adam's passion for Hetty is being defended:

> Before you despise Adam as deficient in penetration, pray ask yourself if you were ever predisposed to believe evil of any pretty woman—if you ever *could*, without head-breaking demonstration, believe evil of the *one* supremely pretty woman who has bewitched you.

Clearly this 'evil' of Hetty's exists simply at the level of assertion, and when Hetty says of herself in prison to Dinah, 'help me ... I can't feel anything like you ... my heart is hard', we feel no depth of imagined reality behind it. We are disturbed by Hetty's treatment because the novel for much of its length demands a response akin to that demanded by realistic fiction, and consequently we ask questions which, in a pastoral art, would never arise.

If, however, we decide to put these questions about innocence and guilt and justice aside, and see Hetty as a conventional victim in a folk tale, then immediately the other characters look distorted and unsatisfactory. And this brings us to Mr. Pritchett's second objection to *Adam Bede*, the marriage of Adam and Dinah. Here again George Eliot has crossed the line between a conventional and a representational art. Unlike Hetty, Adam is a man we *are* called upon to understand in depth; where she is static and bewildered, he is evolving and aware. And the condition of this evolution is that he has to face experiences which bite deeply into him, modifying and altering his attitudes—his father's death, Hetty's desertion and her conviction. As Mrs. Barbara Hardy remarks, 'at the beginning Adam has as much to learn as Lear'.[1] There may be disagreement about the scale of this emphasis, but there can be no doubt that the emphasis itself is correct. When Adam remarks to Arthur: 'I don't see how the thing's to be made any other than hard. There's a sort of damage, sir, that can't be made up for', we feel that this is the fruit of a bitter lesson, which he was learnt with pain and difficulty. It has

---

[1] *The Novels of George Eliot*, p. 37.

The Two Worlds of 'Adam Bede' (1859)

tragic *weight* behind it. Unlike Hetty's, Adam's career cannot be assumed into gesture and mime, it must have a representational reality about it. The marriage to Dinah runs counter to this. Individuality and complexity suddenly become ironed out; our attention is no longer directed towards Adam and Dinah but to 'the bond of marriage', signalizing that the broken community has been made whole again. The sexual element is omitted, not, as Mr. Pritchett suggests, at the dictates of Victorian taste, but because George Eliot has altered her fictional style from moral realism to pseudo-pastoral. Everything in the closing chapters of the novel is designed to accomplish this, the careful placing of the Harvest Supper before the wedding, the stylized meeting on a high hill, surrounded 'by the still lights and shadows and the great embracing sky'. A tableau ending has been given to a novel which, for much of its length, has been concerned with the rejection of appearances. The objection is not to the marriage of Adam and Dinah, but to the facility of its realization. To invoke the 'pastoral pattern' is simply to reduce in status the moral drama which the novel has been concerned to describe. Marriage may fittingly conclude the pattern, but not the marriage of two people who have been presented in the realistic way that Dinah and Adam have, a way calculatedly endorsing George Eliot's earlier irony—'let all people who hold unexceptionable opinions act unexceptionably'. The marriage neutralizes the irony.

Both the things that shock us in *Adam Bede*, the treatment of Hetty and the marriage of Adam and Dinah, proceed from the common defect that George Eliot is extremely uncertain about the *kind* of novel she is writing. She describes the situation and she resolves its conflict by an appeal to a pastoral art; she develops the situation and brings it to a climax by an appeal to the fiction of moral and psychological enquiry. She demands, in the end, a response from the reader which he cannot give, because he cannot feel that the solution admissible in one mode of fiction can solve the problems raised in another. She tries to conceal this final transition from tragedy to serenity by her commentary: 'It would be a poor result of all our anguish, if we won nothing but our old selves at the end of it—if we could return to the same blind loves, the same self-confident blame, the same light thoughts of human suffering. . . . Let us be thankful that sorrow lives in us as an indestructible force. . . .' But what she is building up in her commentary, George Eliot is destroying in her narrative; we see intention outstripping imagination, the moralist 'filling-in' for the artist. Hetty's tragedy does not exist in the world of Adam's marriage; to accept the reality of one is to reject the other. In a letter about *Adam Bede*, George Eliot writes: 'The whole course of the story . . . the descriptions of scenery and houses—the characters—the dialogue—*everything* is a combination from widely sundered elements of experience. . . .' I would suggest that the elements remain sundered; the gap between the world of description and the world of analysis is never bridged so that 'one begins to suspect at length that there is no direct connection between eyelashes and morals. . . .'

The final interest of *Adam Bede* is that it casts its shadow before it. No single novel has the kind of decisive impact that alters the course of fiction, but some novels reveal, consciously or otherwise, a pattern or conflict which later generations come to see as marking a notable change in the art of fiction. Perhaps the novel itself had little influence in such a determination, but looking back we can see that it embodied one in however rudimentary a way. Occasionally we do have a particular novel which seems a landmark in the history of fiction, setting up new possibilities for the artist, but novels like *Emma* and *A la Recherche du Temps Perdu* are extremely rare. Looking at the fiction of George Eliot we feel that it both sums up all that has been done in the world of English fiction before then and yet contains within it the seeds of what is to come. In her best work, *Middlemarch*, *Daniel Deronda*, these two elements are splendidly fused and are an essential part of the distinction of those novels. With *Adam Bede* the fusion is not yet made. But the two elements are clearly discernible. There is the description of a whole social community, presented in such a way that we are asked to look now at this feature and now that. The author's intervention is, in its various

The Two Worlds of 'Adam Bede' (1859)

tones of voice, an indispensable part of the novel, distancing the fiction and ensuring a certain contemplative response from the reader. In Chapter XVII of the novel George Eliot discourses on her art and remarks that her purpose is 'to give a faithful account of things as they have mirrored themselves in my mind'. The image is an interesting one because it gives a peculiar twist to the kind of 'realism' usually intended by users of the mirror analogy. There is no sense of mere passivity here, of a photographic correspondence between the literary work and the reality which it imitates; the mirror is there, but it is the mirror of a particular mind. Though an interpretation of 'the seen' must be the task of every novelist, George Eliot ensures that it is the form of her novels that will make this quite explicit. She acts both as guide and creator. With James and subsequent fiction the guide has become superannuated, and the reader is left to personal exploration. We no longer look at things so much as find them out. With this shift from contemplation to participation, the subject matter itself has altered; the social community in moral action gives way to the individual consciousness in moral reflection. 'Innocence' is translated into 'integrity'.

Before George Eliot we have Tom Jones and Roderick Random and Mr. Knightley and Mr. Pickwick; after her we have Gilbert Osmund and Stephen Dedalus and Paul Morel and Marlow. Obviously there are exceptions, but the drift is plain. In her novels we find both genealogies present. In *Middlemarch* she directs us to 'a study of provincial life', and clearly this is an extension of the Hayslope community in *Adam Bede*; but, accompanying this, is her analysis of the egotistic conscience in Casaubon and Dorothea and Fred Vincy and Rosamund, an enquiry which has begun with Adam and Dinah and Arthur and Hetty. The difference between the two novels is not one of kind, but of success in dealing with the kind. The moral drama finds in *Middlemarch* itself a perfect setting and the dictum of *Felix Holt* is convincingly illustrated, 'there is no private life that has not been determined by a wider public life.' With George Eliot these aspects are equally stressed. With James, however, the enquiry into 'the private life', and with it the development of

The Two Worlds of 'Adam Bede' (1859)

new fictional techniques, begins on a grand scale, and with Lawrence it comes to something like an apotheosis. It is interesting that, looking back, both these novelists see George Eliot's work as marking an end and a beginning. For James, *Middlemarch* 'sets a limit to the old-fashioned English novel', but for Lawrence 'it was really George Eliot who started it all. It was she who started putting all the action inside.' An end and a beginning, an old world and a new—*Adam Bede* in a hesitant and discordant way discloses both, and in doing so marks a distinctive stage, not only in George Eliot's work, but also in the history of English fiction.

It would alter the focus of my discussion if I enlarged on this description of the critical reaction, but reference ought to be made here to particular critics, if for no other reason than that I have profited by reading them, though my conclusions are not theirs. In the first group there are those who see *Adam Bede* primarily as a novel of moral inquiry: Jerome Thale, *The Novels of George Eliot*, 1959, Ch. I; Barbara Hardy, *The Novels of George Eliot*, 1959, Ch. II; Albert J. Fyfe, 'The Interpretation of Adam Bede', *Nineteenth Century Fiction*, 1954. In the second group there are those who see the novel as belonging primarily to a pastoral convention: Van Ghent, *The English Novel: Form and Function*, 'Adam Bede', 1953; G. C. Creeger, 'An Interpretation of Adam Bede', *E.L.H.*, 1956; Maurice Hussey, 'Structure and Imagery in Adam Bede', *Nineteenth Century Fiction*, 1955; R. A. Foakes, ' "Adam Bede" Reconsidered', *English*, 1959.

2

The Novel as Work of Art: 'Madame Bovary' (1857)

A summary of the plot of *Madame Bovary*, together with an account of its publication and reception, might suggest to someone who had not read it that it is a novel in which specific moral issues are raised and treated in a personal and controversial way. The theme is adultery, and adultery not in aristocratic or romantic surroundings, but in the contemporary framework of a Normandy village. Four hundred pages' elaboration of a simple plot, involving the writer in an immensely laboured work of social observation and realistic description—here, if anywhere, one might expect that large moral problems of guilt and innocence must be raised, that the author's purpose must include some sort of evaluation of his main character in her relations with other individuals and with society; indeed it might seem that there could have been little incentive to write the novel unless such issues were to sustain its length and justify the pains expended on it.

That an evaluation had been made, and that it was an immoral one, was the reaction of authority when *Madame Bovary* was published in 1857; with the result that Flaubert was arraigned—and acquitted—on charges of offending against public morality and religion. Exception was taken in the first place to individual passages, such as the seduction scene with Rodolphe and one of the hotel scenes with Léon; to the description of Emma's reli-

The Novel as Work of Art: 'Madame Bovary' (1857)

gious phase, when she addressed to God 'les mêmes paroles de suavité qu'elle murmurait jadis à son amant', and to other allegedly blasphemous scenes such as the administration of extreme unction. More generally it was held that the book glorified adultery and mocked the established order of things; that Emma lives and dies unrepentant and unjudged, so that, in spite of her suicide, morality is not vindicated, and she remains the 'heroine', the vehicle by which the author conveys an immoral and irreligious view of life. Flaubert's counsel had little difficulty in refuting the charges by the same methods, showing *Madame Bovary* to be an improving tract, whose chief purpose was to warn parents against allowing their children to peruse romantic literature; far from being a bad book it was an attack on bad books, since Emma's downfall had its source in such reading.

Such 'proofs' of morality and immorality will seem naïve to the reader of the most modest literary sophistication; we are reminded of the episode in the novel itself where Homais confiscates a handbook on marriage from his apprentice Justin with an angry tirade on the dangers to which his own children would have been exposed if 'ce livre infâme' had fallen into their hands. To reject as irrelevant the majority of the arguments made at the trial is not, of course, to reject the notion that a work of art may have morally subversive implications. But whatever our views on that question, the arguments seem misdirected; and primarily because, when we come to read the novel, we find that Emma's sinful life and edifying death are presented in such a way that the question of individual guilt, as envisaged by Flaubert's accusers and defenders, does not arise. If a case is to be made out for the 'immorality' of *Madame Bovary* it must rest on a much wider criticism of his presentation of life—a presentation governed by his idea of the autonomy and self-sufficiency of Art; it will allege not that he solved his moral problems wrongly, but that in giving an apparently complete account of real life he wrote as though the world of moral distinctions did not exist at all.

It may be instructive here to turn from the history of *Madame Bovary*'s reception to the history of its production. The anecdote has recently been discredited whereby Flaubert's friends,

The Novel as Work of Art: 'Madame Bovary' (1857)

Maxime Du Camp and Louis Bouilhet, having listened in horror to his long-promised reading of the exotic *Tentation de Saint Antoine*, prescribed as a course of literary hygiene the writing of a novel on a topical piece of local scandal.[1] But, when the conception of *Madame Bovary*, and the impulse to write it, have been restored to Flaubert, it is still permissible to see it as in many ways an artistic exercise provoked by disappointment, a self-imposed discipline against which Flaubert himself frequently rebelled. Its composition occupied nearly five years, and Flaubert's correspondence during those years provides an illuminating commentary on his attitude to his subject: endless complaints about its triviality and unsuitability to his talents, tortured accounts of his struggle for words. We see him assailed by every kind of literary danger: lyricism, which would inflate the subject in a way he must resist, the vulgarity of mere reporting, which would defeat his only settled object as a writer—that of writing well. We hear on one day how he has had to write, not for publication, two pages of abuse of one of his characters, in order to clear his mind; on another that he has allowed himself, against his better artistic judgment, an ornate extended simile—'for the sake of my health'.

There could in fact be no greater contrast than that between the Flaubert evoked at the trial, the saloon-bar partisan of adultery, the bohemian enemy of the established order, and Flaubert at work, the lofty misanthropist maniacally pursuing stylistic perfection. 'It will be a haughty, classical book,' Flaubert warns a correspondent. The epithets already prepare us for the moral detachment of the novel and suggest the attitude which secures this neutrality: the artist's untroubled superiority to the whole of his material. But the note of disdain suggests another problem. Flaubert's aim was 'art', an aesthetic illusion from which moral judgment was absent; but, given his views and approach to his work, we may wonder how *Madame Bovary* should have turned out to be anything but a persistent and relentless piece of social mockery. The element of satire is almost continuously present, sometimes flowering into an attempt at a stylized

[1] See R. Herval, *Les Véritables Origines de 'Madame Bovary'*, Paris, 1957.

The Novel as Work of Art: 'Madame Bovary' (1857)

résumé of provincial crassness. 'In two pages', Flaubert remarks, commenting on the discussion which follows Léon's departure for Paris, 'I have brought together all the stupid provincial commonplaces about Paris—student life, the pickpockets who come up to you in parks, and restaurant food, "never as healthy as good home cooking".' Much of the conversation can be checked almost word for word in the *Dictionnaire des Idées Reçues*, the compilation in which, with meticulous cruelty, and a wonderful ear for the rhythms in which they are expressed, Flaubert records alphabetically the opinions of his fellow men. Our analysis will try to show that the whole book is indeed unrelievedly critical—its criticism extending beyond the scenes and characters conceived in terms of open satire to the whole subject; it is so uniformly destructive that it might have become self-destroying. Yet this does not happen; the aesthetic aim is achieved. Flaubert's triumph is so to have spun out and ordered and diversified by his art the limited human interests of the nihilist that the reader still feels engaged in a history of individual beings, and not merely the witness of an exercise in gratuitous and repetitive disparagement. The moral limitations of the novel are implicit in the nature of its success, and in a sense are emphasized by that success: *Madame Bovary* has the proportion, the comprehensive air, the artistic impact of a complete account of human experience; the mechanics and spiritual uniformity of an extremely partial satire.

The novel begins with Charles and his cap, as a communal reminiscence of the writer and his schoolfellows. The technique is curious, and perhaps not very significant for the interpretation of the rest of the novel. But it does allow Flaubert to make what amounts to a personal protest at the triviality of the subject, when he says of Charles that 'il serait maintenant impossible à aucun de nous de se rien rappeler de lui' ('it would now be impossible for any of us to remember anything about him'): an oddly paradoxical statement for the narrator; and we catch another echo of the private Flaubert, of the artist superior to his subject, uncertain of its value and fitfully disgusted by it. The

The Novel as Work of Art: 'Madame Bovary' (1857)

paradox in fact prefigures the paradox of the whole book—the essential, declared insignificance and unmemorability of the subject, and the exhaustiveness with which it *is* remembered and rehearsed over several hundred pages.

The novel, then, starts under as unpromising, nihilistic auspices as it well could. But the implications of Charles's insignificance are not pursued, and the narrative proceeds with a rather playful, abbreviating recapitulation of the early part of Charles's life. We are then introduced to Emma through a series of vignettish glimpses; some of these are connected with Charles's own reactions, others are more purely descriptive elaborations, where the author takes over himself. The first picture is of Emma pricking her finger while sewing up a pad for Charles to use in setting her father's leg:

> Comme elle fut longtemps avant de trouver son étui, son père s'impatienta; elle ne répondit rien; mais tout en cousant elle se piquait les doigts, qu'elle portait ensuite à sa bouche pour les sucer.
> Charles fut surpris de la blancheur de ses ongles. Ils étaient brillants, fins du bout, plus nettoyés que les ivoires de Dieppe, et taillés en amande. Sa main pourtant n'était pas belle, point assez pâle, peut-être, et un peu sèche aux phalanges; elle était trop longue aussi, et sans molles inflexions de ligne sur les contours. Ce qu'elle avait de beau, c'étaient les yeux; quoiqu'ils fussent bruns ils semblaient noirs à cause des cils et son regard arrivait franchement à vous avec une hardiesse candide.
> (As she was a long time finding her work-case her father spoke impatiently to her; she did not reply; but as she sewed she pricked her fingers, which she then put to her lips and sucked.
> Charles was surprised at the whiteness of her nails. They were brilliant, tapering, more polished than Dieppe ivory, and cut in almond shape. Her hand, however, was not beautiful, not pale enough, perhaps, and a little hard at the joints; and it was too long as well, without any softness in its outline. Her most beautiful feature was her eyes; though they were brown they appeared black because of their lashes, and she fixed you frankly, with a look of boldness and candour.)

Several things are suggested by this first presentation: we see Emma out of her element at the farm—her father admits that she has 'trop d'esprit pour la culture'—but unconsciously turning her rather ineffectual practical efforts to good aesthetic advantage.

The Novel as Work of Art: 'Madame Bovary' (1857)

'Charles fut surpris de la blancheur de ses ongles'—a simple, admiring reaction flatly stated, one which even the insensitive Charles could hardly fail to have, since he can rarely have emergency nurses of such distinction. But the following lines are obviously, almost exaggeratedly not his, indeed Flaubert seems to show up the incompleteness of Charles's response by the pedantic minuteness of his own contribution. He elaborates Charles's impression by a deliberately sought-out image, adds a correction which goes beyond the delicate nails to the quality of the hand in general, and finishes by pointing out what, to the refined artistic perception, is the really distinctive feature of Emma's physical attraction.

The first picture is followed by similar ones; physical details are added, though with no attempt at completeness—her neck with the curls falling over it, her parting, her cheeks. But mostly we see her postures: Emma standing on the threshold of the farm at a time when the snow is thawing, holding an umbrella on to which the water drips and through which the sun makes patterns on her skin; or the equally delightful scene where she offers Charles a liqueur and throws back her head to lick the drops off the bottom of her glass. We do not see Emma through Charles's eyes, but what he sees is the starting point. And always implied is the diptych of Charles, clumsy and admiring, Emma artlessly delicate, unable to move without putting herself into some attitude which recommends itself, indistinctly to Charles, explicitly to the artist. The marriage is concluded, and the description of the procession across country from the *mairie* provides a definitive pictorial representation of the Emma-Charles group; the relation of the figures is still the same:

> La robe d'Emma, trop longue, traînait un peu par le bas; de temps à autre elle s'arrêtait pour la tirer, et alors délicatement, de ses doigts gantés, elle enlevait les herbes rudes avec les petits dards des chardons, pendant que Charles, les mains vides, attendait qu'elle eût fini.
>
> (Emma's dress was too long and trailed on the ground slightly; now and then she stopped to lift it up, and then, delicately, with her gloved fingers, she would remove the stray bits of grass and thistle, while Charles, empty-handed, waited for her to finish.)

The Novel as Work of Art: 'Madame Bovary' (1857)

There follow a lively description of the wedding feast, an exact one of the house to which the couple return; and another 'group' depicting the beginning of conjugal life—Charles setting out on his rounds and blowing a kiss to his wife, who stands at the window to see him off and responds, with greater restraint, 'par un signe'.

Up to this point we have had a considerable wealth of physical detail; we have the impression of a willingly protracted, neutral description, of the author selecting and organizing, but not embellishing his material, fixing and painting its most eligible plastic aspects, suggesting a certain recurrent physical grouping. We have hardly noticed that throughout this attractive pictorial introduction we have not heard a word directly from Emma's lips, nor had more than the barest indication of her character or her past or her feelings towards Charles or her reasons for accepting him.

We now have a summing-up of their relations at this early stage of their married life, and the passage is worth quoting in full. Charles is completely happy:

L'univers pour lui n'excédait pas le tour soyeux de son jupon. Et il se reprochait de ne pas l'aimer, il avait envie de la revoir; il s'en revenait vite, montait l'escalier, le coeur battant. Emma dans sa chambre était à faire sa toilette; il arrivait à pas muets, il la baisait dans le dos, elle poussait un cri.

Il ne pouvait se retenir de toucher continuellement à son peigne, à ses bagues, à son fichu; quelquefois il lui donnait sur les joues de gros baisers à pleine bouche, ou c'étaient de petits baisers à la file, tout le long de son bras nu, depuis le bout des doigts jusqu' à l'épaule; et elle le repoussait, à demi souriante et ennuyée, comme on fait à un enfant qui se pend après vous.

Avant qu'elle se mariât elle avait cru avoir de l'amour; mais le bonheur qui aurait dû résulter de cet amour n'étant pas venu, il fallait qu'elle se fût trompée, songeait-elle. Et Emma cherchait à savoir ce que l'on entendait au juste dans la vie par les mots de *félicité*, de *passion* et d'*ivresse*, qui lui avaient paru si beaux dans les livres.

(The universe, for him, was contained in the silken round of her skirt. And he reproached himself with not loving her enough, he could not wait to get back to her; he came home quickly, climbed the stairs with beating heart. Emma would be in her room, at her toilet; he would steal up behind her and kiss her on the back, so that she cried out.

The Novel as Work of Art: 'Madame Bovary' (1857)

He could not stop himself from constantly touching her comb, her rings, her scarf; sometimes he would give her big kisses on the cheeks, and sometimes a string of little ones, the whole length of her bare arm, from the tips of her fingers up to the shoulder; and she pushed him off, with a faintly irritated smile, as one does a child who keeps hanging around one.

Before her marriage she had thought she was in love; but since the happiness which should have sprung from that love had not come she thought that she must have been mistaken. And Emma wanted to know exactly what was meant in life by those words *bliss, passion* and *ecstasy*, which had seemed so beautiful to her in books.)

Another vignette (though a composite, recurrent one), just slightly more active, slightly less exclusively pictorial than the ones we have had so far. But the concluding paragraph, with its bland announcement of Emma's disillusion, is astonishing; it is in no way inconsistent with what has gone before—in reading it we are conscious, perhaps for the first time, that there is nothing for it to be inconsistent with—but it is completely unprepared. Not only is the very first mention of Emma's emotions a bald statement of rapid and complete disillusion, but that disillusion is 'explained' by an equally casual reference to her intellectual status, as evidenced by her reading, her aspirations and her own logic about her love.

Flaubert is content to end his chapter on this sudden, but wholly undramatic résumé. The next chapter elaborates the story behind Emma's disillusion, and fills in some of the blanks of the earlier scenes. But this account turns out to be not the carefully documented psychological history of an individual, but the description of a stock Romantic girlhood, nourished on Scott and Chateaubriand; a girlhood compounded in general of the eternal common places of the imagination and formed in its details by contact with a period of literature and sensibility which was already discredited, and a subject for satire, when Flaubert was writing. We are led up to the marriage with Charles by a different route; but there is a strong contrast between the precision and promise of the physical description and the vague, cursory, ironic quality of the moral. Charles's first visit to Les Bertaux had come when Emma 'se considérait comme fort

The Novel as Work of Art: 'Madame Bovary' (1857)

désillusionnée, n'ayant plus rien à apprendre, ne devant plus rien sentir' ('thought of herself as very disillusioned, with nothing left to learn or to feel'). She accepted him, and her exact reason for doing so is only speculated on—'l'anxiété d'un état nouveau, ou peut-être l'irritation causée par la présence de cet homme'. In the most casual way possible Flaubert has completely devalued Emma; from being the provocative unknown, whose exterior he has allowed us fragmentarily to glimpse, she is shown, the very first time we are allowed to see her more closely, to be a stock figure. What strikes us most is the matter-of-factness with which this is done, the allusive, abbreviating way in which Emma is disposed of. We have moved back, after the physical interlude, to the tone in which Charles's own early life was described. The contrast between the rare physical phenomenon and the ordinariness which it conceals is not emphasized; Emma's life is recapitulated as though it were a mere illustration of something we already knew, her acceptance of Charles as another stock, predictable occurrence, unworthy of detailed motivation. (And this vagueness of motivation continues throughout. For instance, the explanation of Emma's initial resistance to Léon's attractions: 'Ce qui la retenait, sans doute, c'était la pudeur ou l'épouvante, et la paresse aussi' ['what held her back, no doubt, was modesty or fright, and laziness as well']; and of the dying of her love after his departure: 'Cependant les flammes s'apaisèrent, soit que la provision d'elle-même s'épuisât, ou que l'entassement fût trop considérable' ['but the flames died down, whether for lack of fuel or because of too great a piling up of it'].) Yet it would be impossible to call this the showing up of Emma. If she is invalidated as a considerable moral being her exposure is conducted with no trace of triumph (indeed it seems rather to have been delayed as long as possible); nor of regret, nor of surprise, nor of apology. It is stated as the norm. What, in particular, should one expect to find behind a pretty and distinctive provincial exterior? Nothing, is the assumption of Flaubert—and an assumption which he expects his readers to share. The uncommented succession of the highly individualized physical evocation and the 'type' characterization might disconcert the

The Novel as Work of Art: 'Madame Bovary' (1857)

reader looking for the dramatic unfolding of an individual fate; it is framed for the more aristocratic observer, the calm unvindictive pessimist for whom humanity as a whole is pre-judged and pre-classified, whose interest goes to the description of its variants. That reader, had he been led to reflect on the preceding scenes, would have considered what is now confirmed as the most likely interpretation of them; he might even have taken a hint from the one previous mention of Emma's views—also thrown in casually at the end of a chapter—that she would have liked to be married 'à minuit, aux flambeaux', but that her father wouldn't hear of it.

The characterization of Emma is thus offered as an undramatic illustration of a known truth, a circumstantial account of the particular form which Emma's inadequacy takes—one of the two or three forms which human inadequacy *can* take. To return to our diptych: the morally and intellectually blank group of clumsy admiring Charles and pretty provocative Emma is repeated, set in motion, and given meaning for the first time. But its meaning—we begin to see and shall later have confirmed—is only that it has no meaning, no moral content. Charles's appraisal of Emma had already been shown, by contrast with Flaubert's perceptions, to be incomplete and undiscriminating; it is now shown in a less favourable, more nihilistic light, as a sort of fetishistic obsession. Emma's first gesture, an augury of her future bad temper, is her irritated resistance to Charles's continued demonstrations of affection; and her antipathy, like his admiration, is invalidated by the fact that her own ideals are beginning to be seen as only variants of a mediocre norm. Her opposition to him is valid only at the level of physical irritation. This, it seems, is the nearest we can get to an account of human conduct: on the physical plane there is variegated, sometimes intense surface activity and conflict, which can be minutely observed and recorded; behind is the almost equally mechanical world of the mind, and here there is union in intellectual nullity.

In such a world the possibility of a specifically *moral* discrimination is excluded; as regards Emma we have acceptance

The Novel as Work of Art: 'Madame Bovary' (1857)

of the physical fact of irritation, rejection of the philosophical claim of disillusion. The series of descriptions are built up independently, each forming a strong and final impression on our minds; so strong that we accept the writer's confident implication that such descriptions provide a complete account of the characters; for the reader, as for Flaubert, there can be no question of a third, morally differentiating dimension to their conduct. Emma's subsequent relations with Charles are displayed not in terms of a moral progression, a disagreement with its fluctuating rights and wrongs, susceptible of judgment and justification; but merely as elaborations of the first antithetical grouping. Emma-Charles form a unit of discord and incongruity, in exactly the same was as Homais-Bournisien; the incompatibility of the romantic and the unromantic is parallel, as regards its moral status, with the chronic 'intellectual' disagreement of the Voltairean and the priest, which is conceived in terms of pure satire. And the writer's concern is to show his groups in as characteristic and artistically fertile situations as possible. The Emma-Charles group moves away from the purely plastic (Charles watching Emma playing the piano) through the more sinister scenes of domestic frustration (Emma watching Charles eat his food) to the open clash after the episode of the amputation. Even here, at the crisis which precipitates Emma's return to her lover, there is no attempt to show a real and valid interplay of characters. We have the long, objective-ironical accounts of the thoughts of the two characters, Charles accusing fate and wondering what could have gone wrong with his operation when he had taken so much care, Emma considering herself triumphantly vindicated in her contempt for Charles, repenting of her past virtue 'comme d'un crime'; and then the brief, characteristic physical eruptions. Firstly Emma's intense irritation at Charles's person and movements:

> Charles se promenait de long en large dans la chambre. Ses bottes craquaient sur le parquet.
>   'Assieds-toi,' dit-elle, 'tu m'agaces!'
> (Charles was walking up and down the room, his boots creaking on the polished floor.

The Novel as Work of Art: 'Madame Bovary' (1857)

'Sit down, 'she said,' you are getting on my nerves.')

And then the picture of rejected affection:

> Alors, par tendresse subite et découragement, Charles se tourna vers sa femme, en lui disant:
> 'Embrasse-moi, ma chère.'
> 'Laisse-moi,' fit-elle, toute rouge de colère.
> (Then, in an access of sudden tenderness and depression, Charles turned to his wife saying:
> 'Give me a kiss, darling.'
> 'Leave me alone,' she said, red with anger.)

This is only a repetition, a heightened variant, of Emma's very first dismissive gesture—'elle le repoussait à demi souriante et ennuyée . . .'—which we have already discussed; it also recalls very strongly an intervening incident, before the ball at La Vaubyessard:

> 'Les sous-pieds vont me gêner pour danser,' dit-il.
> 'Danser?' reprit Emma.
> 'Oui!'
> 'Mais tu as perdu la tête.'
> ('These straps are going to get in my way for dancing,' he said.
> 'Dancing?' Emma repeated.
> 'Yes!'
> 'But you must be mad.')

Then, when she has completed dressing:

> Charles vint l'embrasser sur l'épaule.
> 'Laisse-moi,' dit-elle, 'tu me chiffonnes.'
> (Charles made to kiss her on the shoulder.
> 'Leave me alone,' she said, 'you are rumpling me.')

Irritation has not advanced, and never advances, to the status of emotional conflict.

The intellectual characterization of Emma, which assimilates her to the characters conceived in terms of pure satire, is completed in the 'cultural' conversation which she has with Léon on the evening of the Bovarys' arrival in Yonville. This, like Homais's remarks on Paris, is a complete repertory of *idées reçues*, in which the whole range of romantic subjects—walks, scenery, mountains, music, poetry, prose, sunsets, solitude—is

The Novel as Work of Art: 'Madame Bovary' (1857)

exhausted in the space of a few minutes. While Homais is discoursing to Charles on the social and topographical advantages of practice in Yonville, Emma and Léon offer just as worthless, just as readily classifiable an intellectual unit in their attempt at a protest. The first prolonged interview between Emma and Rodolphe, on the day of the agricultural show, is the occasion for a similar symphony of banalities, this time on a more elaborate and stylized plane. The grouping is the same—the background of the patriotic and official, of provincial society giving the worst example of how seriously it can take itself, and in the foreground the 'protest' of Emma and Rodolphe, whose conversation is interwoven with the prefectoral speeches blown towards them in the wind; as the orator traces the dignity of agriculture back to Cincinnatus and his plough, 'Rodolphe, avec Madame Bovary, causait rêves, pressentiments, magnétisme'.

But the spiritual sameness of the Bovary world is not only stated in set pieces, it is more pervasively and comprehensively suggested, so that the practical-romantic opposition itself disappears. Charles attempts to contribute to the conversation on the pleasures of travel and change of surroundings with an objection from practical experience: ' "Si vous étiez comme moi", dit Charles, "sans cesse obligé d'être à cheval..." ', but such a mundane intervention is brushed aside by the higher-minded Emma and Léon, who turn Charles over to Homais. Yet, in a wider context, he shares his wife's brand of belief in its efficacy:

> Comme elle se plaignait de Tostes continuellement, Charles imagina que la cause de sa maladie était sans doute quelque influence locale, et, s'arrêtant à cette idée, il songea sérieusement à aller s'établir ailleurs.
> (As she was always complaining about Tostes Charles thought that no doubt her illness was caused by something in the local air, and, fixing on this idea, he seriously thought about going and setting up elsewhere.)

This is a transposition into Charles's terms of Emma's more romantically based notion:

The Novel as Work of Art: 'Madame Bovary' (1857)

Elle ne croyait pas que les choses pussent se représenter les mêmes à des places différentes, et puisque la portion vécue avait été mauvaise, sans doute ce qui restait à consommer serait meilleur.

(She could not believe that things could be the same in different places, and since the part of her life that she had lived had been disappointing, no doubt what remained would be better.)

The *sans doute*, common to both, condemns both, consigns them among the self-deceiving run of humanity, who believe that things could be better. We recall that Charles had been dissatisfied with his first wife, having 'entrevu dans le mariage une condition meilleure'; wherever we drop in on this world we see the familiar pattern of hope and disappointment, the facile diagnosis, the complacently offered panacea:

... souvent Léon se renversait sur une chaise en écartant les bras, et se plaignait vaguement de l'existence.
   'C'est que vous ne prenez point assez de distractions,' disait le percepteur.
   'Lesquelles?'
   'Moi, à votre place, j'aurais un tour!'
   'Mais je ne sais pas tourner,' répondait le clerc.
   'Oh! c'est vrai, faisait l'autre. ...'
(... Léon would often sink back in a chair with his arms stretched out and complain vaguely about life.
   'It's because you don't get enough amusement,' the tax-collector would say.
   'Such as what?'
   'If I were you I should get a lathe.'
   'But I don't know how to use one,' the clerk would reply.
   'Ah, no, that's true. ...')

Emma's two love affairs, both introduced under the sign of open satire, are thus prepared as natural extensions, characteristic illustrations of her now finally categorized personality; and they belong, more generally, to a world in which action is merely the by-product of misguided ideas and ideals. When the ideals have been discounted there remains nothing distinctive but the physical phenomena.

We may consider in this connexion the seduction scene between Emma and Rodolphe. Rodolphe is for Emma the embodiment of chivalrous masculinity, as Charles is the representative

The Novel as Work of Art: 'Madame Bovary' (1857)

of the inadequate and unromantic. He offers to teach Emma to ride, and they soon find themselves in the side-paths:

> De longues fougères, au bord de la route, se prenaient dans l'étrier d'Emma. Rodolphe, tout en allant, se penchait et il les retirait à mesure. D'autres fois, pour écarter les branches, il passait près d'elle, et Emma sentait son genou lui frôler la jambe.
>
> (Tall ferns growing at the side of the path got caught in Emma's stirrup, and Rodolphe would lean over and pull them out as they rode on. At other times he drew up close to her to push back the branches, and Emma felt his knee brush against her leg.)

The fatal ride is described minutely, but the significant detail evoked turns out to be the opposite of significant; it is the normal stuff of sensual attraction, just as Charles's habits are the normal stuff of enervation. The difference between Charles and Rodolphe is seen primarily as a physical one: we remember that we have seen Charles in just the same position with regard to Emma—in the scene of the marriage procession, when he waited, clumsy and incompetent, 'les mains vides', unable to perform for her on foot the sort of office which Rodolphe manages with distinction on horseback. Moreover we have once again, as in the case of the Emma-Léon-Charles 'opinions', not only antithesis, but also a more embracing resemblance. 'Emma sentait son genou lui frôler la jambe'—the most primitive, commonplace physical stimulant, now faithfully recorded on what might be expected to be an individual and highly charged occasion. Had not the birth of Charles's own passion been presented with the same flat, unexceptional detail? Only the setting differs: it is the occasion of his first visit to Les Bertaux, when he returns to look for his whip and, not only inept but uncalculating (here still the opposite of Rodolphe), makes one of his rare attempts at gallantry:

> Mlle Emma l'aperçut; elle se pencha sur les sacs de blé; Charles, par galanterie, se précipita, et comme il allongeait aussi son bras dans le même mouvement, il sentit sa poitrine effleurer le dos de la jeune fille, courbée sous lui. Elle se redressa toute rouge et le regarda par-dessus l'épaule, en lui tendant son nerf de boeuf.
>
> (Mademoiselle Emma saw it and leaned forward over the sacks of

wheat; Charles, trying to be gallant, rushed forward and, putting his arm out at the same time, he felt his chest touch the girl's back, as she bent down under him. She stood up again all flushed and glanced at him over her shoulder as she handed him his whip.)

A final irony, that the Rodolphe-Emma affair is made up of the same constituents as the Charles-Emma marriage; both are seen as natural, predictable, insignificant. A little talk, a little stimulus, the normal desire for something new—these are the elements of human love; behind the accidents of time, place and novelty lies 'l'éternelle monotonie de la passion, qui a toujours les mêmes formes et le même langage'.

We can see the repetitive side of passion further illustrated in the first Charles-Emma and Léon-Emma conversations. Charles for Emma had at first been a welcome auditor to whom she could unburden her imaginary ills and confide her desire for change and travel:

> Elle se plaignait d'éprouver, depuis le commencement de la saison, des étourdissements; elle se demanda si les bains de mer lui seraient utiles; elle se mit à causer du couvent, Charles de son collège, *les phrases leur vinrent.* . . .
> (She complained that since the beginning of the summer she had been having bouts of dizziness; she wondered whether sea-bathing would do her any good; she spoke of her convent, Charles of his school, talk began to flow. . . .)

'Les phrases leur vinrent' is a masterly touch; for Charles at any rate this is one of the few occasions when the words did come; the couple who are to have nothing to say to one another for the whole of their married life are exhausting their modest repertory of ideas and memories. But this is enough to bring them together, to forge a sympathetic alliance 'against' the ordinariness of practical life. The Emma-Léon conversation, as we have seen, is given in greater satirical detail, but when summed up falls into the same persepctive:

> C'est ainsi, l'un près de l'autre, pendant que Charles et le pharmacien devisaient, qu'ils entrèrent dans une de ces vagues conversations où *le hasard des phrases* vous ramène toujours au centre fixe d'une sympathie commune.'

The Novel as Work of Art: 'Madame Bovary' (1857)

(And so, as they sat together, while Charles was discoursing with the chemist, they started on one of those rambling conversations where the chance succession of phrases keeps bringing you back to a fixed point of common sympathy.)

These parallels are not made in order to suggest that Flaubert's *purpose* is systematically to show up the mechanics of human passion; but they demonstrate the range of assumptions on which his depiction of love is based, and confirm the impression which we have while reading that the various stages of the novel are not progressions of a personal fate but variants of a fixed and limited pool of raw material, a succession of episodes in which rightness is all. Flaubert's own observations on the character of the book invite this interpretation. His chief concern is not with the action but with the descriptive 'preparations' and the 'general tone'. 'Drama has little part in it', he remarks, and, though at one point he became worried at the small amount of space occupied by the critical steps forward in the action, he justified himself with the reflection that the novel was 'a biography, rather than a complex dramatic action'. The notion of biography, the filling-in of the life and times of a person already known to the public, the narration of a pre-existing set of facts, is useful; standing apart, as it does, from the notion of a psychological enquiry, or of a tragedy, of the working out of a significant personal fate. Emma is no more fated to love Rodolphe than she is to marry Charles—the most we can say is that both episodes are credible, both entirely and depressingly predictable. It is in this sense, and in this sense only, that Charles's misfortunes can be said to be 'prefigured' in the description of his cap, so beloved of the symbol-hunters. Charles's cap is not symbolic, it is characteristic; every character in Flaubert's world has his Charles's cap. The idea of fatality indeed is invoked only in satirically observed pronouncements, as the pretext for, or the false interpretation of, what happens: 'Oh, n'importe', says Rodolphe to Emma, elaborating his platonic theory of the 'deux pauvres âmes' seeking one another, 'tôt ou tard, dans six mois, dix ans, elles se réuniront, s'aimeront, parce que la fatalité l'exige et qu'elles sont nées l'une pour l'autre'. And he is echoed

The Novel as Work of Art: 'Madame Bovary' (1857)

by Charles, who tries to give a generous, understanding, philosophical air to what is really cowardice or the resignation of fatigue: ' "Je ne vous en veux pas," ' he tells Rodolphe, ' "non, je ne vous en veux plus." Il ajouta même un grand mot, le seul qu'il ait jamais dit: "C'est la faute de la fatalité." '

The repetitive, mechanical pattern acts, then, to secure the narrative at every point against the imputation of a positive, differentiable moral content. But within this uniformly envisaged whole we are not continuously aware of an active attempt to show the characters up. And here we recall Flaubert's aim of *bien écrire*, 'good writing', and the attempts he made to achieve that aim without perverting the subject he had undertaken. The problem is constantly referred to in his letters: 'What I am writing at the moment,' he writes to Louise Colet, 'risks sounding like Paul de Kock unless I can give it a profoundly literary form; but how can one produce trivial dialogue which is also well-written?' The solution to the problem of dialogue is often, quite simply, to avoid it, or rather to concentrate it in stylized satirical fragments. Flaubert *could* have made Emma and Rodolphe appear persistently absurd by retailing their conversations at greater length; yet the extravagant scenes which irritate Rodolphe and elevate Emma, such as the exchanging of miniatures, are mentioned only in passing.

As applied to descriptive writing in general 'good writing' meant a steady fixing of the object, a transmutation into words which would render it completely and uniquely. We do not intend to offer another detailed appraisal of how far Flaubert succeeded in putting into practice what for him was ultimately a mystical belief; we are concerned rather with the conditions under which the attempt was made and its relation to the satirical framework of the novel. Obviously to a certain extent satire and this sort of 'good writing' risk conflicting. As trivial gossip will suggest the artist merely dropping in on life, so too pointed a satirical intent will destroy the poise required in an objective description; and this, as we have seen, was the distortion which Flaubert sought to avoid by writing private satires on his characters before tackling the scenes in which they were to

The Novel as Work of Art: 'Madame Bovary' (1857)

appear. If we return to the seduction scene, to which we have already denied distinctive drama, we find that the preliminaries, though minute, are commonplace; Emma's protests are presented as stagy and routine gestures; and her reactions, when she paces about her room again alone, are nothing more profound than the self-dramatizing 'j'ai un amant, j'ai un amant', trailing off into recollections of the heroines of books she has read, 'la légion lyrique des femmes adultères', of whom she now feels a worthy member; 'la longue rêverie de sa jeunesse' has been realized. Yet the total effect of the episode is not of satirical presentation or of a carefully engineered anti-climax. Rather, perhaps, the opposite. The very circumstantiality of each new description in the novel, the slightly conscious pause that precedes it, suggest not the satirist fabricating a scene to insert into a pattern, but the artist poised for the transcription of an event which he sees germinating in his imagination, and which he hopes will provide a new and worthwhile object for his pen. Thus as Flaubert evokes Emma and Rodolphe setting out on their ride our strongest impression is not of satire but of a willing suspension of satire in the cause of art. That the product is, yet again, an easily recognizable scene, one in fact which the critical observer can link up with previous scenes, is only, we are made to feel, because fidelity to the truth restricts the writer to the depiction of a very limited number of physical groupings. The effect is not so much of calculated irony as of disappointed lyricism, the artist enchained against his own will by a scruple of veracity.

This scene presents in a smaller compass the same succession of promising neutral description and unemphatic satirical devaluation as we saw in the opening chapters. And it engages our interest in the same way by presenting the physical scene in its own right, and not anticipating its conclusion in such a way as to seem a mere schematic exercise of construction and deflation. But the conclusion is none the less relentlessly enforced; and as the book progresses our cumulative certainty that this is the only possible interpretation of events has important effects on our reading. Flaubert has made his point so well from the start that we are not led to look for refinements of meaning under the

The Novel as Work of Art: 'Madame Bovary' (1857)

occasional diversity of the style; we are willing to allow a little latitude to the writer who has made so clear his interest in evoking phenomena and his complete disillusion as to their meaning. In a very different tone from the passages of concentrated satire are the expansive accounts of Emma's daydreams, aspirations and memories: her image of Paris, her memories of the farm, when she receives her father's annual letter with the turkey, her vision of an exotic exile with Rodolphe. For Flaubert the writing of these passages was something of a consolation, a momentary recompense for the lost splendours of *Saint Antoine*; and by no means all of them are punctured with satire. Flaubert entered deeply into these reveries, and lent to Emma an imaginative organization such as even her literary past could hardly have given her. His own yearning for the exotic makes strongest here the temptation to see a subjective identification with the heroine, and the critics who find a latent idealism in the work are encouraged by Flaubert's unhappy aside—'Madame Bovary, c'est moi'. But it is surely wrong to see these passages as running counter to the established sense of the whole work; the nihilistic framework is proof against them, and within that framework Emma's thoughts are so many physical events, their description at its best a permissible embellishment of slightly unresolved status, at its least appropriate a forgivable indulgence of the fine writer. The limited measure of Flaubert's involvement in Emma's feelings, and the sort of approach to them which is predominant with him, is well shown by his use of similes. The simile, which could be an instrument for evaluating or enlarging, is in fact not used in that role:

> Dès lors ce souvenir de Léon fut comme le centre de son ennui; il y pétillait plus fort que, dans un steppe de Russie, un feu abandonné sur la neige.
> (From then on this memory of Léon became the centre of her discontent; it crackled there more brightly than a fire left behind on the snows of the Russian steppes.)
>
> Quant au souvenir de Rodolphe elle l'avait descendu tout au fond de son coeur; et il restait là, plus solennel et plus immobile qu'une momie de roi dans un souterrain.

The Novel as Work of Art: 'Madame Bovary' (1857)

(As for Rodolphe's memory, she had consigned it to the bottom of her heart; and there it remained, more solemn and motionless than the mummy of a king in an underground vault.)

The very resemblance of rhythm of the two examples (separated by over a hundred pages) betrays Flaubert, who is ostensibly analysing key states of mind, in fact pulling out some favourite descriptive stops. The exaggeratedly scientific pretensions of the wording ('centre', 'tout au fond', and in both cases not '*aussi*' but '*plus* fort', '*plus* solennel') make all the more grotesque and dehumanizing the terms of comparison offered; Emma's feelings remain vaguely impressive and moving, but they are primarily, like her body and physical presence, gratefully described *objets d'art*.

The ultimate triumph of Madame Bovary is not to be written in a single style, but to impose its meaning so unmistakably that it can confidently embrace the expansive and the satirical, and steer between their conflicting implications to achieve its main purpose—the exactly neutral presentation of events. This triumph is best illustrated in the closing scenes of the novel. They are not exempt from what could have become a sort of tragic enlargement, or a raising of moral problems of guilt, remorse and repentance; for instance there is the commentary on the administration of extreme unction:

> ... d'abord sur les yeux, qui avaient tant convoité toutes les somptuosités terrestres; puis sur les narines, friandes de brises tièdes et de senteurs amoureuses ... enfin sur la plante des pieds, si rapides autrefois quand elle courait à l'assouvissance de ses désirs, et qui maintenant ne marcheraient plus. ...
>
> (... first on the eyes, which had so coveted all earthly luxuries; then on the nostrils which had sought the warm breezes and the perfumes of love ... lastly on the soles of the feet, so swift in former times when she hastened to the quenching of her desires, and which now would walk no more. ...)

But the last view we have of Emma does not suggest repentance, or any other definitive state of mind, rather it is a last characteristic posture with Charles, a last, ludicrous attempt at communication between two people who have never made contact with one another:

The Novel as Work of Art: 'Madame Bovary' (1857)

'N'étais-tu pas heureuse? Est-ce ma faute? J'ai fait tout ce que j'ai pu, pourtant.'
'Oui . . . c'est vrai . . . tu es bon, toi.'
('Weren't you happy? Is it my fault? And yet I did all I could.'
'Yes . . . that's true . . . you are good, you are.')

'Oh! vous êtes bon', we remember her saying to Rodolphe; and further back still, when she was trying to resist her growing love for Léon, she had praised her husband in the same words:

Alors elle fit la soucieuse. Deux on trois fois même elle répéta:
'Il est si bon!'

As she had moved away from Charles to Léon and Rodolphe, so now, just as predictably, she has returned.

Yet we are neither caught up or moved to reflection by the expansive description; nor do we feel inclined to laugh at the Charles-Emma exchange, for all its stylized and quintessential quality. By this stage our certainty that no new meaning, no distinction of values can make itself felt ensures that we recognize the 'description' for what it is: a rhythmic but uncharged statement of fact. And at the same time our complete familiarity with the characters, the assurance we have that they will act 'in character' to the end, makes us progressively less inclined to laugh at them, more disposed to accept unthinkingly the content of their actions and rivet our attention to the form. Flaubert's narrative has established itself so finally as a description of indifferent and repetitive events that we no longer experience, in these last exchanges, the positive delight of recognition; only an underlying feeling of rightness, a calm certainty that nothing has been overstated and nothing left unsaid.

The narration continues to be interspersed with satire as we move on to the scene of the vigil, with the priest and the chemist renewing, as they do on any provocation, their chronic ideological dispute. There is even a sort of pastiche of the traditional reconciliation in the face of death when they fall asleep and Flaubert, who has so far shown no pity for the human community in weakness, describes them as 'après tant de désaccord se rencontrant dans la même faiblesse humaine'; and to emphasize that it is a parody he soon wakes them up again for

The Novel as Work of Art: 'Madame Bovary' (1857)

their slightly hysterical meal, and makes Bournisien, excited by 'cette gaieté vague qui vous prend après des séances de tristesse', utter the facile *idée reçue* of the optimistic Christian—that all men of good will are really aiming at the same thing: 'nous finirons par nous entendre'. Yet again we do not feel that there has been a wilful satirical intrusion or a gratuitous, distorting prolongation of a story that is really already over. For the point has been made that the *whole* story is gratuitous; and the very exhaustiveness with which these last hours are described is at once an invitation to unreflecting attention to detail and a final illustration of the intention and meaning of the novel. Critical appraisal of the characters gives way to a sort of trance-like absorption in what is going on; so that we can even read such a pointed detail as 'M. Bournisien aspergeait la chambre d'eau bénite, et Homais jetait un peu de chlore' ('M. Bournisien sprinkled the room with holy water, and Homais put down a little chlorine') with little more than a flutter of comic disturbance. It is a virtuoso's performance. What might have been mere satire has justified itself as a transcription of reality. And 'meaning' has been warded off to the end. What we have in *Madame Bovary* is a work of satirical framework drawn out either by suspending satire, giving each new episode the chance to recommend itself to objective description, or going as it were beyond satire, so accustoming the reader to the patterns of its world that he no longer exclaims at recognizing them. Where Flaubert never places himself is this side of satire, in the moral world where the prime interest is to distinguish rather than to assimilate, to enquire rather than to categorize.

The sort of novel *Madame Bovary* might have been but is not may be illustrated by an interesting and rather unexpected intervention which Flaubert makes in favour of Emma. It occurs shortly before Rodolphe's desertion, when his irritation at Emma's extravagant expressions of love is getting more and more acute. After one of these outbursts we are told that Rodolphe had heard such words so many times that they no longer held anything original for him; Emma was no different from all his other mistresses. And Flaubert comments:

The Novel as Work of Art: 'Madame Bovary' (1857)

Il ne distinguait pas, cet homme si plein de pratique, la dissemblance des sentiments sous la parité des expressions. Parce que des lèvres libertines ou vénales lui avaient murmuré des phrases pareilles, il ne croyait que faiblement à la candeur de celles-là; on en devait rabattre, pensait-il, les discours exagérés cachant les affections médiocres; comme si la plénitude de l'âme ne débordait pas quelquefois par les métaphores les plus vides, puisque personne, jamais, ne peut donner l'exacte mesure de ses besoins, ni de ses conceptions, ni de ses douleurs, et que la parole humaine est comme un chaudron fêlé où nous battons des mélodies à faire danser les ours, quand on voudrait attendrir les étoiles.

(He could not distinguish, with all his experience, a difference of feeling under the sameness of the expression. Because he had heard similar phrases murmured to him by licentious or mercenary lips, he had little faith in the sincerity of these. He thought that one had to scale down exaggerated speeches concealing moderate affection; as if the fulness of the soul did not sometimes spill over in the emptiest metaphors, since no one can ever exactly express his needs, his ideas or his sorrows, and human speech is like a cracked iron cauldron on which we beat out tunes fit for bears to dance to, when we wish to move the very stars.)

Here Flaubert is suggesting, as he has done nowhere else in the novel, that there is a third dimension to human conduct, apart from the physical action and the intellectual motive or reaction which is always found on examination to be invalid. The possibility is allowed, indeed insisted on, that behind the unfailingly classifiable repetitions of thought and conduct there are individual moral entities, who can be distinguished, investigated and adjudged of varying worth, instead of being conveniently lumped together through the sameness of a single one of their faculties. Flaubert here seems to be almost making a protest against himself, to be indicating to us the existence of a whole world which he has failed to touch. But the presence of this passage should not lead us to suspect that for Flaubert Emma's love was in any way a *grande passion*, that we should reconsider our interpretation and seek some latent moral content in the relations of the characters. On the contrary the isolation of the passage suggests, and the use to which it is put confirms, that such a search would be in vain. The warmth of the intervention may well come from Flaubert's own strong feeling of the artist's

The Novel as Work of Art: 'Madame Bovary' (1857)

struggle with the inadequate *parole humaine*. But in *intention* it is purely negative and critical, its only purpose is to emphasize still further the defects of cognition of the characters, the reciprocal wrongness and incompleteness with which they judge one another. Flaubert can dismiss Emma as mediocre, a mere type, but if Rodolphe does so he must be taken to task, and the price to be paid by the writer is the allegation of the reality of Emma's passion. Rodolphe is wrong about Emma in the same way as Emma, in the early days of her marriage, had been shown to be wrong about Charles:

> Quand elle eut ainsi un peu battu le briquet sur son coeur sans en faire jaillir une étincelle, incapable, du reste, de comprendre ce qu'elle n'éprouvait pas, comme de croire à tout ce qui ne se manifestait point par des formes convenues, elle se persuadait sans peine que la passion de Charles n'avait rien d'exorbitant.
>
> (After continuing a short time in this way, striking the flint on her heart without getting a spark from it, incapable, moreover, of understanding what she did not feel, as she was of believing in anything which did not take a conventional outward form, she had no difficulty in persuading herself that Charles's passion had nothing extraordinary about it.)

Flaubert had here defended the 'reality' of Charles's love against Emma's attempts to justify her own coldness by casting doubt on the sincerity of her husband's enthusiasm. Thus the reality of love is only used by Flaubert as a neat weapon for rounding off the intellectual destruction of his characters. We have seen them taking their own *idées reçues* for original ideas, elevating their own insignificant disappointments to the status of disillusion; a natural corollary to mistaking one's own trivia for realities is to fail to recognize realities behind the trivia of other people. And in terms of detachment the price paid for such interventions is negligible, since far from involving a *parti pris* in favour of one character it merely contributes to the circular process of devaluation. What is given away—the unappreciated reality of the emotions—is very little, no more than a restatement of what we already know. Charles's passion *is* extreme (or obsessive?), Emma's love is *not* venal but idealistic (or 'romantic'?). We get no nearer, however, to an enquiry into

The Novel as Work of Art: 'Madame Bovary' (1857)

the nature and status of these realities. Their manifestations, their expressions 'par des formes convenues' have been shown, their intellectual background pitilessly revealed; and now, having come forward momentarily to assert his superior understanding of the soul, the artist retires again, gratefully, to the minuteness and variety of the phenomena.

The *formes* fill out the whole canvas to the end. And Flaubert, far from suggesting that he has deliberately restricted himself to painting the outside of events, seems rather to imply that there is nothing further of significance to explore. It would seem permissible, as it is certainly appropriate, to see a justificatory double meaning, a final evaluative epitaph, in the description of the autopsy performed on Charles. Charles had died of a broken heart, without any sign of disease. Homais summons the surgeon, and Charles (who, we recall, is made of the same stuff as all the other characters) is 'looked into' for the only time in the novel:

'M. Canivet accourut. Il l'ouvrit et ne trouva rien.'

A final judgment of *Madame Bovary's* stature as a novel will depend on a criticism of Flaubert's scope rather than of his performance. For any appraisal must fail which does not stress the complete technical triumph of the work and the intense intellectual and aesthetic pleasure which each page of it affords. To Flaubert it represented the winning of a highly problematical literary wager. Formulating yet again the hazards of his subject he writes in a letter:

To try to give to prose the rhythm of verse (while making it remain prose, and very definitely prose) and to write about ordinary life as one writes history or epic, without distorting the subject—perhaps it's an absurd idea . . . perhaps also it's a great and very original undertaking.

As we have Flaubert's sanction for seeing the novel as a successfully solved problem we do him no injustice in exposing the technical basis of this success, or even in expressing it in a negative way, in terms of pitfalls successfully avoided. What these pitfalls were can readily be seen by a look at Flaubert's other novels. After *Madame Bovary* he never again managed effectively to combine and reconcile his divergent artistic aims;

The Novel as Work of Art: 'Madame Bovary' (1857)

and when they operate on their own, not controlling and complementing one another, they lead to inevitable failure. 'Good writing produces the descriptive orgy of *Salammbô*, set in ancient Carthage, the critical spirit finds its ultimate expression in the aimless and desiccated satire of *Bouvard et Pécuchet*. Here, in a novel stripped of all sensuous attraction, we ask from the very beginning the sort of questions which do not occur to us while we are reading *Madame Bovary*: Why should we be interested in the details of this protracted epic of stupidity? What is the point of setting up these two imbecile heroes and expending such immense pains to knock them down? Why should a man like Flaubert want to write about contemporary human beings at all—would he not have done better to have kept to Carthage, that desert, as he said himself, to which disgust with modern life had driven him?

Yet all these questions threatened to raise themselves in the earlier novel, for the basic philosophy was no less simple and ruthless. *Madame Bovary* sustains the paradox of its own existence, but in doing so exhausts Flaubert's whole provision of human material and human interests. Here the patterns, the limitations, the uniformity of Flaubert's world contribute directly to the achievement of his purpose. They give the work its quality of unity and solidity, of completely evoking a certain prevailing atmosphere; they engage the reader's complicity so that he sees events in the way in which the author wants them to be seen, shares to a large degree the vantage point of the detached artistic observer. But the patterns are not so insistent that we see through the mechanism, anticipate the moves, tire of the repetitions. The opening scenes, as we have seen, establish the individual physiognomy of the story, and that capital of reality lasts throughout its length. We have at least the illusion that Flaubert has come to this world with an open mind and is trying to extract the maximum of beauty and interest from it, that he is forced to his conclusions by the evidence itself.

The question already presents itself: why doesn't he look further, or deeper? If there is an inconsistency in *Madame Bovary* it lies, as we suggested, in the dubious status of the descriptions of

The Novel as Work of Art: 'Madame Bovary' (1857)

Emma's reveries. Though their cumulative effect is to emphasize the satirical presentation their detail is, in some cases, too good for her. If we take Emma's daydream provoked by her father's letter and compare it with her ideas and imagination as expressed in the opening conversation with Léon, we find that it is too detailed, too well organized, for her undisciplined and mediocre mind. The only phrase which could be attributed to her with absolute safety is the opening statement of fact—'Comme il y avait longtemps qu'elle n'était plus auprès de lui . . .!', which is paralleled elsewhere in the novel with flat reflections such as 'Comme c'était loin, tout cela!' If she were capable of what follows she would have moved some way towards the condition of the artist, have got sufficiently far outside her predicament to effect her salvation. And in the concluding image we have insensibly but unmistakably moved away from interior monologue to artistic adornment:

Quel bonheur dans ce temps-là! Quelle liberté! Quel espoir! Quelle abondance d'illusions! Il n'en restait plus maintenant! Elle en avait dépensé à toutes les aventures de son âme, par toutes les conditions successives, dans la virginité, dans le mariage et dans l'amour;—les perdant ainsi continuellement le long de sa vie, comme un voyageur qui laisse quelque chose de sa richesse à toutes les auberges de la route.

(What happiness in those days! What freedom! What hope! What abundance of illusions! There were none left now! She had spent them in all the adventures of her soul, in the successive states of virginity, marriage and love;—losing them constantly down the whole course of her life, like a traveller who leaves something of his riches at every inn on the route.)

Flaubert needs this type of writing in order to maintain the 'well-written' quality of his book. Yet in all his work he persistently avoids portraying a sensibility where it would be indisputably in place, and not have to be introduced with a certain amount of technical dexterity. The same contradiction is apparent in *L'Éducation Sentimentale* where a potentially moving representation of real love is inhibited by being tied down to the limitations of another mediocre hero—Frédéric. Conversely, the enthusiastically evoked Dr. Larivière, who bustles into the novel at the height of Emma's agony, dwarfing the characters

The Novel as Work of Art: 'Madame Bovary' (1857)

we have come to accept as norms, seems an intruder from a superior race. This would seem to be a valid criticism of Flaubert's presentation of reality: that the writer is not merely expressing genuine pessimism about humanity, but consciously narrowing his vision in order to suit his artistic predilections. Put in another way—the condition of his art is to portray failures; he must have a subject which will allow him the detachment, the aristocratic disdain, of the artist for art's sake. He must be able uniformly to devalue his human beings and their minds to the status of indifferent material. But this material must be worth describing, or at least provide a starting point for good writing. Emma fulfilled both these conditions. And the lone success of *Madame Bovary* shows how ruthlessly Flaubert lived off Emma's particular brand of failure without giving her the least credit for being what she was. It is on this oversimplification of reality that the case for the 'immorality' of *Madame Bovary* could most properly have been made to rest. Its accusers would have seen, had they looked beyond the details, that the true case was not that Emma had been shown in a favourable light, but that no one had been shown in a favourable light; that the author's apparent objectivity was the product not of scrupulous reporting but of uniform condemnation; that the book contained no positive values, made no distinction between the intellectual and the moral, the imagination and the will; that adultery was seen as a concomitant of stupidity, and stupidity as the whole definition of human conduct. To claim that such a statement as 'Emma trouva dans l'adultère toutes les platitudes du mariage' involved a direct statement of opinion by Flaubert was an easily refuted error of reading. Yet in a wider sense it perhaps coincides with an implication of the whole book—that life itself is a platitude, an endless series of clichés. Significantly, Flaubert is unacceptable even to one of the most pessimistic of Christian critics. For Mauriac his view of men does not go beyond the ability to record 'that collection of pretensions, mannerisms and fads' which strikes us at first sight; we know the absurdities of Homais and Bournisien, but are we sure that we know Homais and Bournisien themselves? Flaubert 'thinks that

The Novel as Work of Art: 'Madame Bovary' (1857)

he is representing life, and he amputates it of everything that does not get on his nerves'. The validity of such a judgment, however, depends in part on the assumption that Flaubert's object was the representation of the whole of life as he saw it. Certainly we may regret (and this was the substance of Lawrence's criticism) that more of the depth and complexity of perception which characterize, for instance, Flaubert's correspondence, did not find expression in his creative work. But we must constantly remind ourselves that such objections to *Madame Bovary* are also a measure of its success. The sub-title, 'Moeurs de Province', suggests satire, and satire with a traditional French butt; that the novel is sufficiently large to be judged by standards with which it did not remotely aim to conform emphasizes its stature as a unique and unrepeatable work of art.

3

The Novel as Social Document: *'L'Assommoir' (1877)*

[i]

Public reaction to the French novel, especially in England, did not distinguish very clearly between the Flaubert of *Madame Bovary* and Zola. Though Zola was more often accused of open materialism both were seen as technically accomplished realists, whose moral attitudes ranged from the indifferent to the subversive. But, though Zola counted himself as Flaubert's artistic disciple, their relationship was tenuous, and the master more than once disclaimed him. The aims of the new 'naturalist' movement, which was being fathered upon him, seemed to him 'puerile' and 'monstrous'. Whereas Flaubert had used 'realism', documentation, only as a means to aesthetic ends, Zola's purpose was that of the dramatic reporter and investigator; while Flaubert was pursuing beauty, Zola, so it seemed, was pursuing scientific truth.

It is not difficult to see what Flaubert objected to in the naturalist programme, or how remote it seemed from his own. The great *Rougon-Macquart* series, to which *L'Assommoir* belongs, has as its sub-title 'Histoire Naturelle et Sociale d'une Famille sous le Second Empire'. Its declared purpose was nothing less than a scientific anatomy of a corrupt society, in which social criticism would be combined with the illustration, through several generations, of the complex, topical, but still very

The Novel as Social Document: 'L'Assommoir' (1877)

dubious 'laws' of heredity and environment. It would be difficult to exaggerate the pretentiousness of theoretical naturalism. Literature was to become a branch of science, a principal agent of positivism. Taine's dictum that virtue and vice were mere products, like sugar and vitriol, was to be taken up for examination and illustration; the Goncourts, though on the aesthetic wing of the movement, described their novel *Germinie Lacerteux* as a pathological experiment—'la clinique de l'amour'. The claim was everywhere implicit that the novelist was going to become an actual assistant of the doctor and the chemist, not a mere publicist or beneficiary of their findings. The obvious objection—that the novelist can only 'discover' in the behaviour of his characters what he has put there himself—was blandly ignored. The results of the method, applied in its purest form, are almost always artistic failure. Germinie and Zola's early heroines, Thérèse Raquin and Madeleine Férat, are all, in varying degrees, physiological monsters, their actions shored up or explained away at every point with scientific and medical commentary. They lack even the semblance of freedom which the fictional character requires in order to come to life.

But there is another side to Zola's choice of programme for his life's work; whatever his public pronouncements on the subject, all the evidence points to a more reassuring fact—that it was made with a strong sense of artistic expediency. The hereditarily depraved family represented neither an intellectual certainty nor the impulsions of a personal moral vision; rather it acted as a starting point (and something of a cover) for the radical commentator's portrayal of a decadent society. Zola remarks very calmly in his preliminary notes for the series that he must choose a 'tendency' in order to hold his work together, and that 'materialism would probably be the best' for his particular aims and talents. In short an avowed weakness in psychological invention and discrimination led Zola to the choice of violent and rough-hewn characters; and the inclinations of the impressionist, the poet of humanity in the mass, presided at the conception of his novels rather than any doctrinaire scientism. Zola's most successful novels are those where the individual is

The Novel as Social Document: 'L'Assommoir' (1877)

less important than the society, and can be seen primarily as a product of it. It is in the panoramas of working-class life that the liberal observer can feel at his most secure. Here materialism can be implicit, without being dogmatic or restrictive; in depicting a homogeneous, highly-conditioned society of victims he can stop well short of examining the individual conscience, without implying that it does not, or at least could not, exist. Thus *Germinal* has no character who is studied in his own right; it is concerned with individuals only in so far as they contribute to a portrait of the society. The structure of the novel declares this preoccupation. It starts with a long evocation of the mining country, seen through the eyes of a newcomer; and the action which follows is largely amplification, we are taken closer to the picture and shown the details. There is *variety* in the characters, but no concern for moral appraisal; in that what there is to condone appears to be condoned, and what virtue and humanity survive under such appalling conditions are held up for our wonder rather than for our admiration.

Essentially the world of *L'Assommoir* is the same sort of homogeneous, impressionistically conceived world as that of *Germinal*. Though it follows out the fate of a single character, Gervaise is not the tragic heroine chosen and set in action because she embodies some particular vision of human destiny or human nature. She is followed because she is illustrative not so much of a human or cosmic as of a social truth. She is not a tragic victim, but a casualty, in a particular milieu where the casualty rate is high. Given the world as it appears in *L'Assommoir*, we can imagine other accounts of the same field of events, taking other characters as their centre, which would be equally valid for making Zola's point, if less interesting and efficient. Gervaise's is only one of the disasters that take place in *L'Assommoir*, all of them of the same 'status'; she is an example of what is happening, less tellingly, all over the novel. The point being made is a general sociological one, Gervaise is chosen to give it undogmatic illustration. And the manner in which this is done represents perhaps the only successful conversion of the naturalist idea of 'scientific' study of the individual fate to effective creative purpose. The Goncourts' story of Germinie Lacerteux, which profoundly influenced Zola, had attempted a complete and systematic exculpation, and had inevitably foundered in medical terminology and other forms of pleading inimical to the novel. Zola is not concerned with excusing the individual or examining the question of freedom, only with dramatizing and making irrefutable a relationship—the interdependence of the individual with the forces which play on him in a particular situation. By comparison with *Germinol*, *L'Assommoir* is a fragmentary and unsystematic plea for moral relativism. Gervaise is not documented from birth to death but is introduced to us already deeply implicated in life, the victim of a violent and unhappy home and mother of two children by the age of eighteen; she is a reclaimed drinker, capable of hard work, but easy-going and a lover of pleasure. Zola sets her down to enact her fate in a society—the working world of Paris—which has precisely her own tendencies. The novel can thus succeed because it has no case to establish, no exact apportioning of responsibilities to perform. This undogmatic quality allows it to produce not a scientific account but a vast and detailed working out of a sociological proposition which is also, in this case, an uncontroversial moral tautology.

A moral tautology rather than the history of an individual fatality—this notion brings us back to something resembling the moral world of *Madame Bovary*, a world where nothing is anticipated but nothing shocks, which is presented in its apparent openness but has nothing to reveal but its own homogeneity. The purpose of *L'Assommoir* includes a much more dramatic engagement of the reader, but in a series of studies devoted chiefly to novels whose concern—however variously interpreted—is moral discrimination, it is well to emphasize the similarities of Flaubert and Zola, and their common remoteness from the English tradition. Those similarities can perhaps be seen at their clearest in *Madame Bovary* and *L'Assommoir*. Both Flaubert and Zola are committed to aesthetic principles in which there is no place for the raising of moral issues or the recognition of moral distinctions: while Flaubert's ideal novel was one which would

The Novel as Social Document: 'L'Assommoir' (1877)

be 'about nothing' Zola's was one which explained away everything; neither has any use for the distinctive 'hero'—indeed, as Zola put it himself, to 'kill the hero' was the first task of naturalism. Yet both embark, in *Madame Bovary* and *L'Assommoir*, on the scrutiny of a single character, a concern which never slackens into the purely descriptive or panoramic. In each case moral neutrality can only be secured by assimilating the main character to a homogenous world, and so confining our response to the representative rather than the individual; and in each case the character is studied with an exhaustiveness which such simple mechanics might seem hardly able to sustain. We have seen that Flaubert's solution consisted in serious, uncharged descriptive writing, whose meaning was controlled by an unemphatic but embracing satirical framework. Zola faces a similar problem of involving us dramatically in an action in which nothing is to disconcert or move us to moral reflection, of making us always acquiesce but never anticipate. The 'scientific' novelist is particularly aware of the problem of enforcing the necessity of his action without destroying its vitality. Zola remarks in his preliminary notes to the *Rougon-Macquart* series, no doubt with his early failures in mind, that he must 'stop using the word fatality' which would be 'ridiculous in ten volumes'. His task is to have resilience without suggesting responsibility, to engage the reader in the apparent autonomy of his actors while keeping him at just the right distance from the central character, making him concur in the dominant sociological perspective. Zola's solution can best be studied in what have been the most admired and the most controversial aspects of the novel—its structure and its narrative and linguistic technique. The symmetrical structure—the thirteen chapters with the great central episode of the birthday feast—have been appreciated in terms which suggest that *L'Assommoir* is a heroic commercial tragedy, a parabola of success and failure in the manner of Balzac's *Grandeur et Décadence de César Birotteau*; while the narrative technique was the subject of various dissensions over linguistic innovation and literary propriety. In fact these two features serve Zola's purpose in a much more distinctive way,

The Novel as Social Document: 'L'Assommoir' (1877)

and provide a key to an achievement no less remarkable—and no less open to attack—than Flaubert's own successful literary wager.

[ii]

The first presentation of Gervaise offers a dual and inconclusive image. Though her personal fortunes are at their lowest ebb she is by no means abandoned to despair. Her routine acceptance of misfortune, her unreflecting pursuit of her daily tasks, her physical strength and courage—all these give an impression of resilience. But at the same time we see, in suggestive impressionistic terms, that dwarfing of the individual which is to be the theme of the novel. As Gervaise waits for Lantier to come home she looks down on a sight still relatively new to her—the vast flow of workers trooping from the faubourgs into Paris; and already, in the tableau of her isolated silhouette against the unknown crowd, we get the sense of the individual only just succeeding in remaining distinct in the larger flux of life. That impression is strengthened by the ensuing scene of the fight in the wash-house, which, while it emphasizes Gervaise's courage, also prefigures much of what is to follow—with its overripe atmosphere, its vulgarity and raucousness, its incidental personal struggle overshadowed by the more permanent reality of the machine, suggesting here the grinding routine of everyday life, the basic communal struggle against dirt. As Gervaise trudges back to her room, 'derrière elle le lavoir reprenait son bruit énorme d'écluse' ('behind her the wash-house returned to its huge monotonous noise, as of a rushing weir'), and as she looks out again on the street she feels a dull fear at the sight of the two landmarks which seem to bound her life—the abattoir and the hospital. The first day recounted establishes an image of Gervaise's fate—it is a buoyant, unreflecting sortie against life, whose symbols, however, are threateningly and incontrovertibly evoked.

The dual image of the contender for mastery and the potential victim is reinforced, and remains unresolved, in the following episodes, which, while they advance the action, repeat the struc-

The Novel as Social Document: 'L'Assommoir' (1877)

tural pattern. Thus in the second chapter a 'new start' seems to have been made. The lyrical enlargement on which the previous episode closed seems to have been discounted, and with no reference to intervening hardships we have the almost idyllic scene of Gervaise and Coupeau sitting in the *assommoir* together; she now has a job, and Coupeau wants to marry her. But again the scene widens out so that the precarious security of the individual is threatened. As Gervaise prepares to involve herself with Coupeau so the implications of that involvement are impressionistically suggested by a further evocation of the constituents of 'life'. The couple sit, significantly, only just inside the sinister dram-shop, enjoying its most harmless commodity, a plum steeped in brandy; the room is almost empty. But as the lunch hour approaches the crowds flood back—'c'était un envahissement du trottoir, des ruisseaux, de la chaussée'—and the neatly contained idyll is disturbed by the arrival of Coupeau's boisterous workmates, who have come for the stronger products of the silent distilling machine at the back of the bar. As the atmosphere thickens Gervaise has to go outside to breathe. The picture of the milieu, its pressures and oppressiveness, fills out further, after the marriage has been decided, with the visit to Coupeau's relatives in the vast, pullulating tenement-house, which we see through Gervaise's eyes, and which she feels as something bearing down on her physically, 'écrasante, glaciale à ses épaules'. This time, however, she herself discounts her fears as childishness —'c'était toujours sa bête de peur, un enfantillage dont elle souriait ensuite'. We concur in the rejection of fatalism, while retaining the indication of sociological probabilities.

That rejection is apparently confirmed with the beginning of the next episode—the marriage day. We are back in the world of autonomy, the forward-looking world of routine planning: 'Gervaise ne voulait pas de noce. A quoi bon dépenser de l'argent?' While the scene is essentially pictorial, the description of a characteristic working-class celebration, it is also functional, its structure again moving from the contained, purposeful opening to a wider prospect weighted with threats of invasion and disaster. The dinner is the sort of scrappy festivity, with bad

The Novel as Social Document: 'L'Assommoir' (1877)

service, mediocre food, squabbles about the bill, which would probably be looked back on as a notable family event. But in spite of Gervaise and Coupeau some of the men start drinking and quarrelling; the party disintegrates in bad humour; and when the couple go out into the streets they are caught up in the drunken uproar of Saturday night. The episode closes on the encounter with the drunken undertaker's assistant, Bazouge, whose lugubrious imprecations frighten Gervaise and spoil for her a whole day of quiet pleasure. Again in terms at once realistic and discreetly symbolic individual enterprise is confronted with the larger and less manageable flux of life.

The opening episodes establish the pattern of action of the whole novel. Gervaise's career is not a regular curve of success and failure, but a series of discontinuous and unco-ordinated sallies against life; and her buoyancy depends in a large measure on her inability to make a synthesis, an assessment of probabilities. Thus the threatening image of the slum-house is subsequently discounted, and Gervaise brought over to Coupeau's own cheerful optimism—their greatest wish, we are told without any corrective explanation, was to get a room there. Though the fortunes of the family rise substantially the imagery remains of involvement rather than ascendancy. Indeed the normal line of the success and failure story is deliberately broken: Coupeau's accident precedes the leasing of the shop, and he is already a drinker and waster by the time the laundry establishes a moderate success. When she enters on the lease Gervaise feels she is throwing herself 'au beau milieu d'une machine en branle'; and the image is apposite. Life had threatened from outside; Gervaise, by her very enterprise, draws it closer around her. The alternation of hard work and indulgence, the constant gossip, the stench of clothes and the fumes of the stove, all these work a destructive effect on her will. The laundry, in fact, is only a variant of the *assommoir*, both toxic and anaesthetizing in its effect; Coupeau and Gervaise succumb to the composite fumes of the *quartier*, 'l'air de Paris, où il y a une vraie fumée d'eau de vie et de vin'.

The Novel as Social Document: 'L'Assommoir' (1877)

There is much more to *L'Assommoir* than the impressionistic outline, and we shall have to return to its detailed portrayal of relations, to the way in which it gives 'life' a more precise definition. But the recurrent, uncommented pattern of enterprise and engulfment, autonomy and invasion, is what gives meaning to, and makes acceptable, the positive steps in Gervaise's downfall. If we examine the presentation of her yielding to Lantier and her return to drinking spirits, we find that each occurs at the end of an episode (and at the end of a day), under conditions of fatigue and pressure amounting almost to physical vertigo. And each is superseded, and as it were ignored, by a return to the world of the practical—in the first case Maman Coupeau's illness and death, in the second the question of Nana's future. The inexorable recurrence of the pattern seems to level out the significance of the individual features, to make them mere variants, outward and not in themselves very momentous signs, of another less personal process. That process could be called organic decay. Gervaise is not seen as an individual with an unbroken moral consciousness, but rather as a willing machine, constantly restarting and redirecting itself, but gradually running down, getting worn out. 'Worn out', indeed, is the definition she finds for herself—'oui, Coupeau et Lantier l'*usaient*, c'était le mot'. For Gervaise the demands of living are so urgent that events are easily assimilated, positions hastily improvised; as action squeezes out awareness, degradation consolidates its hold, almost unfelt. The adequacy of such an account from the moral point of view remains to be discussed; from the point of view of artistic strategy we may note that it is precisely the vitality and sense of freedom which Zola gives his characters that allows him to enforce a materialistic pattern in which moral questions cease to be asked.

Since the later part of the novel relates an obviously irreversible decline it is not without its *longueurs*. But by following up the long chapter devoted to Nana we can see how the structure continues to be exploited both to animate and to neutralize the scene, to give it life and to establish a framework in which the consciences of the characters have diminished significance. At

The Novel as Social Document: 'L'Assommoir' (1877)

the end of the previous chapter Gervaise's return to drink had reduced her finally to Coupeau's own state of moral insignificance. We now turn to another part of the scene, where life is proceeding normally:

> Nana grandissait, devenait garce. . . . Oui, c'était ça, quinze ans, toutes ses dents et pas de corset. . . .

Nana's activities are not recounted merely in the interests of the novel series, in order to form a transition to the work that bears her name; their significance lies in the reactions they provoke in her parents. For Gervaise and Coupeau exercise the severest moral authority on her at a time when they themselves have forfeited all right to respect. But the account of their accompanying Nana to the workshop and making elaborate arrangements for her surveillance is related without irony. We do not feel the moralist's comparative intention; there is no attempt to use Nana's conduct in order finally to appraise Gervaise's, and Gervaise herself cannot be recalled to an appraisal of her own position. When she openly accuses Nana of selling herself she iss tunned by her daughter's retaliation—'tu as fait ce que tu as voulu, je fais ce que je veux'—and her reaction is purely physical: 'Gervaise restait toute pâle, les mains tremblantes, sans savoir ce qu'elle faisait'. And later, when the household have become resigned to Nana's delinquencies Gervaise still makes a moral restriction—Nana can do what she likes, but she musn't come home dressed in fine clothes, 'qu'elle s'habillât au moins comme une ouvrière doit s'habiller' ('she must dress at least in a way fitting for a worker'). Their attitude towards Nana is not so much a revival or survival of the Coupeaus' old *honnêteté*, as a sign of the fact that they have not fully registered their own decline. Certainly it is not conscious self-defence. In a sense they approach this episode with the same self-confidence as they have previous phases of their life. But we feel that this moral activity is growing more and more ritual and meaningless. Indeed Zola, in these last episodes, engages the reader in the same way that Flaubert engages us in Emma's death: his narrative, having finally categorized the characters, treats them without irony; and

The Novel as Social Document: 'L'Assommoir' (1877)

we give a sort of numb attention to the detail of what we know to be moral nullities. The Nana episode finally shows the interplay of character, moral conflict, the survival of virtue and conscience, as miniature and automatic features within a wider and more impersonal process. Reminders of the workings of that process may evoke sentiment, but not invite moral reflection. Thus, the precise feelings of Gervaise for Coupeau in the last stages are not investigated; but we are told that when she goes to see him in the asylum she buys a couple of oranges at the door, so as not to go in empty-handed. There is a touch of pathos in the survival of an ingrained working-class habit. But the pathos arises from a spectacle of unresolved status; it is not determined by a consideration of the state of mind of the character. Our reaction is not moral or evaluative; for this is less goodness combating life, than habit ignoring it. Gervaise's very decency is a sort of independent mechanism, a token of how little she has made a synthesis of events, of how much more powerful life is than she to control or keep up with or analyse it.

The structure of the novel, then, suggests a Gervaise acting with only apparent purposefulness inside a larger pattern of pressures and probabilities visible to the sociological observer; and eventually within a process of decay visible to all, but only sporadically to herself. But our analysis so far may have suggested a rather vague and selective impressionism, concerned to distract moral judgment in order to impose a more poetic, humanitarian interpretation of the facts. This, however, would be a completely misleading description of the texture of *L'Assommoir*. If Zola places his heroine in a wider perspective, the other characters of the novel subject her to myopic scrutiny. In few other novels do we have such a continuous impression of a life lived in the public gaze, wholly composed of fluid social relations, the subject of unrelenting moral comment and speculation. And, to see how this 'close-up' view of Gervaise both fills out and confirms the broader outline, we must turn to what is perhaps the most distinctive feature of *L'Assommoir*—its narrative technique.

The Novel as Social Document: 'L'Assommoir' (1877)

[iii]

The narrative technique, like the structure, has been widely noticed; and it brought Zola criticism from two opposing quarters. While a conservative public objected to the idiom on grounds of brutality and obscenity, Flaubert regarded the style as an artistic aberration. Zola, he said, thought that there were 'strong' words in the same way that the salon blue-stockings of the seventeenth century thought there were 'noble' ones. Zola's general apology, contained in his preface to the novel, was that he had been engaged on a scientific enterprise, 'un travail purement philologique'; in a novel about the people he had to use the language of the people. The argument, however, never went beyond a superficial level of moral and artistic propriety. As in all questions of style much larger issues are involved—and in this case the whole sense of the novel. The nature of the vocabulary is less important than the way in which it is used. For it is not only in the reporting of direct speech that the popular idiom is reproduced; it spreads to, and substantially takes over, the whole narration.

Two pairs of brief quotations, from the beginning and the later part of the novel, will serve to introduce a discussion of the style. The first pair involve Gervaise and her family. At the very beginning of the story Gervaise and her children are waiting for Lantier:

> Cependant, couchés côte à côte sur le même oreiller, les deux enfants dormaient. Claude, qui avait huit ans, ses petites mains rejetées hors de la couverture, respirait d'une haleine lente, tandis qu'Étienne, âgé de quatre ans seulement, souriait, un bras passé au cou de son frère. Lorsque le regard noyé de leur mère s'arrêta sur eux, elle eut une nouvelle crise de sanglots, elle tamponna un mouchoir sur sa bouche, pour étouffer les légers cris qui lui échappaient. Et, pieds nus, sans songer à remettre ses savates tombées, elle retourna s'accouder à la fenêtre....
>
> (The two children were fast asleep, with their heads on the same pillow. Claude, who was eight years old, drew in long breaths, his little hands outside the quilt, while Étienne, who was only four, smiled in

The Novel as Social Document: 'L'Assommoir (1877)

his sleep, one arm round the neck of his brother. As the mother's tear-filled glance rested on the children she burst out sobbing afresh, then pressed a handkerchief to her mouth to stifle the little sobs that she could not keep down. And barefooted as she was, without thinking of putting on her slippers again, she went back to her post at the window. . . .)

In the period of their decline the Coupeaus' relations with their daughter Nana are described as follows:

> Les parents avaient dû s'y accoutumer. Les roulées n'y faisaient rien. Ils la trépignaient, ce qui ne l'empêchait pas de prendre leur chez-eux comme une auberge, où l'on couchait à la semaine. Elle savait qu'elle payait son lit d'une danse, elle venait recevoir la danse, s'il y avait bénéfice pour elle. D'ailleurs, on se lasse de taper. . . . Elle rentrait, ne rentrait pas, pourvu qu'elle ne laissât pas la porte ouverte, ça suffisait. Mon Dieu! l'habitude use l'honnêteté comme autre chose.
>
> (Her parents had had to get used to it. The hidings she got made no difference to her. They gave her a good drubbing, but that did not prevent her from making use of their lodgings as a sort of inn, where one could put up by the week. She knew that she would have to pay for her bed by a thrashing, and she came and took her thrashing, when there was anything to be gained by it. And then, you get tired of dealing blows. . . . She came in or she didn't come in; as long as she didn't leave the door open it was all right. Good heavens, decency, like anything else, wears out in time.)

The second pair are descriptions of slum lodgings, respectively the room in which Gervaise had lived with Lantier and the attic to which the Coupeaus move after the ruin of the laundry:

> Et lentement, de ses yeux voilés de larmes, elle faisait le tour de la misérable chambre garnie, meublée d'une commode de noyer dont un tiroir manquait, de trois chaises de paille et d'une petite table graisseuse, sur laquelle traînait un pot à eau ébréché. On avait ajouté, pour les enfants, un lit de fer qui barrait la commode et emplissait les deux tiers de la pièce. La malle de Gervaise et de Lantier grande ouverte dans un coin, montrait ses flancs vides. . . .
>
> (And slowly, her eyes clouded with tears, she looked all round the wretched little lodging-house room, with its walnut chest of drawers in which one of the drawers was wanting, its three cane-bottom chairs, and its greasy little table on which stood a delapidated water jug. They had put in an iron bedstead for the children, which filled up two thirds of the room and blocked up the chest of drawers as well. Gervaise and

The Novel as Social Document: 'L'Assommoir' (1877)

Lantier's trunk, wide open in the corner, stretched out its empty sides. . . .)

Enfin, contre Bazouge, c'étaient les Coupeau, une chambre et un cabinet donnant sur la cour. . . . Une chambre et un cabinet, pas plus. Les Coupeau perchaient là, maintenant. Et encore la chambre était-elle large comme la main. Il fallait y faire tout, dormir, manger et le reste. Dans le cabinet, le lit de Nana tenait juste . . . et on laissait la porte ouverte pour qu'elle n'étouffât pas. . . . Le lit, la table, quatre chaises, le logement était plein.

(Then, over against Bazouge, was the Coupeaus', a room and a little room looking on the court. . . . One room and a little room, that was all. The Coupeaus had to perch there now. And the larger of the two rooms was a mere handbreadth. Everything had to be done in it. You had to sleep, eat, and all the rest. In the little room there was just space enough for Nana's bed . . . and they left the door open at night so that she shouldn't suffocate. . . . The bed, the table, four chairs; the place was quite full.)

What is striking in each case is not so much the change in what is described as the change in narrative standpoint, one might almost say in the very identity of the narrator. The earlier passages are serious and objective, perhaps even with a tendency to sentiment, the later are familiar, confidential, even amused, with no sense of tragedy and a certain moral nonchalance. The transition is significant. Clearly the events of *L'Assommoir* are not, for the most part, directly related and interpreted by the author as omniscient observer. Nor, on the other hand, do we have a purely 'dramatic' presentation, narrated by identifiable observers distinct from the author. A novel could, of course, be put together in this latter way, as a traveller might piece together recordings from a distant tribe, not in order to distinguish its individual members but to chart its beliefs and moral standards. Such a novel would in fact imitate the anthropological documentary in being willingly removed from concerns of evaluative morality. But our impression of *L'Assommoir* is of something more serious and more authoritative. Just as the structure shows the individual in a wider perspective of social and physical pressures, so the narrative form actually illustrates the proposition that the relative judgment is the only meaningful one. We are

The Novel as Social Document: 'L'Assommoir' (1877)

not just set down in the *assommoir* world to listen to the local gossip. Rather the start is in the manner of objective narration: Gervaise is the unknown heroine of a new environment, held up for our inspection and whom, it seems, we are to follow and appraise. When she has her fight in the wash-house it is remarked that she is at a disadvantage in the battle of insults, 'n'ayant pas encore le coup de gosier de Paris' ('she had not got into the Paris way of slanging'). But the burden of what follows is that she becomes so much a conditioned part of her milieu that she can only properly be described in its own colloquial terms. We get not appraisal, but the impression of a forced withdrawal from the attempt at appraisal; we witness a gradual retreat by the novelist, a handing over of his role to a succession of appropriate narrators. The novel is a dramatized admission, and demonstration, of the impossibility of an absolute moral judgment.

The stages of this process, and its precise effect on the reader, are difficult to illustrate in detail; only the broad outline can be indicated. Though the narrative begins in conventional descriptive manner, characterization is from the first built on and limited to the observable; there is no 'inside' information on Gervaise, no authoritative comment. Our picture of her is built up solely through the reactions and opinions she provokes. She is, we gradually learn from her own revelations, already deeply compromised with life; but she is primarily the newcomer to a society, about to make a new start. And it is a society for whom character is equated with performance, whose moral judgments are avowedly discontinuous, continually remodelled in the pattern of experience, expediency and oblivion. As Coupeau says when he strikes up the friendship with Lantier—if one kept grudges for nine or ten years one would end up by not talking to anybody. And as her world does not seek final moral realities, so Gervaise herself willingly disclaims any permanent moral growth—'l'expérience l'avait corrigée un peu, voilà tout'. The novel thus establishes itself as working legitimately in the realm of the provisional. For Coupeau Gervaise is 'joliment courageuse' in her struggle; after their marriage the couple become

The Novel as Social Document: 'L'Assommoir' (1877)

popular 'à cause de leur gentillesse'; and admiration for Gervaise increases when she insists on nursing Coupeau after his fall—'elle boitait, mais elle avait du chien' ('she limped, it was true, but she had guts'). Her faults too, as her prosperity increases, are noted, but generally excused:

> Elle devenait gourmande, tout le monde disait ça; mais ce n'était pas un vilain défaut, au contraire. Quand on gagne de quoi se payer de fins morceaux, n'est-ce pas? on serait bien bête de manger des pelures de pommes de terres.
>
> (She was getting fond of good things to eat; on that everyone agreed, but it was not a bad fault, quite the contrary. When you have the income to pay for delicacies it would be silly indeed to eat potato peel.)

This last judgment already points to the relative quality of Gervaise's virtue, the way in which her popularity tells us as much about her society as about herself. But a more definitive judgment does not seem to be precluded. In general the early characterization, though fragmentary and speculative, seems at any rate to admit the possibility of a synthesis, of a final portrait. The various views of her are in general clearly attributed, and—even when incorporated in it as indirect speech—remain distinct from the objective narrative. We are invited to assess their validity, to continue our *own* work of appraisal.

But quite early the distinction between narrative and reported opinion begins to be blurred. Thus maxims of common currency begin to appear in the text, without any obvious attribution. When the numbers for the wedding feast are fixed at fifteen the decision is approved by the observation that 'quand on est trop de monde, ça se termine toujours par des disputes'. Goujet's temperance is approved, but so is his refusal to condemn wine, 'car le vin est l'ami de l'ouvrier'. It is in the framework of this proverbial wisdom, the expression of a philosophy by turns realistic and fatalistic, sceptical and superstitious, moralizing and indulgent, that Gervaise's conduct is recounted and that her moral status comes to be gauged. The narrative viewpoint itself is getting imperceptibly closer, becoming inextricably identified with a sort of composite local opinion. In consequence, from

The Novel as Social Document: 'L'Assommoir' (1877)

being someone whom we are to judge *in the light of* her society's judgments, Gervaise becomes more and more a manifestation of that society, a factor in *its* characterization, a sounding-board for *its* scale of values and reactions. Not, however, exclusively: Zola's achievement is so to have evoked the homogeneity of the milieu, the necessary conditioning of all its inhabitants, that we also recognize these judgments as the only possibly valid ones; they are the nearest we can get to a true perspective. Thus we have the impression of a sharp authoritative focusing of Gervaise, the feeling that Zola has delegated the narration to the only competent observers; yet every judgment points back to the society making it, we watch the judges watching and are made conscious that judge and defendant are part of a larger organism, which is being 'studied' disinterestedly from above.

By the time the Coupeaus take their most controversial moral step—the setting up of the *ménage à trois* with Lantier—the status of the narrative has shifted to that of an anonymous, almost uniformly colloquial commentary. And the comments themselves are inconclusive, precisely because Gervaise's fate is so familiar, so typical of her world, that, though its mechanics can be endlessly annotated, judgment invariably trails off into the relative and the comparative:

> Tout ça, d'une façon comme d'une autre, ne semblait guère propre; mais il y a tant de saletés dans la vie, et de plus grosses, que les gens finissaient par trouver ce ménage à trois naturel, gentil même, car on ne s'y battait jamais et les convenances étaient gardées. Certainement, si l'on avait mis le nez dans d'autres intérieurs du quartier, on se serait empoisonné davantage.

> (All that, however you took it, hardly seemed the thing; but there are so many unpleasant things in life, and much worse than that, that the neighbours came to look on the *ménage a trois* as quite natural, quite decent even. For there were no quarrels, and propriety was never outraged. Certainly, if you were to pry into other houses in the neighbourhood, you would get some much nastier shocks.)

As the Coupeaus' decline continues judgment may get more severe, but its expression remains reluctant, the nature of its comparisons tendentious:

> Sans doute les Coupeau devaient s'en prendre à eux seuls. L'existence

The Novel as Social Document: 'L'Assommoir' (1877)

a beau être dure, on s'en tire toujours, lorsqu'on a de l'ordre et de l'économie, témoin les Lorilleux qui allongaient leurs termes régulièrement, pliés dans des morceaux de papier sales; mais ceux-là, vraiment, menaient une vie d'araignée maigre, à dégoûter du travail.

(No doubt the Coupeaus had only themselves to blame. However hard life may be you can always make your way, with order and economy, like the Lorilleux for instance, who sent in their quarter's rent punctually, folded in bits of dirty paper; but then, the Lorilleux lived like starved spiders—enough to disgust you with work.)

A last recapitulation seems to place the blame finally on the Coupeaus and to reject their fatalistic excuses:

Oui, c'était la faute du ménage, s'il dégringolait de saison en saison. Mais ce sont des choses qu'on ne dit pas, surtout quand on est dans la crotte. Ils accusaient la malchance, ils prétendaient que Dieu leur en voulait. Un vrai bousin, leur chez-eux, à cette heure.

(Yes, it was their own fault, no doubt, if they went on from bad to worse. But people don't say those things, especially when they are on their beam-ends. They declared it was their bad luck, that God had it in for them. They kicked up a regular shindy now, indoors.)

But the tone of this only serves to mark a final shift in the narrative viewpoint—from inconclusive criticism to acceptance. The Coupeaus' fall loses even its blurred moral contours, and ceases to engage the sustained interest of the *quartier*; not only for us but for them the Coupeaus become intractable to moral comment. They become, rather, local phenomena, an accepted part of the landscape, like the recumbent drunks whom the inhabitants step unthinkingly across on the pavements. They are regrettable, picturesque, sometimes pathetic, but their case is well-known and requires no explanation. The moral 'fall' moves into perspective as a striking case of the familiar social 'downfall' (*dégringolade*)—'enfin un plongeon complet'. The narrative gives up even its sporadic attempts at analysis; as the course of the action becomes more disastrous the account of it becomes, on the whole, coarser, more superficial, more familiar, more garrulous; the tone is by turns resigned, head-shaking, amused, deprecating. Now that they have been categorized the Coupeaus' behaviour is readily explicable, it is allusively referred to popular 'laws'. 'Naturel' and 'naturellement' become the recurrent

The Novel as Social Document: 'L'Assommoir' (1877)

explanatory terms: 'Naturellement on ne peut pas nocer et travailler'; 'naturellement, à mesure que la misère et la paresse entraient, la malpropreté entrait aussi'; 'naturellement, lorsqu'on se décatit à ce point, tout l'orgueil de la femme s'en va'. In the same way Lantier's progress is followed with amusement and without surprise—'enfin il n'y a que les hommes de cette espèce qui aient de la chance'—his sort have all the luck. Nana's flight causes as little impression—'dans la maison où chaque mois des filles s'envolaient comme des serins . . . l'accident des Coupeau n'étonna personne' ('in the house, from which girls flew off every month like canaries, the Coupeaus' misfortune surprised no one'). Eventually the Coupeaus become, in another characteristic phrase, something 'qu'il fallait voir'—which you ought to have seen; Gervaise's imitation of Coupeau's delirium becomes, in her last days 'une des curiosités de la maison'. So, when Bazouge finally comes to collect her, we remember that when he was summoned at the time of Maman Coupeau's death he thought, for no particular reason, that it was for Gervaise. Reasonably; for Gervaise's fate is only a foreground feature in a picture littered with death and misery—she follows Maman Coupeau, Mme Bijard, Mme Goujet, Lalie, Coupeau and Père Bru.

The insistence on naturalness alternates with other responses equally remote from moral adjudication. Thus turns in the Coupeaus' fortunes are frequently introduced by the words 'heureusement' and 'malheureusement', which suggest not appraisal but a sort of unreasoned, *ad hoc* sympathy, the subdued encouragement accorded to the losing side. Or else statements are introduced with phrases such as 'il faut dire que', 'le pis était que', 'le plus triste était', 'la vérité était', 'à la vérité'. These do not, of course, introduce the author's interpretations or corrections; indeed their recurrence suggests almost a parody of the definitive narration. Rather they are the glosses of a somewhat knowing raconteur, prompted in his reminiscences to attempt to organize and estimate what he is describing: 'Gervaise appelait ça la paillasse; mais à la vérité ça n'était qu'un tas de paille dans le coin' ('Gervaise called it the mattress, but really

The Novel as Social Document: 'L'Assommoir' (1877)

it was only a pile of straw in the corner'). The very casualness and lack of vindictiveness of the comment makes it not an arresting pointer to the state of Gervaise's consciousness, but another token of the pathetic ordinariness of the situation. To have sold the bed is 'natural', to refuse to admit it equally so— 'ce sont des choses qu'on ne dit pas, surtout quand on est dans la crotte'.

But the growing 'frivolity' of the account can only be appropriate provided that there is no suggestion that it conceals or distorts reality, that there is a 'real' Gervaise behind the seen one whose moral life would require a more serious account. Otherwise the narrative technique would be openly seen as an evasive trick to avoid facing the moral issue. In fact, however, the sardonic narrative corresponds exactly to an increasing coarseness, a decaying awareness, on the part of the characters themselves. And the expression of that correspondence finally secures Gervaise from the focus of an outside moral judgment. Not only does narrative progressively merge with local opinion; ultimately, in certain key passages, it becomes difficult to distinguish the character's reactions from the comments of the observer. When Gervaise goes to see Coupeau in the padded cell the account seems partly to reproduce her own bewildered but unsentimental impressions. But we also feel the presence of the local narrator, looking for words to describe a situation which is by no means a rarity but which one does not often see close up—'Oh! les dames enceintes faisaient bien de rester dehors! ... un drôle de démolition quand même, s'en aller en se tordant, comme une fille à qui les chatouilles font de l'effet' ('Oh! it was well that women with child were not there to see! ... a funny way to break down, wriggling about like that, like a girl who is ticklish'). The overlapping, and substantial identity, of the reactions of actor and narrator is such that Gervaise's feelings are not and cannot be examined for their dignity or adequacy; they are merged with those of her world, they acquire the atoning seal of typicality. Or rather we could say that the view of Gervaise has become so close-up that the possibility of a critical focusing is denied. Having moved nearer out of a scruple for

The Novel as Social Document: 'L'Assommoir' (1877)

justice, a respect for the relative context, the narrative standpoint is reduced to a mere acquiescence in the facts; the distance necessary for judgment has been whittled away to nothing.

By the same token Gervaise forfeits the claim to personal tragic stature. While tragedy must concern itself to a point with the consciousness of its characters, must assess their own view of their predicament, *L'Assommoir* is the story of a decaying, rather than an errant or a suffering conscience. Gervaise is only fitfully aware of her own degradation, for long periods her reactions are blunted and trivial. The final literary advantage of the narrative technique is that, relieved of the necessity of offering events for possible tragic interpretation, it can remain piquant and exhilarating in disaster. Coupeau's drinking bouts with 'ce farceur de Mes-Bottes', 'cet animal Lantier' grown fat off the two shops he has ruined, Nana's drift into prostitution, all these are the objects of racy comic observation. But the possibility of pathos is not thereby excluded. Gervaise's pathos, however, belongs strictly to her lucid intervals of reflection and reminiscence —notably in the finely sustained scene where she is reduced to soliciting; and here, quite appropriately, the narrator is, as it were, sobered into respect. But, with equal propriety, there is no attempt to make the whole cohere into a tragic portrait, because there is no continuous moral consciousness in the subject. The change of tone is no more than a change of expression on the face of the familiar spectator, to whom all is within the field of the natural, who is ready to respond to the phenomena in all their variations.

By his manner of presentation Zola avoids either judging the Coupeaus or fitting them into a dogmatic scheme of necessity. The former would infringe his theoretical, the latter destroy his artistic pretensions. It is significant that 'natural', the keyword of the movement which Zola founded, is here exploited in its colloquial, not its scientific acceptation. The Coupeaus' fate is seen as natural not in a deterministic sense, but in the light of experience, almost even of statistics. They are neither judged nor excused; they are imperceptibly demoted from the status of individual moral beings to that of sociological specimens. And if

The Novel as Social Document: 'L'Assommoir' (1877)

the stages of the process are elusive and discontinuous this only reinforces the realism of the account. It is remarked at one point that it is no longer any use treating Coupeau as a 'père sans moralité' since drink has taken away from him 'toute conscience du bien et du mal'. And this only states a fact of which we have been becoming increasingly aware as we read. There is in 'real life' a point at which the alcoholic, the criminal or the social wreck ceases to interest the moralist and engages the doctor or the sociologist; and the impossibility of fixing that point does not make the transition from one state to the other any less real; nor need it raise the problem of freedom. Zola has not explicitly denied the existence of the moral world; he has merely dramatized the transition.

[iv]

A dramatized transition—perhaps the force of the drama has failed to come over in the rather technical discussion to which Zola's own very calculated methods have led us. It may act as some sort of corrective to introduce the final part of our discussion with a fairly detailed account of one of the most famous 'set-pieces' of the novel—Gervaise's birthday feast, which occupies the whole of the central chapter. In addition to being one of Zola's most vigorous pieces of description it illustrates better than any other scene the rigorous subordination of the pictorial to the functional, and provides material for a final and more precise definition of Gervaise's fate at the hands of 'life'.

Though the birthday feast represents Gervaise's moment of triumph in the *quartier* it is in no sense the high point of a continuous curve of happiness and prosperity. The previous chapter had faded on a note of despair and disintegration, with Gervaise's discovery that Coupeau is drinking brandy—'alors elle resta toute froide; elle pensait à son mari, à Goujet, à Lantier, désespérant d'être jamais heureuse'.

The birthday episode starts, as usual, in the unreflecting world of the practical: 'La fête de Gervaise tombait le 19 juin.' And the fame of the Coupeaus' parties, from which one came away

The Novel as Social Document: 'L'Assommoir' (1877)

'ronds comme des balles' is condoned by the amused colloquial narrative. There is also explicit moral approval from Virginie:

> Lorsqu'on a un mari qui boit tout, n'est-ce pas? c'est pain bénit de ne pas laisser la maison s'en aller en liquides et de garnir d'abord l'estomac.
>
> (When a man drinks all you have it's fool's labour to let everything run away in drink, and not fill your own stomach first.)

The prospect of the feast provides an effective basis for a social *entente*. The Lorilleux agree to a reconciliation, the Boches make their peace, Maman Coupeau is good-natured and co-operative —'l'idée de la fête attendrissait tous les coeurs'. Gervaise's generosity answers a 'sacrée envie de nocer' in the whole society; her popularity is a function of its own philosophy of life. And on Gervaise's side good-nature is complemented by a desire for revenge—the Lorilleux are to be readmitted, but they are also to be 'écrasés', put to shame by the splendour of the feast. In this Maman Coupeau is Gervaise's willing accomplice, and an undercurrent of malice sustains their solidarity during the preparations.

But as soon as these start they are overshadowed by threats of disruption: Virginie reports that Lantier has reappeared in the district. Gervaise's reaction is of fatalistic self-pity:

> Que lui voulait-il donc, ce malheureux? Et justement il tombait en plein dans les préparatifs de la fête. Jamais elle n'avait eu de la chance; on ne pouvait pas lui laisser prendre un plaisir tranquillement.
>
> (What did the wretched man want of her? And just now, when she was in the midst of the preparations for the party; she had never had any luck; she couldn't even have a little pleasure in peace.)

Another incident loaded with significance, but to which Gervaise makes the stock reaction of indignation and self-pity, is the arrival of an irate customer demanding her washing. Gervaise pretends they are closed to clean the shop:

> Puis, lorsque l'autre fut partie, elle éclata en mauvaises paroles. C'est vrai, si l'on écoutait les pratiques, on ne perdrait pas même le temps de manger, on se tuerait la vie entière pour leurs beaux yeux! On n'était pas des chiens à l'attache, pourtant.
>
> (As soon as she had gone, Gervaise burst out into abusive language. If you listened to your customers, sure enough you would never have

The Novel as Social Document: 'L'Assommoir' (1877)

time to eat a mouthful; you would slave out your very life for their precious sakes! One wasn't a dog on a leash, was one?')

She plunges back with renewed enthusiasm into the preparations. When they run out of money Gervaise cannot think what to do; the pawnshop has not been mentioned since the first scene of the novel, and Maman Coupeau is the first to suggest it. Gervaise laughs at herself for not thinking of it, and even calls Maman Coupeau back to give her her wedding ring:

> Et quand maman Coupeau lui eut rapporté les vingt cinq francs, elle dansait de joie. Elle allait commander six bouteilles de vin cacheté... les Lorilleux seraient écrasés.
>
> (And when Maman Coupeau had brought back the twenty-five francs she danced for joy. She would buy six bottles of vintage wine ... the Lorilleux would be squashed flat.)

Encouraged by this prospect they complete the preparations; and the party begins with an almost ritual procession of tribute to Gervaise as the guests arrive with their potted plants. The reconciliation with the Lorilleux is ceremoniously carried out, but they have not brought any flowers, and the party spirit does not prevent Gervaise and Maman Coupeau from eagerly watching their reactions to the magnificently laid table, and making pained reflections on the existence of such people. But it is the Lorilleux who are finally condemned in an anonymous comment, which sees their resentment, characteristically, as 'natural', but blames their lack of self-restraint:

> Personne, bien sûr, n'aime à être écrasé; dans les familles surtout, quand les uns réussissent, les autres ragent, c'est naturel. Seulement on se contient, n'est-ce pas? on ne se donne pas en spectacle.
>
> (No one, certainly, likes being taken down a peg; and in a family especially, when one succeeds, the others are furious, it's natural enough. Only one keeps it in, one doesn't display it for everyone to see.)

The dinner is now ready, but again disaster threatens. Coupeau is missing, and when Gervaise, Virginie and Goujet go to look for him, they see Lantier in a restaurant. When they find Coupeau in the *assommoir* he makes a scene, refusing to be fetched home by women; and when they finally get him out he

The Novel as Social Document: 'L'Assommoir (1877)

too sees Lantier and accuses Gervaise of going out specially to attract him. And, though he calms down, the party returns less gaily than it had set out.

Gervaise's fatalistic premonitions receive further support when she finds that there are thirteen people at the table. Seeing a convenient remedy to an urgent situation she calls in from the street Père Bru, the destitute old house-painter who often comes to warm himself by her stove. Not only are their numbers made up, but they can now overeat with a good conscience. The gesture receives sentimental approbation:

> Goujet avait les yeux humides, tant il était touché. Les autres s'apitoyèrent, trouvèrent ça très bien. . . .
> (Goujet's eyes filled with tears, he was so touched. The others too were moved, thought she had done very well. . . .)

For us, Gervaise's spontaneous good nature, without being appraised, is firmly linked with the superstition and self-indulgence of her world.

The company's humour is restored, though Mme Lorilleux is not too pleased at being placed next to the grubby old worker. And another momentary annoyance, Coupeau's renewed disappearance, is swept away when he returns with a pot of flowers under each arm and embraces his wife: a touching moment which, however, is again placed firmly into naturalistic perspective by Clémence's comment:

> 'Il est très bien, M. Coupeau, ce soir,' murmura Clémence à l'oreille de Boche. 'Il a tout ce qu'il lui faut, juste assez pour être aimable.'
> ('Monsieur Coupeau's in good form tonight,' whispered Clémence in Boche's ear. 'He's had just enough to put him in good temper.')

The dinner can now begin; the past is for the moment forgotten, the future can be put out of mind. The door of the shop is closed to keep the neighbours from prying; and the establishment of harmony and domestic security is signalized by the eruption of a more healthy, everyday quarrel among the children; the courses succeed one another, the initial awkwardness of the guests wears off, the wine circulates freely. For a precarious moment they are at peace and safe from the world. They

The Novel as Social Document: 'L'Assommoir' (1877)

will remain safe only as long as the door is shut, life as it were excluded, the escapist moment judiciously prolonged. But before the giant goose is eaten the ladies complain of the heat, and Coupeau, who no longer cares what the neighbours think, throws open the door on to the street. Gervaise stuffs herself, but Goujet is still touched by her solicitude for old Bru—'dans sa gourmandise elle restait si gentille et si bonne'. The narration reflects the growing mood of harmony, vivacity and self-justification:

>Quand on y est, on y est n'est-ce pas? . . . Vrai, on voyait les bedons se gonfler à mesure. . . . La bouche ouverte, le menton barbouillé de graisse, ils avaient des faces pareilles à des derrières, et si rouges qu'on aurait dit des derrières de gens riches, crevant de prospérité. . . . Et le vin donc, mes enfants, ça coulait autour de la table comme l'eau coule à la Seine. . . . Ah! Dieu de Dieu! les jésuites avaient beau dire, le jus de la treille était tout de même une fameuse invention. . . . Avec ça que l'ouvrier, échiné, sans le sou, méprisé par les bourgeois, avaient tant de sujets de gaieté, et qu'on était bien venu de lui reprocher une cocarde de temps à autre, prise à la seule fin de voir la vie en rose.
>
>(When you're at it, you're at it eh? . . . Why, you could see the corporations getting larger every minute. . . . With their mouths open and their chins bedabbled with grease, they had faces for all the world like backsides, and so red too that you would say they were rich people's belongings, rich people bursting with prosperity. . . . And the wine too, my friends, the wine flowed around the table as water flows in the Seine. . . . Devil take it all! the Jesuits might say what they like, the fruit of the vine was a famous find all the same. . . . As if the workman, downtrodden, penniless, despised by the bourgeois as he was, had so much fun in his life that anyone had a right to complain if he got a bit boozed from time to time, for the sake of seeing things look rosy.)

Even Goujet, normally so sober, is letting himself go; Poisson proposes a toast to Gervaise, and she is loudly acclaimed. In the meantime the feast has attracted the attention of the street; a good-natured crowd assembles, and the Coupeaus' triumph is only increased as they call out to their friends and toast the passers-by.

But the unreal security is already undermined. Eating has given way to singing, but as the company join in the choruses

The Novel as Social Document: 'L'Assommoir' (1877)

Virginie, who has been out reconnoitring, comes in to warn Gervaise, not without a certain relish, that Lantier is in the area; and shortly after they see him in the crowd which has collected on the opposite pavement. The company are completely immersed in their maudlin emotion at Mme Lerat's ballad; but Coupeau, noticing Gervaise's anxiety, sees what she is looking at, and goes out to deal with Lantier. As the factitious emotion inside the shop increases Gervaise watches with real terror what is going on outside. Coupeau, struck by the fresh air, is not steady enough to fight Lantier, and after several minutes, to Gervaise's surprise, their verbal dispute begins to change tone; the insults give way to friendly banter. At length Coupeau pushes Lantier inside to join the party. The company, hardly recovered from their effusion of tears, look on curiously, but not very comprehendingly. Gervaise herself can hardly believe what has happened; and then, quite suddenly, 'elle avait trouvé ces choses *naturelles*'—just another of life's tricks. Why should she bother herself or make a scene? She welcomes the physical torpor which deadens her moral response, and her pretexts, as she words them to herself, are in harmony with the whole fatalistic and indulgent philosophy of the evening:

> L'oie la gênait un peu; elle en avait trop mangé, décidément, et ça l'empêchait de penser. Une paresse heureuse l'engourdissait. . . . Mon Dieu! à quoi bon se faire de la bile, lorsque les autres ne s'en font pas, et que les histoires paraissent s'arranger d'elles-mêmes, à la satisfaction générale . . . il n'aurait pas été convenable, bien sûr, de troubler la fin du dîner.
>
> (The goose had not quite agreed with her; she had certainly eaten too much; and it hindered her from thinking. A pleasant idleness weighed upon her. . . . Good Lord! what was the use of getting worked up when other folk didn't, and things seemed to settle down of themselves to the general satisfaction. . . . It would really have been out of place to break up the harmony of the dinner, right at the end.)

Lantier pays very little attention to her, and he is soon forgotten as Coupeau effects a return to the former atmosphere by striking up *Qué cochon d'enfant*; he adopts a rusty old woman's voice, the ladies poise their knives ready to beat time, the song

The Novel as Social Document: 'L'Assommoir' (1877)

continues 'au milieu d'une gaieté formidable'. And now the whole neighbourhood joins in:

> 'Le quartier chantait *Qué cochon d'enfant*. En face le petit horloger, les garçons épiciers, la tripière, la fruitière, allaient au refrain, en s'allongeant des claques pour rire. Vrai, la rue finissait par être saoule; rien que l'odeur qui sortait de chez les Coupeau faisait festonner les gens sur les trottoirs. Il faut dire qu'à cette heure ils étaient joliment saouls là-dedans. Ça grandissait petit à petit, depuis le premier coup de vin pur, après le potage. A présent c'était le bouquet, tous braillant, tous éclatant de nourriture, dans la buée rousse des deux lampes qui charbonnaient. La clameur de cette rigolade couvrait le roulement des dernières voitures. . . . Coupeau était à ce couplet:
>
> L'dimanche à la P'tit'-Villette,
> Après la chaleur . . .
>
> Alors la maison craqua, un tel gueulement monta dans l'air tiède de la nuit que ces gueulards-là s'applaudirent eux-mêmes, car il ne fallait pas espérer de gueuler plus fort.
>
> (The whole street now joined in *Qué cochon d'enfant*. Across the road the little watchmaker, the grocer's boys, the tripe-seller, the fruiterer, all took up the refrain, slapping themselves in chorus. The whole street seemed to be drunk—the very smell of the feast had set them reeling. And it must be said that the party itself was by this time awfully boozed. It had come on little by little, from the first glass of wine after the soup to now, the finishing touch, when they all bawled together, all crammed with food, in the reddish haze of the two smoking lamps. The immense jollity deadened the very sound of the last vehicles passing in the street. . . . Coupeau was at this verse:
>
> L'dimanche à la P'tit'-Villette
> Après la chaleur . . .
>
> At that they fairly raised the roof, and so loud a burst of voices went up into the warm air of the night that these roisterers fell to applauding themselves, feeling that it was an effort impossible to beat.)

On this climax the scene fades out. The last paragraph is a postscript: nobody ever managed to remember exactly how the feast ended, but the next day there are some embarrassed attempts at self-justification, and all are able to concur in condemning Clémence, 'une fille à ne pas inviter, décidément', who had finished by showing 'tout ce qu'elle possédait' and being sick over the muslin curtains. The men, at least, had gone out in the

The Novel as Social Document: 'L'Assommoir' (1877)

street, while Virginie had lain down just for a moment, to guard against any consequences. We hear nothing of Gervaise's excuses, and her memories are very vague; she seems to remember Goujet sobbing as he left, and Lantier must have stayed to the end; at one moment she had felt a warm breath in her hair—'mais elle ne savait pas si ce souffle venait de Lantier ou de la nuit chaude'.

The next chapter opens in the usual meticulously circumstantial way, but for the first time it does not focus Gervaise's enterprise:

> Le samedi suivant, Coupeau, qui n'était pas rentré dîner, amena Lantier vers dix heures. . . .

It ends with Gervaise, now a resigned physical victim, being pushed towards Lantier's bed, while Coupeau, disgusting and insensible on the floor, 'roulé dans son vomissement', blocks the way to her own.

Clearly the episode is in no sense gratuitous description, since it prepares and enacts a critical incident in Gervaise's fortunes. The structural pattern of previous episodes is repeated, and for the first time with decisive effect. The disastrous infiltration of Lantier takes place at a moment when individual consciousness and power of decision are in abeyance, anaesthetized by the pressure of the milieu; whereas the sober wedding feast ended with Gervaise brought up against the symbols of disaster she is now, literally, invaded by them. The particular quality of this scene is to define more precisely and realistically the nature of this individual helplessness, without sacrificing impressionistic and representative power. Certainly it has that power—in a sense it could be said to be a final image of Gervaise's life, to sum up the fruitless struggle for happiness and success in which she is engaged, to define the terms and narrow limits in which they are possible. The very 'detachability' of the episode is significant. It is a 'set piece', but only in the sense that every episode in Gervaise's life is a set piece, an attempt to carve out an improvised happiness in the face of all the evidence. It supersedes a moment

The Novel as Social Document: 'L'Assommoir' (1877)

of despair. It is conceived in a mood of resigned self-indulgence. From its very beginnings it is threatened with disaster. It establishes a moment of precarious success, but a success founded on rough-and-ready or impermanent bases—the Lorilleux' greed, Coupeau's propitious dose of alcohol, the general desire to shut out realities; the moment is achieved only by calling on all the resources of the society, exploiting all its most dangerous virtues. And as soon as it is achieved it begins to be undermined: the opening of the doors marks the reassertion of life, the situation passes out of Gervaise's control, personal responsibility and identity dissolve in a haze of fatigue, intoxication and confusion.

The recurrent structure is consummately exploited here: viewed in one light the feast seems a splendid gesture of resilience, a come-back against despair, which ends in unforeseeable disaster; another example of the relentless processes of life which cheat and by-pass the individual will. But the detailed working out of the scene defines the nature of 'life', as well as evoking its movement. The action is rigorously realistic; the dramatic enlargement itself is generated from within—it is alcoholic, rather than lyrical or tragic. And 'life' is not some mysteriously compulsive pressure outside Gervaise, which can only be understood in symbolic terms. Rather here it is little more than the sum of interacting personal weaknesses, which may or may not have a remoter social cause. The very harmony which the idea of the dinner provokes, the conspiratorial escapism, make it a characteristic and conscious gesture of an organically decayed society. And Gervaise in freely proposing it is seen to be a typical constituent part of the organism that destroys her. Her enterprise is a product, not a transcendence of her social condition, her very ability to conceive and manage the dinner is a token of potential disaster.

Gervaise's inherent weaknesses exactly dovetail with the debilitating influences of her society; and both her popularity and her decline are seen as almost automatic functions of that correspondence. Thus even in this scene of triumph and disaster it is clearly enforced that Gervaise has no *moral* ascendancy over her world; indeed the feast presents a uniformly low moral tone, in

The Novel as Social Document: 'L'Assommoir' (1877)

which Gervaise is scrupulously included. No one is swayed or 'reformed' by Gervaise, and she herself is seen to be made of exactly the same sort of stuff as her fellows. Not only in the case of Coupeau's *bonhomie* is the idealistic and sentimental interpretation discounted; Goujet's view of Gervaise is also implicitly corrected. Gervaise is successively grouped with various characters to point what she shares with them of malice, extravagance, complacency and superstition. In this scene, more strongly than anywhere else in the novel, we have the impression of urban humanity not as a collection of individuals, but as a pool of highly-conditioned materials merely made up in different permutations; the particular blend which constitutes Gervaise happens to be the 'recipe' both for popularity and defeat. An intimate, almost mechanical connection between the two is strongly suggested in visual terms—the same door which serves to publicize Gervaise's triumph to the *quartier* also serves to admit Lantier. So that if the absolute of goodness is demoted into the relative of popularity, the absolute of responsibility is also attenuated. Since Gervaise is called on to act as an individual at a moment when the society are as one man, responsibility radiates out on to them. The postscript is perhaps intended as a last reminder of the moral homogeneity of the society. All the members of the party feel the need to justify themselves, to claim that they remained responsible, retained their individual identity throughout. And the fact that these claims are so obviously invalid stresses the primacy of the group as the irresponsible unit. Their life, in a less spectacular way than the dinner, is a moral orgy from which each saves what face and stature he can; Gervaise's being posed a specific moral problem is an incidental—and representative—piece of bad luck.

[v]

'A totally represented world ... a world practically workable with every part as functional as every other, and with the parts all chosen for direct mutual aid.' Henry James's description of Zola's achievement stresses the density of the realism, the feeling we have of having covered all the ground, of having had the whole subject revealed to us in all its scenic and personal detail. But 'direct mutual aid' also provides an unexpectedly appropriate definition of the moral interdependence, the spreading of the moral burden, which we have seen as characterizing the presentation of Gervaise and her society. And it points to an intimate connection between the aesthetic aim of making the whole take shape from the parts, and the moral implication that the parts can be finally explained in terms of the whole. James goes on to describe the profuseness of the social evocation as 'perpetually delaying access to the private world, the world of the individual'. That limitation, though of little importance in novels whose chief purpose is panoramic, assumes greater significance in *L'Assommoir*, where an individual fate is the centre of interest. And the 'delay' is made more striking by the fact that there is some appearance of expedition. Zola seems to want to get at the 'truth' by every available means, the whole air of the novel is serious, comprehensive, authentic. But every approach to Gervaise, as we have seen, dissolves as if inevitably into the relative and inconclusive. The moral objector might assert that Zola, having promised us the scientific truth in all its complexity, restricts himself to means which effectually stop him providing it; that he has merely simplified his world in such a way that he can remain on the surface without appearing superficial.

To such a critic the technical accomplishment of the book would seem a distortion of reality, a concealing of what he most wants to know. The aesthetic impact of the novel's structure is to convey the all-absorbing demands of living, to present Gervaise in her resilience, to temper her irresponsibility by denying her leisure for self-inspection. And, though this may be a legitimate image of working life, it does remain a telescoping of the real, where the margin for reflection, however diminished, is never completely negligible. Moreover, when it *is* studied, the personal consciousness still appears in such a way as to make a moral discrimination impossible; and it would be possible to see this presentation as something of a technical sleight of hand.

The Novel as Social Document: 'L'Assommoir' (1877)

There is every appearance, in the close scrutiny applied to Gervaise, that her state of mind, her moral stature, are being made the object of critical study. At every moment, for instance, we are reminded of the difference between statement and truth. Thus Gervaise's fatalism and rationalizations about her conduct are not meant to be accepted at their face value; we are not called on (to return to the birthday scene) to believe that what she had to eat *really* prevented her from thinking, or that God was *really* against her. But the possible lines of inquiry which such a self-deception offers are not followed up; in fact all we are allowed to feel about it is its 'typicality'. What Zola does is to give a scrupulous appearance of discounting individual illusions, but only to make way for a broader sociological interpretation which, by implication, substantially repeats the characters' self-deceiving claims. 'Qui dit psychologue', declares Sandoz, Zola's mouthpiece in *L'Oeuvre*, 'dit traître à la vérité.' But here the rejection of analysis is conveniently extended to the presumption that the individual conscience has nothing individual to reveal, its expressions are only significant as elements in the characterization of a larger unit. Looking back on *L'Assommoir* we are certainly aware of a spiritual homogeneity in excess of what strict realism would allow. It is a world, for instance, where no one is misunderstood and no one shocked, a world full of scandal but devoid of mystery. And the reason for the uniformity of this world, and the apparent completeness of our knowledge of it, is that every one in it has the same sort of mental life; each is placed equally distant, in conformity with a sociological axiom, from self-knowledge and truth. In a different cause from Flaubert, but with some of the same results, Zola too forbids his characters to stray beyond the bounds of the cliché. In such a world attention is easily diverted from questions of personal responsibility to considerations of typicality, without the issue of freedom being specifically faced.

Zola might retort that such criticism was largely irrelevant, since his aim was not a study of freedom and responsibility but an urgent social portrait, which justified and acknowledged the 'delay in access to the private'. He is not proposing the philo-

The Novel as Social Document: 'L'Assommoir' (1877)

sophical: 'This had to be'; but the sociological: 'This was, and the measure in which it was typical is its most important aspect.' Zola was much concerned to reject the generalizing speculation which *L'Assommoir* provoked, and in his preface he answers, rather inconsequentially, the many critics who had complained that he was betraying the working-class movement by his uniformly unflattering portrayal:

> It is a work of truth, the first novel with a real tang of the people. And it must not be concluded that the people as a whole are bad, for my characters are not bad, they are only ignorant and corrupted by the atmosphere of hard work and misery in which they live.

But the charge of materialism arises precisely out of the invitation which a work makes to generalization. And in this sense the predicament of the naturalist is that the more accomplished his artistic achievement, the more immoral its implications can be held to be. Thus it is the very congruity of Gervaise with the world she lives in which permits the symmetry, the undogmatic assurance and dramatic power of the birthday scene; but the choice of the easily movable object to meet the barely resistible force is hardly a very searching way of 'studying' the complex question of the interaction of personal and social forces. In this respect the realist (like the popular newspapers today) could be held accountable not only for his presentation of events, but also for his choice of materials. 'On what authority', asked James of *Nana*, 'does M. Zola present nature to us as a combination of the cesspool and the house of prostitution? On the authority of his predilections alone.' After the play he had made of the scientific basis of his works Zola could hardly be surprised if their content was seen as the description of 'nature' and not as historical symbolism or political satire.

But the fact that the artist in Zola appealed against the implications of his own scientific theory is itself significant; and our final impression of him is not of the militant materialist. His best novels are completely undogmatic, their morality is the preliminary humanitarian morality of the liberal reporter; and his rejection of 'psychology' is so clearly seen to be a function of an artistic weakness that it has little power to harm. When carried

The Novel as Social Document: 'L'Assommoir' (1877)

to excess the 'physiological' approach always defeated itself: thus *La Bête Humaine* strikes us not as a complacent demonstration of the necessary depravity of railway workers, but as an improbable horror story against a superbly evoked background for which it is largely a pretext. When *L'Assommoir* appeared Edmond Goncourt welcomed it as carrying on the 'clinical' work that he and his brother had started in *Germinie Lacerteux*. But he said that the battle for scientific modernity in the novel was only just starting: only when the method had been applied to every human species and every stratum of society would victory be achieved. That would, indeed, involve a definition not only of 'the people as a whole', but of human nature. Zola may have started with that ambition—and certainly *L'Assommoir* is still a by-product of comprehensive scientific intentions; but perhaps he is better described by his own words in the preface to the work, where he protests that he is not 'the brutal novelist, the gorger of blood', but 'a worthy bourgeois, a studious artist keeping quietly to himself, and whose one ambition is to leave behind him as broad and living a work as he can'. 'Large et vivant' describes *L'Assommoir* more nearly than the abstract labels of materialist or determinist; like *Madame Bovary* it is the supreme product of an aesthetic which proved to have strictly limited potentialities.

4

The Case of 'Esther Waters' (1894)

[i]

One is made aware by certain passages that Mr. Moore would fain imitate the methods of Zola and his odious school, but two obstacles are in his path, the faith of a Christian and the instincts of a gentleman; the author recognises and respects goodness, purity and disinterestedness, and if M. Zola or any of the hogs of his sty could write such an episode as that with which the story opens, the work-girl's sacrifice for the penniless artist, one would have as much hope for their future as for that of Mr. Moore.

It was with these words that the *Spectator* received George Moore's first novel, *A Modern Lover*. And though few readers today would claim that he fulfilled the *Spectator*'s hopes we have nevertheless, for various reasons, considered his best-known work as worthy of a full-length study.

Esther Waters does not approach in stature the other novels examined in this book; its interest is primarily that of a literary 'case'. Moore was an avowedly imitative writer, and looked to France for his models. Having first aimed to be 'Zola's ricochet in England', 'a dagger in the heart of the sentimental school', he was won over to the pursuit of formal beauty and became equally vocal in his enthusiasm for Flaubert; while Zola is dismissed as lacking in style, 'his very name is tawdry'. *Esther Waters* is, among other things, the product of a rather uncertain and incomplete change of direction; and purely as an instrument of comparison it is interesting for the way in which it throws into

The Case of 'Esther Waters' (1894)

relief the achievement of the great French writers. Because the work of Flaubert and Zola must be described so largely in terms of technique, discussion tends to be restrictive in tone, to suggest, even when praising, that it is all 'only' a triumph of professional artistry. The example of Moore at least serves to show up in a more positive light how consummately the French writers understood their art, how precise and exacting were their formulae—and also how irrelevant any sort of criticism must be which suggests that their novels would be the better for an injection of the English literary virtues.

For *Esther Waters* is also significant for the measure in which it is a native product. Its sub-title is 'An English Story', and the admirer of France thought of himself also as a successor to George Eliot and an easy superior to Hardy. Moore's example reminds us that, though the English novel learnt much from the French in terms of technical rigour and impersonality, their paths never really converged. Though he described his literary evolution in terms of allegiance to various French writers his very waverings of taste suggest a dissatisfaction, prompted in its turn by the weight of a completely different tradition. It was not only the *Spectator* which found Zola uncongenial; and *Esther Waters* testifies to the fact that, for the English novelist—even the Francophile—with a long tradition of ethical preoccupation behind him, both the novel of social degradation and the novel of pure art seemed from the first a limited and unpromising field. Moore's attempt to find a way out resulted in a blending of the naturalistic, the formally artistic and the ethical—a predictable but unhappy combination.

However it must also be said that Moore's ethical concerns did not take him far from the Francophile world of 'art'; they reflect in the main certain attitudes and interests of the loosely defined English 'aesthetic' movement which reached its height in the nineties. Despite the *Spectator*'s diagnosis of his basic decency Moore was not a Christian, nor perhaps, by some standards, a gentleman. And like that of Wilde (though the two had little personal sympathy for one another), his interest in ethical and social problems existed primarily at the level of the iconoclastic and the paradoxical—the only possible public attitude in a movement which prided itself on its indifference to morality. But this in itself gives the novel an added claim to our attention. No account of changes in moral sensibility in the last hundred years is complete without some mention of the 'nineties', which, in spite of their many absurdities and the relative sparseness of their artistic achievement, nevertheless played an important part in the change from Victorian to modern ideas, and hence from Victorian to modern artistic preoccupations.

It is therefore a triple aim which guides the following study: to analyse a curious literary hybrid; to illustrate the scope and the limits of French influence on the English novel; and to recall a neglected but important phase in the transition from nineteenth- to twentieth-century social and artistic attitudes. It is hoped that *Esther Waters*, viewed in these various lights, will be thought to deserve the title—rather too freely conferred by literary historians—of an 'interesting failure'.

The plot of the novel is perhaps worth setting out in some detail:

When the story opens Esther is emerging from a hard youth with a drunken stepfather and numerous brothers and sisters; she has not, however, had a completely careless upbringing, as her mother belongs to the Plymouth Brethren and she herself has been brought up as a devout member of the sect. She goes to work at Woodview, a country house where racehorses are trained, and where the lives of everyone revolve around riding and gambling; the one exception in this household is its mistress, who also turns out to be a Plymouth sister and who takes an interest in Esther and tries to teach her to read. Esther however makes little progress and is soon seduced, on promise of marriage when his winnings improve, by the cook's son, William Latch, whose aspiration is to escape from menial employment and become a bookmaker and publican. Esther now suffers a violent access of pride, virtue and temper, with the result that William drifts away from her and elopes with Peggy, one of the young ladies of the house. Esther discovers that she is pregnant and is dismissed with a good character: 'Mrs. Barfield . . . paused at the word reliable, and wrote instead: "I believe her to be at heart a thoroughly religious girl."' We then follow her through her confinement and the hardships of domestic

The Case of 'Esther Waters' (1894)

service, watch her dismiss with horror the usual offer to let her child die quietly away in the 'baby-farms', and eventually see her reach comparative security as the servant of Miss Rice, a gentle and understanding (though agnostic) women's novelist. She considers marriage with Fred Parsons, an evangelical stationer's clerk, who takes her back to the brethren, but William meets her by chance and survives her initial indignation. For the sake of the child, and with her mistress's encouragement, she goes to live with him, so that he can get a divorce from the worthless Peggy, who has separated from him after a childless marriage. William has become rich through bookmaking and they settle down to run a pub in Soho. After several years of comparative happiness things begin to turn against them. Their house gets a reputation for demoralizing the whole district; children pawn their parents' property, one of the customers commits suicide on the premises, Sarah, who had been a fellow-servant at Woodview, steals from her employers to place a bet for her lover. After warnings from Fred and the Salvation Army they are fined for their betting activities and finally lose their licence. William contracts tuberculosis by going to the races in all weathers and dies repentant of the evils of gambling, and Esther, after further hardships, goes back to her first employer, herself now alone at Woodview, the only survivor of a family ruined by racing. The novel ends with Esther presenting her son, now a fine soldier, to Mrs. Barfield.

This outline already points to affinities with the French naturalist novel; there is, for instance, an obvious parallel between the Latches' pub and the *assommoir*, each at once the symbol and the agent of demoralization. The obvious peculiarity of *Esther Waters* is that it is also a success story. Esther is both victim and victor, and the disparate approaches involved in such a presentation constitute a positive reason for the novel's failure. This is not, of course, to maintain that the novel fails primarily because it breaks the rules. Failure in itself requires no technical explanation—just as consistency and coherence can never make up for a lack of creative power. But though Moore's work might be rejected on more fundamental grounds this does not mean that structural analysis is irrelevant, the mere description of a failure within a failure. The imaginative and the technical are interdependent, in that creative poverty both promotes, and is aggravated by, theoretical 'misunderstandings'; and that relationship is demonstrable in Moore's case. Nevertheless it seems

The Case of 'Esther Waters' (1894)

advisable to preface the rather scientific account which follows with a note of reservation: what is attempted is a description using certain literary parallels, and not a diagnosis of a sick novel assuming the possibility of an ideal state of health.

A look at the opening episode of Esther's fall will both give an idea of the texture of the novel and illustrate the duality which runs right through it. Esther's disaster is prepared in terms of an insidious—and inevitable—contamination by the society she lives in; and it is repeatedly implied that however strong the character, however repellent the example, our lives, and particularly the woman's life, the servant's life, are circumscribed by our 'lot'. The ruling mood, not only in the action but in the most casual asides, is that 'life'—the pressures of instinct, society, circumstance—works irresistibly on the individual and provides an almost complete definition of his conduct. The themes of general depravity, social necessity and Esther's own contamination are woven together in exchanges of the calibre of this one— Esther is listening to the cook's account of how the butler misled those who tried to get stable information from him, and how a man committed suicide after putting all his money on a horse that didn't even start:

> 'John Randal has that man's death on his conscience. But his conscience don't trouble him much; if it did he'd be in his grave long ago. Lies, lies, nothing but lies. But I dare say I'm too hard on him; isn't lies our natural lot? What is servants for but to lie when it's in their masters' interests, and to be a confidential servant is to be the prince of liars!'
>
> 'Perhaps he didn't know the 'orse was scratched.'
>
> 'I see you're falling in nicely with the lingo of the trade.'
>
> 'Oh', replied Esther smiling, 'you never hears anything else; you pick it up without knowing.'

William increases the the pressure of the milieu by inviting her to go to the pleasure gardens with him:

> 'You've never been to those Gardens, have you? Dance-hall, theatre, sorcerers, every blessed thing. But you're that religious, I suppose you wouldn't come?'
>
> 'It's only the way you're brought up.'
>
> 'Well, will you come?'
>
> 'I don't really think I should like those gardens. But I dare say they

The Case of 'Esther Waters' (1894)

are no worse than any other place. I've heard so much since I was here that really....'
'That really what?'
'That sometimes it don't seem much good to be too particular.'
'Of course not—all rot. Well, will you come next Sunday?'
'Certainly not on Sunday.'

He next tempts her to join in a sweepstake, and again social pressure and a 'sudden impulse to oblige him' overcome her scruples, and 'before she had time to think' she had put her hand in the hat and taken a number:

'So they've gained you round to their way of thinking', said Mrs. Latch straightening her back.
'I know very well indeed that it's not right to bet; but what can a girl do? If it hadn't been for William I never would have taken a number in the sweepstakes.'
'Do you like him very much then?'
'He's been very kind to me—he was kind when....'
'Yes, I know, when I wasn't.'

The life of pleasure goes on from the sweep to the ball to evenings in the fields:

.... listening to the sheep bells tinkling they often lay together talking of love and marriage, till one evening, putting his pipe aside, William threw his arm around her whispering that she was his wife. The words were delicious in her fainting ears. She could not put him away, though she knew her fate depended on her resistance, and swooning away she awakened in pain....

The world has taken its toll—and Esther, though she accepts responsibility, recognizes the nature of the process in her confession to her mistress. Her will is being corroded from without—'... I shouldn't have touched the second glass of ale.'

This is the world and these are the processes of the naturalist novel. But already the explicit insistence on the defeat of character by life points to a difference—and a flaw. Esther's conduct is expressed in terms of conflict and paradox, and 'life' is merely the opposite of what one would expect from her character, of what she thinks right, of what she had intended to do. For Esther is not a passive figure, a blank sheet ready to be written on by life; she also has a *positive* character, described in static

The Case of 'Esther Waters' (1894)

terms and conceived of as a constant; and it is one which seems to offer a singularly unpromising target for 'life'. She is proud, strong-willed, puritanical, and 'that religious' that we might be surprised at her rather routine fall, were it not for the tendentious commentary which prepares and accompanies it. That commentary, which includes Esther's own remarks, is both necessary to the novel's intelligibility and a token of its certain failure.

At this stage the extreme contrast between known character and behaviour need not in itself be disastrous—what would be easily credible in real life is at least acceptable in fiction. But if the artist uses paradox he must know and demonstrate what purpose it is to serve. Esther, the strong girl who acted 'against her will', the puritan who felt 'a sense of liberation' in her new home but 'returned to her true self' when she saw one of her fellow servants drunk, presents urgent logical as well as pyschological problems. The choice has to be made between autonomy and necessity, between character and life. If 'life' is pursued 'character' must be dropped, or rather it must be allowed that character has no meaning unless it can be constantly redefined in terms of behaviour; you cannot be theoretically strong and weak on each particular occasion. If, on the other hand, 'character' is to take over then Esther's fall—the victory of life—becomes an isolated oddity, telling us nothing of significance about Esther or the world in which she operates; it becomes a mere premiss, a contrivance to get her into the field. Either course, rigorously pursued, would to some extent discredit the presentation of the opening episode: the former would show the reference to Esther's 'true self' to be premature and misleading; the latter would make the cumbrous naturalistic mechanism seem, in retrospect, singularly out of place, like an important character in a drama whom the author forgets to bring back after the first act. A single act of violence (such as happens to Tess) would have been a less disconcerting way of launching the good girl into the world of social injustice. What in fact happens is that having set himself the problem Moore continues to evade it, and to run the two themes independently, extracting as much

The Case of 'Esther Waters' (1894)

as he can from each. It is in the central episode of the novel—the rejection of Fred for William—that the breakdown becomes overt and complete.

The second section of the book, describing Esther's years of struggle as a domestic servant, belongs entirely to the world of character and personal responsibility. It is an edifying account of the triumph of devotion and hard work over cruelty and injustice. Esther's virtue has its reward in the stability of her post with Miss Rice, and it is at this point that the chance meeting with William takes place. She immediately interprets it as a symbol of her defeat by life, the last straw which crushes her in her precarious struggle for survival. And the naturalistic language is brought out again to enforce this interpretation:

> Never had she felt more certain that misfortune was inherent in her life, and remembering all the trouble she had had she wondered how she had come through it alive; and now just as she seemed like settling down everything was to be upset again.

The language of the victim of life rings completely false, and shows up decisively the moral discontinuity of the novel. For the incident to make any sense Esther must be, as Gervaise always is, near a moral and physical breaking point. But Esther's experiences, if they have tired the body, have left the will unimpaired. In fact they have served to strengthen and confirm her original character. Every episode—the baby-farmer's offer, the dispersal of her family, the injustices of her various employers—roots her deeper in her determination to keep straight and succeed in her task of bringing up her son. She has no temptations, no irrational fears, no suppressed physical desires, she has a pleasant job and a prospect of marriage with a man of her own religion who has forgiven her past. She would appear to be very well equipped to deal with William's importunities. But Esther is completely overwhelmed, and her crisis is expressed, suggestively, in terms of the contrast between her two suitors:

> William's great square shoulders had come between her and this meagre little man. She sighed and felt once again that her will was overborne by a force she could not understand or control . . . she was overwhelmed by a sense of sorrow which she could not understand,

and she was aware that life was proving too strong for her, that she could make nothing of it, and it seemed to her that she didn't care much what happened to her. She hadn't even the strength for blame, and merely wondered why she had let William kiss her.

Fred understandably thinks this force is something very simple:

'You're in love with this man, though you may not know it, and you've invented this story as a pretext to overthrow me.'

Esther's thoughts roam along similar lines:

. . . if she were to marry William she would go to the King's Head to stand behind the bar and serve the customers. She had never seen much of life; and felt somehow that she would like to see a little life; there would not be much life in the cottage at Mortlake; nothing but the prayer-meeting. She stopped thinking, for she'd never thought like that before, and it seemed *as if some other woman she hardly knew was thinking for her.*

But having led us up to the brink of a naturalistic interpretation with almost wilful explicitness Moore pulls us back at the last moment from the logical conclusion; Esther's integrity is saved, her rejection of the 'other woman's' thoughts as alien to her is confirmed. And it is the virtuous Esther, the 'true self', who, in the face of all the evidence (including the caricatural description of Fred), is deemed to be acting here. No wonder that a direct editorial intervention is necessary to make it clear: 'Her sincerity was unmistakable and Fred doubted her no longer.'

Esther, then, freely chooses to go back to William, arguing that he will settle money on her child, whereas Fred, despite all his protestations and his exemplary character, might turn against him if they ever had children of their own. At the same time the naturalistic constituents have not been assembled merely in order to be discounted—they are enrolled to add to Esther's pathos and confusion, so that in defiance of logic she is seen both as lucidly choosing and inevitably succumbing. 'Fred, I can't help myself —can't you see that. Don't make it harder for me by talking like that' is her truculent reply to her fiancé's objections; while to Miss Rice she explains that though 'it don't look right to go and live with a married man' she is only doing it 'because it seems for the best'. In his need to explain Esther's behaviour and preserve

The Case of 'Esther Waters' (1894)

the consistency of her character Moore invokes the 'overwhelming force' but must reject any definition of its components. The definition (partly offered by Fred) would include, in indistinguishable combination, love, the relaxation of the will, a materialism produced by long hardship, the natural desire for something new after years of monotony; it would also include the expression as a duty of what is really a covert desire. But this would presuppose an interaction between character and life such as has nowhere been shown in the novel; Moore at this stage has little option but to sustain the glaring paradox, and this he does to the end. The last section of the book moves back to the world of character; Esther's integrity is ensured by the re-definition of her duty to include the selfless care of her husband. Like her position as an unmarried mother her position as the wife of a betting man becomes a mere oddity, a premiss, a change of scenery for her virtue. She continues, from the vantage point of her principles, to register fitful protests against gambling, but the contradictions of her situation make no moral impact on her, they serve only to confirm her belief that our destinies are beyond our control:

'... I suppose this betting and drinking will always seem to me sinful and wicked. I should 'ave liked a quite different life. But we don't choose our lives, we just makes the best of them. You was the father of my child, and it all dates from that.'

In short Esther's religion guarantees her virtue, while 'life' accounts for the shady places in which she has to practise it and her apparent insensitivity to moral issues. It is only a final token of the unreality of Esther's conflict with life that she returns to Mrs. Barfield almost the same person as when she first arrived at Woodview as a girl:

Esther was stouter and her face kept that look of blunt honest nature which had always been her charm in years gone by, and was attractive in the thick-set working woman of forty, who stood holding the hem of her skirt in her rough hands.

She has worn well because, if life has been hard, her author has treated her delicately. Esther is innocent because with two strings to her bow she has never been in a position to be guilty—and the good woman's duties have been defined in such a way that it was impossible for her to fail.

[ii]

Such an outline account does not of course characterize the novel fully; *Esther Waters* like *L'Assommoir* is a social portrait as well as an individual drama, and it would require further illustration and analysis to show how Moore's evocation of 'low life' compares with Zola's. Our account has tried to show the basic contradiction of the work. The décor of the naturalist novel is there, more or less vividly described—the scenes of hardship, the seediness and corruption of working life, the drinking and betting and their attendant tragedies; but these cannot be harnessed directly to the theme of Esther's personal fate because Moore no longer wants to face the full rigour of the naturalist equation. *L'Assommoir* illustrates that equation in its greatest purity. Here 'character' and 'life', in the sense in which we have used the terms, are not in conflict but merely aspects of the same thing, interchangeable ways of talking about the world as it is. Life's victory is Gervaise's defeat; internal weakness and external pressure are exactly complementary, or rather they provide definitions of one another. Zola's triumph is to have dovetailed the two elements so perfectly that we are never tempted to seek the join; to talk about Gervaise doing something against her will is to make a dubious linguistic usage more than usually meaningless. The naturalistic scheme eliminates the notion of the autonomous will; action alone defines will, and weakness is not a psychological concept but a descriptive term for those who have been beaten by life.

The technical corollary to Gervaise's passivity is the absence of any description of mental conflict. Zola's is a purely surface presentation, materialistic in that Gervaise's moral and physical lives are not distinguished, her moral defeats are mere variants of physical capitulation. He is not concerned with analysis— 'Qui dit psychologue dit traître à la vérité'—and the novel of

The Case of 'Esther Waters' (1894)

defeat offers him no temptation to indulge in it. *Esther Waters* demonstrates that even the mention of mental processes is inimical to a naturalistic effect. When Moore tells us that Esther acted 'before she knew what she was doing' or 'on a sudden impulse' he is directing us to that very no-man's-land between freedom and necessity which the naturalist should narrow away to nothing. The conflict between character and life means that the novel must lean heavily on such statements; and apart from these glosses on motivation the naturalistic tone is established largely through Esther's own feelings and appraisals. While Moore extols her character she herself must be responsible for presenting her quality of victim. Again we see that the formula of *L'Assommoir* cannot be successfully modified. Since the inevitability of Gervaise's fate is not a matter of psychological adjudication her own words and feelings do not play any vital role in indicating the sense of the novel. Rather self-deception is a part of her condition of victim. Her own pronouncements are to be taken as indulgent self-justifications, and there is no more authoritative verbal commentary on her behaviour than the idiomatic narrative which expresses the consensus of local opinion: 'Tout ça, d'une façon, comme d'une autre, ne semblait guère propre; mais il y a *tant de saletés dans la vie*, et de plus grosses, que les gens finissaient par trouver ce ménage à trois naturel, gentil même . . .'. In Moore's novel the same remarks put into Esther's mouth have to be the sole vehicle of the meaning—and inevitably misfire. When Esther reflects that it 'don't do to be too particular' or (almost exactly reproducing the italicized French phrase) that there are *'many things in life one couldn't approve of'* but which one can't help being involved in, the paradox of her moral status is emphasized rather than explained away. What is meant to give her coherence seems almost an invitation to convict her of duplicity.

If Esther is disqualified by her will as a naturalistic heroine she is also pallid as an autonomous personality. This of course is only to re-state in terms of imaginative failure what has already been illustrated as logical contradiction. Esther is raised above the level of passive victim—and her 'character' must be substan

The Case of 'Esther Waters' (1894)

tiated, it demands that Moore describe her consciousness and give her a rudimentary imagination. But at the same time she must, as it were, be left within the grasp of 'life', the portrait must not be so complex as to sever or obscure her ties with the naturalistic world; she starts as, and remains, a simple illiterate at the mercy of society. The result of this uncertainty of purpose is that Esther forfeits Gervaise's status of representative victim without achieving that of an intrinsically interesting individual. In attempting to give her some sort of inner life Moore has constantly risked making her and her problems seem insignificant. Thus we hear how, on arriving at Woodview, Esther admired the dresser with its 'multitude of plates and dishes' and 'thought how she must strive to keep it in its present beautiful condition'. Her fall to William is set against her resolution to make good—'she must learn to control that temper of hers—she must and she would'—a resolution which grows with her confidence so that, in spite of the hardness of the post, she became 'determined to stay at Woodview till she learned to make jellies and gravies'. It is on this heroic ground, between the lure of the pleasure gardens and the ambition to conquer the minor skills of the kitchen, that the battle for Esther's destruction takes place.

The problem of social realism, of the novel of 'ordinary' people, could hardly have a clearer illustration. Moore fails where Zola and Flaubert succeed; and a condition of their success is seen to be that, however much their primary aims differ, they both appeal to and satisfy our critical intelligence. Gervaise and Emma Bovary are both 'ordinary' heroines, but what they feel and say has importance by reference to something outside themselves. If either of them says, for instance, that she is destined never to be happy, our response is to be (in differing degrees) a critical one. Gervaise is self-dramatizing, but in a wider sense ironically right; Emma is stupid, yet echoes, in a particular key, the refrain of the whole run of bovaristic mankind. Esther, on the other hand, has to bear the whole burden of her own banalities—which have been given her precisely in order to distinguish her as a significant individual.

It is surely this sort of flat realism which Wilde is reacting

The Case of 'Esther Waters' (1894)

against when he dismisses Zola's characters as leading lives 'absolutely without interest' and criticizes Bourget for the mistake of thinking that 'the men and women of modern life can be infinitely analysed for an innumerable series of chapters'. But it is in diverging from Zola, and not in following him, that Moore has been led into error. Moore (as we shall see later) was substantially in agreement with Wilde's own aesthetic, and the spirit in which he undertook *Esther Waters* had something in common with Flaubert's attitude to *Madame Bovary*. The starting point was not a positive belief in the parity of the classes as artistic material, but the doctrine of the indifference of subject matter, of the ability of art to describe everything—and the adequacy of description to make a work of art.

We have so far considered *Esther Waters* as a modification of the naturalist novel; it may also be seen in the light of Moore's return to Flaubert, of a too hopeful belief in the interest and efficacy of detached well-written description. If we compare Moore's novel with *Madame Bovary* we find that the presentation of the two heroines is not dissimilar: both are put briefly on the stage and then 'explained' by a flashback sketch of their early life. In each case the character is conceived statically and the adventures are illustrative rather than formative. Acceptably so in Emma's case, since the novel is primarily satirical, the pleasures are chiefly those of recognition; Flaubert's unique success derives not from his fidelity to Art for Art, but from a subject which protects him from the worst of the doctrine's implications. But Esther's illustrative adventures fail artistically for two reasons: first, because they illustrate something dull, they lack the bite of a representative reference; secondly, because if they are to have any structural function they *ought* to be formative. This is only to state again what we have already emphasized—that Esther's adventures are dislocated from her fate because, unlike Gervaise's years in the laundry, they leave her will intact. But it is to approach that dislocation in a slightly different way, not only as a distortion of the naturalistic scheme, but as the product of a *positive* ideal of pure description. 'Picturesque comfort or picturesque misery, l'un vaut l'autre dans l'art', Moore had remarked, speaking of the potentialities for the artist of the Irish scene. And undramatic, illustrative description plays a considerable part in *Esther Waters*. If the definition fits Esther's years of domestic service it is even more clearly applicable to the long Derby Day scene. Moore was very proud of this scene and pointed to its purely artistic preoccupations when his admirers imputed humanitarian motives to his work. Flaubert had a similar affection for his description of the agricultural show—'mes comices'—and it hardly seems likely that Moore was unaware of the parallel. Moore's episode also has affinities with the birthday scene in *L'Assommoir*—it shows the society at its most characteristic, it marks the high point of the Latch family's fortunes, and it ends in a drinking orgy in which one of the party, Esther's friend Sarah, starts on the downward path to crime and degradation. But the immediacy of the danger only serves to emphasize Esther's immunity, her character as a spectator; the whole fifty pages thus remain a detachable impression, unrelated to the main theme and therefore not rising above the level of (to use Moore's own term) the picturesque. Flaubert's great scene is a variation on a theme, Zola's a dramatic turning point, the dramatic framed in the characteristic. Moore's piece of virtuosity points to the imitator who would have seen the two models merely as samples of fine impressionistic writing. At least his own rather imprecise pronouncements on his predecessors suggest a failure both to understand the naturalistic mechanism and to distinguish the conditions in which Flaubert's description succeeds: Moore's final remark on *L'Assommoir* was that it was Zola's only great novel because it was the last in which he had aimed, above all, at style, the last which he had written in the manner of Flaubert.

[iii]

While there is much in *Esther Waters* that can be discussed in terms of its literary antecedents the novel remains, in other respects, a typical product of its times. Such an assertion may seem odd of a work pervaded by a sort of half-hearted, plaintive

The Case of 'Esther Waters' (1894)

religiosity. But paradox was a major literary tenet of the nineties, and *Esther Waters* is not the only work of the aesthetic period in which religion makes an unexpected appearance. It is not the task of the critic to enquire historically into the 'sincerity' of a writer in order to arrive at a judgment of his work; but a look at the social attitudes of Moore and his times will help us to understand and characterize more clearly the sort of thing that is being done in *Esther Waters*. Those attitudes hardly seem at first sight propitious to the flowering of a working-class heroine. All the conventional responses to the poor and the problem of suffering are rejected, and the emotions normally involved in such responses consistently depreciated. Beauty is the ideal, and humanity, says Moore, a second best: 'Men of inferior genius, Victor Hugo and Mr. Gladstone, take refuge in it.' Philanthropists and humanitarians are despised as sentimentalists who help to perpetuate a bad social system by their guilty efforts at relieving individual hardship. Moore denounces pity as 'that most vile of the virtues', and Wilde protests that it is easier and less fruitful to sympathize with suffering than to sympathize with thought. Descriptions of the poor are characterized by a peculiar, brutal violence of language, and a calculated avoidance of sentiment. The tone is remarkably consistent—whether it is Moore describing the Irish peasants (his tenants):

> Some of the men are down on their hands and knees grovelling . . . their hearts are full of the gross superstition of the moment, they address God in the coarse language of the cabin: out of their torn shirts, revealing the beast-like hair of their breasts, rises the rancid sweat of the field. . . . They cough and groan as they pray, and the spittle splashes on the floor.

Or Moore again, on the charwoman who was to have been the model for a novel:

> Dickens would sentimentalize or laugh over you; I do neither. I merely recognize you as one of the facts of our civilization. . . . You are a beast of burden, a drudge too horrible for anything but work. . . .

Or Wilde forecasting the benefits of a socialist utopia:

The Case of 'Esther Waters' (1894)

There will be no people living in fetid dens and fetid rags, and bringing up unhealthy and hunger-pinched children in the midst of impossible and absolutely repulsive surroundings. The security of society will no longer depend, as it does now, on the state of the weather. If a frost comes we shall not have a hundred thousand men out of work, tramping about the streets in a state of disgusting misery, or whining to their neighbours for alms, or crowding round the doors of loathsome shelters to try and secure a hunch of bread and a night's unclean lodging.

But the insistence on squalor and degradation already points to a more positive social attitude; though the poor may be rejected as disgusting and uninteresting, and pity condemned as the conscience money of a *laisser faire* society, there is in much of this writing a homogeneous strain of real feeling; the aesthetic attraction of the horrible, which had been exploited in France by the Goncourts and others, gives way to a fierce intellectual pleasure in exposing the paradoxes and hypocrisies of a complacent, philistine civilization. Hatred of the ideals and rationalizations of the bourgeois and the capitalist, rather than sympathy with their victims, is the animating force.

The extent to which writers like Wilde are 'engaged' remains doubtful, though it might be rash to deny them as much clarity and humanity as socialists of a more overtly emotional brand. What concerns us here is that, though their attitude may produce unsentimental journalism of attractive modernity, it is an unfertile one from the artistic point of view, and especially for the social novel. Not only are its bases aesthetic and intellectual rather than ethical; but it is directed away from the victim, indeed it positively recoils from the imaginative consideration of individual predicaments. The aim is to expose an undifferentiated degradation. Or else the desire to startle may lead to an equally comprehensive idealization. Thus, in a famous and powerful attack on prison conditions, Wilde begins by agreeing with the common protest that life in prison is corrupting for children; but he goes on to say that it is the prison authorities that are the agents of contamination; and their meticulous segregation of the children is useless because 'the only really humanizing influence in prison is the influence of the prisoners.

The Case of 'Esther Waters' (1894)

Their cheerfulness under terrible circumstances, their sympathy for each other . . . their gentleness, all are quite wonderful, and I myself learnt many lessons from them!' Again we have conscious paradox and simplification. And though Wilde's remarks are partly the product of experience and observation they owe much to a prior hatred of the authoritarian society, an urge to turn upside-down conventional judgments and standards. The interest of the 'nineties' writers in morality springs not so much from a positive urge to make ethical re-appraisals, as from a negative certainty that current standards are bankrupt, that, in another of Wilde's sweeping phrases, the man-made law 'But straws the wheat and saves the chaff/With a most evil fan'.

Such a moral viewpoint may naturally be expected, when translated into literary terms, to produce the social melodrama with a rather simple, functional centre; the critical attitude to society is ready for use, the victim remains a (to the writers) not very interesting, even rather embarrassing gap to be filled in. *Esther Waters* fits this description in many respects: it is essentially a partisan story of a good girl fighting a bad society; and the good girl is given an odd, makeshift portrayal—but one which is not without parallel in the literature of the time. The presentation of the oppressor class is always simple, sometimes caricatural. All Esther's employers before Miss Rice are more or less cruel and insensitive, and the woman she serves as a wet-nurse, and who refuses to let her visit her own child when he is ill, is a rather stylized butt for Esther's invective. The hypocrisies of justice are also directly satirized in the account of Sarah's trial, where the judge's address to the prisoner is glossed by a heavily ironical commentary on his lordship's own betting and drinking habits. Though Esther cannot approve of betting her own misfortunes are echoed in William's repeated protest that there is 'one law for the rich and another for the poor'. Inhumanity is also linked with puritanical religion—Esther leaves the Bingleys, 'Dissenters who exacted the uttermost farthing from their customers and their workpeople', with the reflection: 'It's a strange thing that religion should make some people so unfeeling.' And this hostility to conventional religion and puritanism

The Case of 'Esther Waters' (1894)

brings us back to the central problem of Esther's presentation as a girl with a 'pure religious mind' who never disowns the strict moral views in which she was brought up. That the agnostic votary of Art should write in this way is at first sight disconcerting; but a look at another work of the period may help to explain the spirit in which *Esther Waters* was conceived, and the difficulties into which Moore was inevitably led.

Wilde's *A Woman of No Importance* was first produced in the year before *Esther Waters'* publication; it has survived chiefly for its verbal comedy, but it is also a melodrama with a moral and social theme. The heroine, Mrs. Arbuthnot, is, like Esther, the good religious woman who has sacrificed her life to the bringing up of her son. Hester, the visiting American puritan who is disgusted with the shallowness and immorality of English upper class society, is attracted towards her—seeing her as the embodiment of virtue and chastity—and invites her to agree with her own stringent moral views. It turns out that the son, Gerald, is illegitimate, and his father one of the chief figures in the sparkling society which Hester so much despises. Unable to think of Mrs. Arbuthnot as a sinner Hester is obliged to modify the rigidity of her standards of judgment, to admit that good and bad cannot be defined so easily. The play ends, of course, with Hester's engagement to Gerald and the three starting a new life together. Here we have goodness posited by reference to 'character' and works, a distant infringement of the moral law discounted, religion enrolled to give stature and respectability to the heroine. At the level of melodrama no problems of characterization or consistency arise; moreover, Wilde's chief interest is not in presenting the central character but in showing the puritan confounded and converted, proving the inadequacy of rule-of-thumb moral judgments. The distant fault, discovered and forgiven by the puritan, is also the theme of *Lady Windermere's Fan* and *An Ideal Husband*. The attack on convention and hypocrisy is the primary aim, the central figure is given a 'good' character which is little more than a mark to distinguish the victim of a social law which 'straws the wheat and saves the chaff'. This critical aim also means that Wilde feels under no obligation to

The Case of 'Esther Waters' (1894)

identify himself with the standards of his main character. Mrs. Arbuthnot is made 'religious' in order to recommend her initially to Hester, to heighten the paradox of her position. But Wilde, the self-proclaimed amoralist, never clearly dissociates himself from the witty society which treats her and her virtue as rather a joke.

Is not Esther conceived in the same melodramatic, paradoxical terms? For long stretches of the book she is simply the good girl with a single distant fault, which still counts against her, but which is in strong contrast with what is permanent in her character and behaviour. But what is acceptable as the premiss for a social melodrama becomes problematical when filled out and presented as a complete account of a life. There is no need to consider the question of Esther's religion in isolation—it is only the most obtrusive aspect of her 'character' in the character-life conflict already discussed. The opening section of the novel may now be seen as a rather piquant ninety-ish episode, with Moore disingenuously trying to rout the conventional moralists by, as it were, taking a victim out of their own camp. See how strong life must be, he says in effect, since even the religious girl falls so quickly! Introduced at the level of paradox, retained as a token of character, Esther's religion cannot fail to appear insubstantial and contradictory as the action progresses. After her marriage her moral code consists, to judge by what she does and says, in a blind devotion to her husband, combined with a vague mental reservation whereby she witholds approval for his way of life. It is these theoretical views which constitute her superiority, which are the mark of her uncompromised conscience. But what psychological status can they have which would distinguish them from mere lip-service to virtue, or regret for lost innocence? Though Esther argues against betting with William she is even more touchy with the accusing Fred. 'I must do my duty to my husband' is her mechanical reply when she meets him by the mission tent at the Derby. And when he tries to present the conflict of human and religious duties as a moral problem we feel that a relation between belief and action must be established and Esther's old and new religions shown to be mutually exclusive.

The Case of 'Esther Waters' (1894)

But once again her integrity is saved, though in words that almost openly admit the oddity of the situation. Esther hasn't forgotten her upbringing and joins Fred in the tent, 'prayer being so inherent in her that she felt no sense of incongruity'. Whether Moore thinks it is incongruous he does not tell us, but it is difficult to imagine what Esther prays for—perhaps that, since her husband insists on betting, he shall at least do well enough to keep their son on at school. This, at any rate, is the sort of situation we have later, when William is betting for the money which will enable him to go abroad and save his life: Esther prays that the horse he backs may win—'though it did not seem right to address God on the subject'.

All these oddities would of course fall into place if *Esther Waters* were a naturalist novel which admitted the confused consciousness, the notion of the religious sense warped by the pressures of life. The interview with Miss Rice, for instance, where Esther watched another candidate for the job go in before her and 'breathed a prayer that she might not be engaged' could be touching if presented in this way; offered as a testimonial to the *survival* of Esther's 'true self' in a hard world it is merely ridiculous, and invites the reader to substitute his own interpretation for the author's.

But while the melodramatic conception of virtue prevents Moore from adopting a directly critical attitude to his heroine's consciousness, criticism disrupts the novel in a more oblique way. The melodramatic formula has involved Moore in a full-scale portrait of a woman with whose ideals he has nothing in common, who is to him essentially indifferent, 'of no importance'; and, with results more serious than in Wilde's case, his natural sympathies seem to lean away from the world of virtues which Esther represents, to align him more closely with William, whose philosophy of life—that betting is inevitable and puritanism just humbug—Esther must reject. This conflict between the ostensibly 'straight' narrative and the author's private judgment is clearest in the portrayal of the two men. Fred is the subject of a gratuitous caricature, and we feel that the Salvation Army point of view hardly has a fair chance when conveyed by

The Case of 'Esther Waters' (1894)

the clerk with his 'high round forehead, his weak eyes, his whole face expressive of fear and hatred of the evil a falsetto voice denounced'. Moore manifestly saw reasons for Esther's returning to William which he could not possibly let her approve of, yet which he equally obviously wants to suggest are valid. So that the episode seems to be an elaborate tongue-in-the-cheek rigmarole in which Esther comes to a reluctant decision—and is criticized for her reluctance. Thus she is unwilling to negotiate with William until persuaded by the agnostic sage Miss Rice, who says that she is protecting Esther against her own acknowledged obstinacy, a quality which has been shown to be a product of her puritan upbringing. Having, in the interests of her integrity, her 'character', refused Esther a 'natural' reaction, Moore cannot avoid the temptation to suggest the emancipated anti-puritan's criticism of the very source of her virtue! The same ambiguity surrounds the presentation of Esther's first fall. She is the aggrieved party, and her respectability is guaranteed by her immediate moral reaction; but at the same time it is suggested, and repeated when they reunite, that an *excess* of moral indignation or puritanical temper on Esther's part was responsible for the well-meaning William's abandoning her. In short, the anti-puritan novel with a puritan heroine leads not only to psychological curiosities but to inevitable ambiguities and waverings in the writer's own attitude. The religious character, which looked a promising convenience, proves too near to the narrowness the book is attacking to remain immune from its shafts. The conception has an appealing audacity, it belongs very recognizably to the gay youth of militant anti-Victorianism; but *Esther Waters* proves that the paradoxical is a bad basis for a novel.

[iv]

Moore has poured such ideas as he has into a mould unsuitable for them. The traditions and theories on which he draws cannot provide a formula for a successful novel when adapted to his idiosyncratic purposes. And the French masterpieces themselves

The Case of 'Esther Waters' (1894)

may be seen as isolated successes, which fully exploit, but at the same time exhaust, the possibilities of their own theory. Thus the comparison with Zola shows that the scheme of his world is not capable of modification; it also reminds us that within that world the scope for the portrayal of an individual fate has narrow limits. The theme of drink in *L'Assommoir* produces the perfect social tragedy of the interplay of personal weakness and corrupting environment; but it is a theme which admits of few variants, and—basically—of only one sort of character. From here the naturalist novel can extend downwards to the portrayal of mass victimization, but in doing so it must (as in *Germinal*) shift its emphasis from the individual to the epic and panoramic. *Esther Waters* is the proof that it cannot move upwards, even in a small degree, towards the world of personal responsibility. The formalistic aesthetic ideals of the period, deriving from Flaubert, also help to lead Moore astray. 'To write well without humour is the supreme test', he observed; he might have added that the minimum requirement for doing this is a subject which the writer can take seriously. But the complementary heresy of the indifference of subject matter allowed him to take a heroine whom he felt tempted to mock at but dared not. The school of Flaubert might have been much smaller if it had been understood that his greatest masterpiece was largely due to the fact that its subject admitted and provoked satirical treatment.

But Moore is not primarily an incompetent imitator. His error lies rather in not abandoning completely ideas and forms which are no longer valid for him. If he does not follow Zola it is because he wants to go beyond the small world of the novel of defeat, an aim which was already apparent in the paradoxical twist he gave to his direct imitation of Zola, *A Mummer's Wife*, where the 'innocent' seducee dies a depraved alcoholic, while her seducer is redeemed by his devotion to her. Though his masters were French Moore also liked to see his work as an injection of modernity into the tradition of social tragedy in the English novel. His denunciations of George Eliot and Hardy are violent and contemptuous, even for a critic in whom violence is a stock reaction. A 'true moulding' of the subject of *Adam Bede*,

The Case of 'Esther Waters' (1894)

he says in calmer mood, would have been Hetty not murdering her child but living to save it. In *Esther Waters* he supplied this new 'moulding' in defiance of the moral code of the circulating libraries; and, if he did not make a good novel by it, Moore probably judged well in thinking that only the addition of the naturalistic rhetoric about 'life' and the religious element could make it acceptable. If it was strategy it worked: while Hardy had to fight a long battle with the self-appointed censors, Moore, with a novel openly condoning adultery and reintegrating its heroine into society, won the approval of no less a critic than Mr. Gladstone. The failure of the enterprise should not obscure what is bold and original in it: under the pietistic and melodramatic surface there is at least a suggestion of standards very different from those of the laborious exculpation. Esther talks of sin and repentance, but such words are little more than descriptive terms for her 'lot'. She knows little of that world. At her most typical—when moral issues are raised—she is obstinate, truculent, self-righteous. She's 'had enough of reproaches', as she tells Fred with unexpected violence when she first makes her 'confession'. If Esther is formally the most religious of our nineteenth-century heroines she is also the angriest, and there is in her touchiness a foretaste of some of the axiomatically 'pure' figures of the modern theatre. While Esther's fate is geared for the most part to the social background and the social judgment it contains the hint of a smaller and more private novel, independent of the borrowed 'lower-class novel' framework. The presentation of Esther's duty to her son and her husband suggests a more subjective appraisal of personal fulfilment, of the life well lived. It is a suggestion only, at variance with the main tendency, but insisted on in a number of incidents and details. When Esther sees William dressed up in his 'betting togs' at the Derby the great argumentative sophistries of the earlier part of the book seem to fall away as irrelevant preliminaries; from not knowing whether Esther chose William as the lesser of two evils, or whether she was forced back on to him by life, we now find their union proposed as a good in itself. Esther is looking after her husband's needs while he shouts

The Case of 'Esther Waters' (1894)

the odds—but the pre-Lawrentian implications are hardly supported by the quality of Moore's performance:

> There was a nice piece of beef in the basket, and Esther cut several large sandwiches, buttering the bread thickly and adding plenty of mustard. When she brought them over William bent down and whispered:
> 'My own duck of a wife, there's no one like her.'
> Esther blushed and laughed with pleasure, and every trace of the resentment and suffering he had occasioned her dropped out of her heart. For the first time he was really her husband; for the first time she felt that unity of life which is marriage, and knew henceforth he was the one thing she had to live for.

The *fin de siècle* writers may have little to say about the landscape of the private moral world; but they help to ensure that it will be the chief concern of their successors.

5

The Novel as Moral Protest: 'Tess of the D'Urbervilles' (1891)

> ... who was the moral woman? The beauty and ugliness of a character lay not only in its achievements, but in its aims and impulses; its true history lay not among things done but among things willed.
>
> TESS OF THE D'URBERVILLES (Ch. XLIX).

[i]

In 1874 Henry James was invited by the *Nation* to review *Far from the Madding Crowd*, and in the course of his article he remarked: 'Hardy describes nature with a great deal of felicity and is evidently very much at home among rural phenomena. The most genuine thing in this book is a certain aroma of the meadows and lanes—a natural relish for harvestings and sheep-washings.' Twenty years later, in June 1895, the Bishop of Wakefield wrote to the newspapers to announce that he had thrown Hardy's last novel, *Jude the Obscure*, into the fire. Taken together these two comments eloquently indicate what Hardy has in common with the author of *Adam Bede*, and where he differs from her. Both writers are very much 'at home among rural phenomena', but whereas George Eliot, in writing her 'country story', was able to believe in the vitality and serenity of the community she created, Hardy, writing thirty years later, could find only a community in decay, a tragic vision inviting moral protest. For George Eliot the story of Hetty, close though

The Novel as Moral Protest:

it was to the genesis of the novel, was only an element in a wider context. She exists in her communal relationships, and questions of personal innocence, personal guilt, are never allowed to catch our attention. It is not that these questions are deliberately set aside, in the way that Flaubert and Zola set them aside, but rather that they have no place in this particular story. For Hardy the story of Tess was the only story, it could accommodate within it everything he wanted to say, and in telling it he could reveal poverty, class privilege, cruelty, hypocrisy—it could be the substance of his moral protest.

The difference of temper between the two books can be illustrated by looking at the way each concludes. In *Adam Bede*, Adam is speaking about Arthur Donnithorne:

'He'd never heard about poor Hetty till Mr. Irwine met him in London, for the letters missed him on his journey. The first thing he said to me, when we'd get hold o' one another's hands, was: "I could never do anything for her, Adam—she lived long enough for all the suffering—and I thought so of the time when I might do something for her. But you told me the truth when you said to me once, There's a sort of wrong that can never be made up for!"'

'Why, there's Mr. and Mrs. Poyser coming in at the yard gate', said Seth.

'So there is', said Dinah. 'Run, Lisbeth, run to meet Aunt Poyser. Come in, Adam, and rest; it has been a hard day for thee.'

'Come in, Adam, and rest'—that is the note on which the novel ends; there has been misunderstanding, sorrow, tragedy, but these things belong to the past and they will live in the memory; the broken community has now been restored, and Hetty's story must give way to the welcome news that the Poysers have arrived. The belief in the new day is all the more confident because it does not seek to forget Hetty; but it accepts her fate for what it is, one of the inevitable sorrows that life will bring.

At the end of *Tess of the D'Urbervilles* the fate of another tragic woman is being described:

A few minutes after the hour had struck something moved slowly up the staff, and extended itself upon the breeze. It was a black flag. 'Justice' was done and the President of the Immortals, in Aeschylean phrase, had ended his sport with Tess. And D'Urberville knights and

'Tess of the D'Urbervilles (1891)

dames slept in their tombs unknowing. The two speechless gazers bent themselves down to the earth, as in prayer, and remained thus a long time, absolutely motionless; the flag continued to wave silently. As soon as they had the strength they arose, joined hands again, and went on.

'There's a sort of wrong that can't be made up for' would indeed be a pertinent comment on this sombre scene, but how differently it sounds when read in this context. Here there is no question of letters arriving from a distant colony bearing the tragic news, rather a black flag announcing to all the countryside that justice has been done. At the end of *Tess* it is not 'the day that is hard', but the whole process of living, which is as relentless as it is inscrutable; there is no farmhouse to enter and rest in, surrounded by family and friends, only an empty road, stretching out as far as the two wanderers can see, to nowhere. *Adam Bede* ends with the social group, *Tess* with two exiles.

It would however be misleading if this description of the way in which Hardy differs from George Eliot was taken as implying that he was anything other than a profoundly traditional novelist. The fact that his work, in its last phase at least, ran to moral protest, so that he could be an embarrassment to the serial proprietors and cause anger to a bishop, should not obscure the fact that at heart he was a simple teller of stories. Had he possessed a greater sophistication, a greater mastery of the 'art of the novel', *Tess* and *Jude* would not have caused the stir they did. Looking back, we can see the gaucheness as an intrinsic part of the power, but for Hardy this kind of fiction was against his natural bent and, after the public hostility to *Jude*, he was glad to abandon the writing of novels. Essentially he was very much the novelist of Henry James's description in his review of *Far from the Madding Crowd*, a man thoroughly at home in the country, but also a man who felt increasingly that there was becoming no 'country' to belong to. When Hardy wrote of the dying agricultural community in *Tess* he was not writing simply out of personal observation and reminiscence, as George Eliot was in *Adam Bede*, but rather about the death of a whole tradition of local life, local folklore, a tradition in which he found the source of his artistic power. George Eliot may have written a 'country story' in

The Novel as Moral Protest:

Adam Bede, but her imaginative home was in the pages of the *Westminster Gazette* and in the conversation of Lewes and Herbert Spencer. To find comparisons with Hardy we have to look back to the beginning of the century, and outside the novel altogether, to poems like Wordsworth's *Guilt and Sorrow*, composed in the Wessex region, and to the tales of Crabbe. 'The uncommonness must be in the events', Hardy once wrote, 'not in the characters', and that remark should check any tendency to see in his note of moral protest an artistic dissatisfaction with the traditional novel. If that note marked him off from George Eliot, it marked him off much more fundamentally from Henry James, and it is between these two novelists that we find Hardy creating his own highly personal mode of fiction.

We could begin to describe this mode by saying that Hardy's stories, considered as such, have, like ballad literature, a great anonymity about them;[1] they proceed from a strongly individual mind which it is important to recognize, but it is not an individuality which can usefully be explained in terms of autobiographical detail. Even in those parts of his work where his personal interests might be thought to be most openly declared he resented the inference being made: 'Nothing irritates me so much as the mania of those writers who want to find at all costs something autobiographical and to identify me with the character of Jude or Stephen. I assure you nothing is further from the truth. The elements from which I have derived the idea of a novel are often manifold, sometimes strange and incongruous. Imagination and invention play a greater role than people recognize.'

Just as his stories may have a startling juxtaposition of action, so, allied to this, they may reveal a startling juxtaposition of mood. The kind of experience which lies behind such a verse as this from *The Unquiet Grave*:

> *Cold blows the wind on my true love,*
> *And a few small drops of rain;*

[1] For a good discussion of this aspect of Hardy's fiction see Donald Davidson's article 'The Traditional Basis of Thomas Hardy's Fiction', *The Southern Review*, Summer, 1940, pp. 162–78.

'Tess of the D'Urbervilles' (1891)

I never had but one true love,
And in the greenwood he was slain.

lies behind scenes in a Hardy novel. The sudden access here to a world of feeling at once remote and bleakly true recalls the strange emotional pitch of such episodes as the desperate card game played on the heath by the light of the glow-worms in *The Return of the Native*; of Henchard in *The Mayor of Casterbridge* looking over the bridge as his own corpse floats by in the shape of an effigy; of Troy's sword flashing round Bathsheba in *Far from the Madding Crowd*; of Angel sleepwalking with Tess and laying her in the empty coffin. The ballad verse, like the poem from which it comes, is a tragic one, but it is interesting to note that a narrative of this kind is so distanced that we don't ask the kind of questions which would be provoked by a similar situation in a novel: Who is the lover? What is the reason for the situation? Is the view of life a pessimistic or a tragic one? To ask these questions is to fail to respond to the peculiar power of this kind of poetry. It is the power partly of juxtaposing startling narrative statements and moods, so that we are made to feel, quite simply, 'this was so'; as with Hardy, 'the uncommonness lies in the events and not the characters'. Speculative questions arising out of the narrative can only be said to emerge from a more sophisticated treatment of material.

No one would want to argue that the Wessex novels may be considered as a number of prose ballads; their relationship with the ballad exists only at their inception, at the first and elementary stage of composition. As Hardy begins to 'work-up' his initial material—fragments of conversation, stories, anecdotes—two things, in particular, happen. The first is that it was quite impossible to contemplate this 'ballad-world' without realizing that it was passing away. In describing Hardy's attitude to this we must be alert to the dangers of over-simplification. On one side, it is tempting to see him as a latter-day Cobbett recording the final decline of the English peasantry, on the other, to think of his attitude as antiquarian, a nostalgic report on the passing away of old customs and crusted characters. Hardy's art overlooks, without ever invading, the territory occupied in one direction by the tract and in the other by the pastoral, and it is because he keeps to the space between that his art is a living thing. It would be a mistake to translate literally the social attitudes of his article on 'The Dorsetshire Labourer' into the social attitudes of the novels. The latter are more accurately glimpsed in his remarks to Rider Haggard:

> Changes at which we all must rejoice have brought other changes which are not so attractive. The labourers have become more and more migratory—the younger families in especial . . . the consequences are curious and unexpected. For one thing, village tradition—a vast mass of unwritten folk-lore, local chronicle, local topography, and nomenclature—is absolutely sinking, has nearly sunk, into eternal oblivion. . . . Thus you see, there being no continuity of environment in their lives, there is no continuity of information, the names, stories, and relics of one place being speedily forgotten under the incoming facts of the next.

This is not the accent of a social reformer, or a historian, or an antiquarian—it is that of a novelist whose work draws its stimulus from the understanding of a precise historical scene; and the vitality of the art is in proportion to the depth of the understanding. The ballad world and, flowing inevitably out of that, the gradual disintegration of that world, these are the basic elements of Hardy's fiction, and wholly within the compass of his art.

To these elements, however, he adds another—and to put it in that deliberate, external way, doesn't seem to misrepresent the process. This is when his artistic material begins to cohere firmly enough to become the object of his philosophical speculation. The sharp twists and turns of the ballad-narrative, together with its frequent and pervasive irony, provide natural channels in which a deterministic philosphy can set. The tragedy of a maid seduced in a wood becomes the sport of the gods, the wheels of the migratory carts along the Wessex roads become the wheels of Fate. Why did Hardy build into this fairly simple narrative material these philosophic amplifiers, which he never managed to conceal, or indeed felt the necessity of concealing? Obviously, Hardy had a naturally speculative as well as an artistic cast of

'Tess of the D'Urbervilles' (1891)

mind—the tendency to 'follow through' was ever present, so that the time-honoured 'changeless' character of balladry comes also to exemplify for him Schopenhauer's tenet that 'no real change of character is at all possible in a world in which man is from his birth controlled by irresistible influences'. Alec D'Urberville is cut from this cloth, as well as being, simply, The Seducer. Hardy seemed to feel that he needed his 'high thinking' and elaborate mythological references in order to obtain for his novels the kind of serious attention he wanted.

After this abstract description of the staple material of a Hardy novel, I would like to turn to the opening of *Tess* for a brief illustration. The book begins at night with a rather drunk John Durbeyfield meeting Parson Tringham. After some reluctance the Parson tells Durbeyfield why he called him 'Sir John'. The story of the old D'Urberville family is related, and how they are now extinct and lie in the vaults at Kingsbere. Overcome with this tale of the grandeur of his ancestors, Durbeyfield thanks the Parson, and orders a boy to get him a horse and cart, so that he can ride home with a dignity becoming to such a family. This fragment of conversation is the germ of the whole novel. One day, during the months that Hardy was making the jottings and notes for *Tess*, he was standing at a street corner in Dorchester when a drunk man staggered past, shouting, 'I've got a great family vault at Bere Regis'. Weber describes the incident:

> Hardy's curiosity was aroused. Bere Regis is not far from Dorchester and, upon investigation, he discovered that the drunkard's statement was correct. Not only were many of the old Turberville family buried at Bere Regis, but there is a fine Turberville window of stained glass there. Hardy also made the interesting discovery that, although the name 'Turberville' had died out, there were still a number of very humble families living in Dorset who were descended from the ancient Turbervilles, and who unwittingly hid their honourable name under various corruptions.[1]

There we have the genesis of the novel, and we can see the admixture of local gossip and local placing that goes to make it up. That is the first stage—a pure tale.

[1] Carl Weber, *Hardy of Wessex*, pp. 122-3.

The Novel as Moral Protest:

To return to *Tess*. The action now shifts to the unspoiled village of Marlott where Tess is taking part in the annual club-walking. This Hardy describes as a survival of the May Day dance, and, although we have the white gowns and the peeled willow-wand, the celebration is only a disguised form of a custom that has died. Into this world which can now only play-act the customs it follows, 'Sir John's' carriage arrives, together with loud proclamations about his illustrious ancestors. A focusing lens has been quietly slipped in front of the 'pure tale'. And this is the second stage.

The dance continues; three strange young men, apparently on a walking tour, take a mild interest in the proceedings. One in particular, who wishes to join in, encourages the other two to continue on their way. The reason why the latter wish to hurry away from the 'country hoydens' is to get another chapter of *A Counterblast to Agnosticism* read before the end of the day. The third member, who is Angel Clare, stays only briefly with the dancers, though as he leaves he notices Tess and is sorry that he did not see her before. Here, very lightly sketched in, is the third element in the novel—the 'intellectual' in the 'world of the natural'. Two pass it by altogether, the other engages but not really happily. It is a very minor episode and only a hint of the development to come, but even here, in this extremely sure opening of the novel, the only discordant and forced note is the book-title, which is just too pat for the occasion.

It would be foolish to make too much of these incidents in *Tess*, but they serve in a schematic way as an illustration of the general pattern of Hardy's novels, and they provide a pointer for a detailed discussion of the novel. Before I take that up, however, I want to turn aside to consider something of the background which urged Hardy to make a 'moral protest'. The most convenient way of doing this is to describe the difficulties he had in getting the book published as he wrote it.

'Tess of the D'Urbervilles' (1891)

[ii]

Following the great success of *The Woodlanders* in 1887, Hardy received numerous invitations during the early part of the following year for his next novel. He accepted the invitation of Tilotson and Son. They were the owners of a group of Lancashire weekly newspapers, who in 1871 had established the Newspaper Fiction Bureau, the aim of which was to syndicate serial fiction to provincial newspapers. Having accepted Tilotson's offer, Hardy turned down requests first from *Murray's Magazine* and then from *Macmillan's* for the serial rights of his novel. In the autumn of 1888 Hardy set to work, first with elaborate notes and jottings, and then, in the spring of the following year, with the novel proper. On 23rd August 1889 he sent his first MS. to Tilotson, 'a list of some scenes from the story that your artist may choose which he prefers'. A week or two later he followed this up by sending a section of MS., 'equal to about one half, I think'. So certain were the publishers of the general nature and quality of Hardy's work that it appears they never bothered to examine the MS. before sending it off to the printers. Not, in fact, until the artist had made three illustrations and they had received sixteen chapters in proof from the printers, did Tilotson seriously examine the novel they had undertaken to publish. As the first sixteen chapters contained all the contentious material, the drift of the novel was perfectly—and disturbingly—clear. Alarmed, Tilotson's wrote to Hardy suggesting he recast the story. Hardy refused. In the face of this, Tilotson's withdrew their offer to publish, but offered to fulfil their obligation to pay for the serial. The unhappy wrangle was concluded with Hardy's suggestion that the whole arrangement should be scrapped. Tilotson's thanked him for his generosity, and, in September 1889, returned the MS. together with the three illustrations and the sixteen chapters of proof.

Hardy now felt in a position to turn to some of the other pressing offers for publication rights which he had received the year before. In October he sent it to *Murray's Magazine*. A week or so later, the MS. was returned 'on the score of its improper explicitness'. Shaken but persistent, Hardy sent it to *Macmillan's*, and on 25th November the MS. was returned once again, with apologies for refusal. He now realized that, if *Tess* was ever to be published, he would have to accept the suggestion that he had turned down three months earlier and recast the story. Accordingly, he went to work, and throughout 1890 he was trimming the novel, 'with cynical amusement', to match the moral expectations of his reading public.

By a pleasant stroke of irony he had been invited to contribute at the beginning of the year to the *New Review* an article on 'Candour in English Fiction'. Hardy certainly had reason for thinking that he was an authority on the subject, and, as letters of rejection from three publishers were arriving virtually while he was composing the article, it must have been an overwhelming temptation to point his argument with particular illustrations. He resisted, however, and the argument is a general one. Beginning with the observation, which his recent editorial encounters made heavily ironical, that 'even imagination is the slave of stolid circumstance', he goes on to consider how a novelist's sincerity is constantly being compromised by the machinery of the publishing world, by which he means the magazine and the circulating library, and also by the expectations of the novel-reading public itself. The latter,

acting under the censorship of prudery rigorously exclude from the pages they regulate subjects that have been made, by general approval of the best judges, the bases of the finest imaginative compositions, since literature rose to the dignity of an art. The crash of broken commandments is as necessary an accompaniment to the catastrophe of a tragedy, as the noise of drum and cymbals to a triumphal march. But the crash of broken commandments shall not be heard. . . . More precisely, an arbitrary proclamation has gone forth that certain picked commandments of the ten shall be preserved intact—to wit, the first, third, and seventh; that the ninth shall be infringed but gingerly; the sixth only as much as necessary; and the remainder alone as much as you please, in a genteel manner. . . . The writer may print the '*not*' of his broken commandment in letters of flame; and it makes no difference. A question which should be wholly a question of treatment is confusedly regarded as a question of subject.

'Tess of the D'Urbervilles' (1891)

The interest of Hardy's article is chiefly autobiographical, coming just when it did, and when he turns to offer solutions to solve the novelist's dilemma they are sketchy and half-hearted. Encouragement should be given to the purchase, rather than the borrowing of novels; indiscriminate family reading in newspapers and magazines should be broken down by the publication of special magazines aimed exclusively at an adult audience, and supplements, similarly aimed, should be issued with newspapers. But these recommendations are hurried into a final paragraph, and Hardy's main interest is to state as forcibly as he can the *crise de conscience* that faces the serious contemporary novelist. It is certainly a situation which exposes the kind of grip that serial publication and the circulating library had on a writer's work, even at this comparatively late date.

Having had an unexpected opportunity to express his views on public taste directly, Hardy now returned to consider the ways in which *Tess* could overcome the 'stolid circumstance' of continuous editorial rejections. Two incidents, in particular, were causing the trouble—the seduction scene, which was obliquely presented, and the baptism of Tess's child. Hardy decided to replace the first by a mock-marriage with Alec, so Tess's story to her mother appeared in this form to serial readers:

'He made love to me, as you said he would do; and he asked me to marry him, also just as you declared he would. I never have liked him; but at last I agreed, knowing you'd be angry, if I didn't. He said, it must be private even from you, on account of his mother; and by special licence; and foolish I agreed to that likewise, to get rid of his pestering. I drove with him to Melchester, and there in a private room I went through the form of marriage with him as before a registrar. A few weeks after, I found out that it was not the registrar's house we had gone to, as I had supposed, but the house of a friend of his, who had played the part of the registrar. I then came away from Trantridge instantly, though he wished me to stay; and here I am.'

The letter of the law is preserved; Tess's seduction is made socially acceptable by the fact that she thought she was marrying Alec. In fact, Tess is morally obtuse here in a way she is not in the book, committing herself to marrying a man she despises, because she is afraid of her mother's anger and his pestering. And

The Novel as Moral Protest:

on these inadequate and rather shoddy moral and dramatic motives the serial version is built.

In this version there is no child, and consequently the second troublesome incident, the baptism, is by-passed. After these major changes, the rest of the 'moral' adaptations are small; perhaps the most interesting occurs in the final section. In the serial, we are made to realize, by various touches, that Tess is not living in Sandbourne as Alec's wife. This time defence of the letter leads actually to the creation of a morally perverse situation. If Tess is simply living in Sandbourne, as the serial says, 'to be friends with him', there can be no dramatic catastrophe when Angel Clare arrives. Further, Tess's killing of Alec then becomes gratuitous in a way that *is* morally shocking. Now that the novel had been made by the strict observance of conventional relationships both morally dubious and dramatically false, the way was clear to acceptance for serial publication.

Accordingly, Hardy sent it to the illustrated weekly newspaper, the *Graphic*, and there, flanked by pictures of the Kaiser's visit to London and the building of the Manchester Ship Canal, it appeared in twenty-four illustrated weekly instalments from 4th July to 26th December 1891. Once publication had started everything went smoothly, except for one of the August numbers. The editor objected to the scene where Clare carries the three girls over the flooded lane. He suggested a wheelbarrow would be more fitting. Hardy, obedient to the last, complied, and accordingly readers of the serial read: ' "I'll wheel you through the pool—all of you—with pleasure, if you'll wait till I get a barrow. . . . There's a barrow in the shed yonder." ' Even in questions of transport 'imagination had been made the slave of stolid circumstance'.

Although Hardy had excised from the serial the crucial scenes of the seduction and of the baptism of Tess's child, he was reluctant to leave them unprinted. Consequently, he 'de-characterized' them and turned them into episodic sketches. The baptism scene appeared under the heading 'The Midnight Baptism: A Study in Christianity', and was published in the *Fortnightly Review* in May 1891; that is, just over a month before the serial version began in the *Graphic*. Chapters X and XI, containing the revels scene in Chaseborough and the seduction of Tess, were published in an abridged form in a Special Literary Supplement of the *National Observer* in November 1891, under the title 'Saturday Night in Arcady'. No reference was made to the serial currently running in the *Graphic*. This scene was clearly rather a complicated one to edit, and in doing it Hardy lost three or four pages. They were subsequently found, but not printed until 1912.

While the serial was running its course in the *Graphic*, Hardy was getting ready for the publication of the book by reassembling the original structure and making certain small stylistic revisions. Hardy's last act before returning the final proofs to the publishers was to redraft the title page, and add the sub-title 'A Pure Woman', together with the quotation from *Two Gentlemen of Verona*:

'Poor wounded name! My bosom as a bed/Shall lodge thee.' In his preface to the 1912 edition Hardy wrote: 'Respecting the sub-title... it was appended at the last moment... as being the estimate left in a candid mind of the heroine's character—an estimate that nobody would be likely to dispute. It was disputed more than anything else in the book.' During the last week of November—a month before the serial ended in the *Graphic*—*Tess of the D'Urbervilles* was finally published in volume form.

Such was the tortuous course into print of the first novel to allow a seduced woman to appear as an unqualified heroine. It was now given over to the reading public at large—and to the critics.

[iii]

On 16th January 1892 the *Saturday Review* printed the first substantial review of the book, and it was highly unfavourable. They laconically repeated the plot and then went on to say quite coolly: 'It matters much less what a story is about than how that story is told, and Mr. Hardy, it must be conceded, tells an unpleasant story in a very unpleasant way.' No evidence was offered. Hardy, with justifiable irritation, wrote to his publishers: 'You will be surprised to hear that they alter my preface and omit the second title, *which is absolutely necessary to show its meaning*...'¹ (my italics). This judgment is, I think, a sound one, and to overlook it, or even not to place it at the centre of one's examination and understanding, is to invite a charge of irrelevance. When Mr. Arnold Kettle, beginning his essay on *Tess*, writes: 'The subject ... is stated clearly by Hardy to be the fate of a "pure woman"; in fact it is the destruction of the English peasantry,'² he slants his analysis in a way from which it never recovers. It is interesting, and rather characteristic, that a novel like this must first of all be shown to be socially and historically significant before it can be considered 'important'. The significance and the importance are not equated, but they are near allied. To suggest the limitations of Mr. Kettle's point of view is not necessarily to rehabilitate the *Tess* of the older critics as providing an opportunity to discuss social and personal morality or the workings of the Immanent Will. We have to seek a vantage point which will take in both views and see their relationship not only to each other, but to the point from which the overall view is taken. I described earlier in general terms how I saw Hardy's novels: the work of a ballad writer, conscious that the ballad world is disintegrating, and played upon by the intellectual speculations of his age. I now want to consider how far this general description illuminates *Tess*, and in particular what light it casts on Hardy's attitude to the central character of the 'pure woman'.

To examine the novel in any detail is to be made more than usually aware of two things—the varying levels of imaginative intensity which it contains, and the way in which these levels disappear to leave the reader with a dominant impression of unity. There is the art of the ballad writer: the beautiful village maid, seduced in the green wood, who rallies to find her true lover, only to be rejected by him when he discovers her 'past' and brought to a tragic end. There is the art of the writer who feels

[1] Quoted by R. L. Purdy, *Thomas Hardy, a Bibliographical Study*, p. 75.
[2] *Introduction to the English Novel*, Vol. II, p. 49.

'Tess of the D'Urbervilles' (1891)

that such a world is dying in the shadows of the new industrial society which is growing up round it. And finally there is the writer who reflects philosophically on these things. The effect of this intervention was acutely observed by Lionel Johnson as early as 1895. Talking of these reflections, he comments: 'At times, they read like quaint modern imitations of those marginal glosses, which adorn the *Pilgrim's Progress* and the *Ancient Mariner*: "Here Tess illustrateth the falling out betwixt Nature and Society," or "In this place did Angel mock at Giant Calvinist, for that he taught an untenable redemptive theolatry." '[1] Nevertheless, the total impression that Tess leaves on the reader is undeniably one of unity. And we must start by asking how *that* is done, before going on to isolate the various elements that make it up.

The first thing to be noted is the extraordinary vividness and imaginative density with which Tess herself is presented. With her cheeks as 'smoothly chill as the skin of mushrooms', and with 'the stopt diapason note which her voice acquired when her heart was in her speech', Tess is continually before the reader as a living presence. She is the heart of the novel, giving it all the life it has, and that life remains a personal life; it doesn't transform itself into symbolic terms so that she becomes 'the agricultural community in its moment of ruin'. If an enlargement of the character takes place, it is to increase the force of the character, not to point out its significance. Tess 'felt akin to the landscape' —this is Hardy's way of providing a dramatic notation for material which, in another novelist, would have been handled psychologically. At every stage of the tale interior states are visualized in terms of landscape.

Tess's childhood is spent in the village of Marlott, 'an engirdled and secluded region, for the most part untrodden as yet by tourist or landscape painter'. When she goes to visit Alec she sees 'The Chase' for the first time, 'a truly venerable tract of forest land, one of the few remaining woodlands in England of undoubted primeval date, wherein Druidical mistletoe was still found on aged oaks. . . .' Here, under these emblems of the

[1] *The Art of Thomas Hardy*, p. 219.

Druids, she is ruined, and five years later she is to lie sleeping in the Druid temple of Stonehenge, while the police gather round to arrest her. On their wedding day Angel hangs mistletoe above the bed, but Tess confesses her past and the mistletoe is to overhang the place where she tries to kill herself. Weeks later Angel revisits the house, finds the mistletoe discoloured and wrinkled; he crushes it into the grate. In this way it is entwined with every emotional climax of the book. In the shadows of 'The Chase' is the D'Urbervilles' house, where 'everything looked like money —like the last coin issued from the mint'. It is precisely the need for money which drives the Durbeyfields to take up Alec's invitation to live there. And Tess's ruin is complete.

The fatal party on the day of her seduction is at Chaseborough, 'a decayed market town', and from there it moves to 'The Chase'. Tess begins her rally in 'the Valley of the Great Dairies where milk and butter grow to rankness . . . the waters were as clear as the pure River of Life shown to the Evangelist'. It is at Wellbridge, in a crumbling manor of the old D'Urberville family, that she goes to spend her honeymoon with Angel and the fatal confession takes place. Wellbridge stands as a pivotal point between the scene of recovery in the Froom Valley and the scene of growing despair at Flintcomb Ash where 'the whole field was in colour a desolate drab; it was a complexion without features, as if a face, from chin to brow, should be only an expanse of skin'. That face is now also Tess's, and the interchangeable image shows the kind of fusion that has taken place between the landscape and the person, without either losing identity.

If these are the dominant unifying images running through the novel, both saturating it with a sense of place and giving body to the central character, there are numerous others which lock into the structure of the tale just as effectively. The initial disaster is brought about by the death of Durbeyfield's horse, which is killed by an oncoming mail-coach. Appalled at what has happened, Tess tries to check the flow of blood, 'with the only result that she became splashed from face to skirt with crimson drops'. Later, she looks at the road: 'The huge pool of blood in front of her was already assuming the irridescence of coagulation; and

'Tess of the D'Urbervilles' (1891)

when the sun rose a hundred prismatic hues were reflected from it.' When the family come to bury the horse, Tess stands by the grave 'dry and pale as though she regarded herself in the light of a murderess'. The horse was the sole wealth of the Durbeyfields, his death leaves them economically vulnerable, and drives Tess to make acquaintance with the D'Urbervilles and with Alec, 'who stood fair to be the blood-ray in the spectrum of her young life'. Eventually it is Alec who becomes, like the horse, the financial support of the Durbeyfields. And, obliquely, it is this which is to lead to the morning when a landlady in a seaside boarding-house notices a spot on her ceiling: 'It was about the size of a wafer when she first observed it, but it speedily grew as large as the palm of her hand, and then she could perceive it was red. The oblong white ceiling, with this scarlet blot in the midst, had the appearance of a gigantic ace of hearts ... she touched the spot ... it was a blood stain.' The tale which is precipitated by the shedding of blood closes with it also. But for all this there is no sense of violence in the novel; the note which is struck is one of passivity, of acceptance. How this is achieved is suggested if we look at a related and more subtle series of images—which is largely responsible not only for giving unity to disparate material, but for controlling the novelist's attitude towards it.

The final scene in the book, Tess's arrest at Stonehenge, has been frequently praised, and the praise has usually found expression in terms similar to Mr. Kettle's: 'The symbolism is obvious, one might almost say crude. And yet the very clumsiness, the almost amateurish manipulation of the mechanics of the scene, contributes something to its force. . . .'[1] About this scene two things should be kept in mind. It belongs to what we might think of as the ballad world of the novel, and consequently has the stark, visual stylization which would provide a fittingly dramatic conclusion to a tragic ballet. The quiet sleeping figure on the altar-tomb, the bowed, protective form of the lover, and the dawn gradually coming up behind the Sun-Stone to reveal the encircling arm of the law. The visual 'staginess' of the scene

[1] *Introduction to the English Novel*, Vol. II, p. 61.

enforces the ironical commentary that the President of the Immortals 'had ended his sport with Tess'. It is not in any way a naturalistic presentation. The second point we ought to remember is that the peculiar power of the scene's central feature, Tess lying still on the altar-tomb, is due partly to the fact that it has been prepared for throughout the novel.

At the beginning of the tale John Durbeyfield describes his ancestors as lying under the church—'hundreds of 'em, in coats of mail and jewels, in gr't lead coffins weighing tons and tons'. In a sense, it is precisely the weight of that nobility which drags the Durbeyfields down to their ruin. Again and again Tess tries to shake it off by seeking to join them in death. When she realizes the tragedy that Alec has made of her life, 'her depression was terrible and she could have hidden in a tomb'. On two occasions Fate taunts her in separate ways, with biting irony. Angel sleepwalks and places her in the empty stone coffin of the abbot and she has to rise and lead him back and prevent him being 'chilled to certain death'. Later, unable to secure lodgings at Kingsbere, the desperate family decide to spend the night in the church over the family vault. Wandering round in the gloom of the building, Tess notices an effigy lying on one of the altar-tombs. It appears to move and then 'as she drew close to it, she discovered all in a moment that the figure was a living person . . . she recognized Alec D'Urberville in the form'. The living join forces with the dead in the final conspiracy against Tess. As Alec leaves, Tess 'bent down upon the entrance to the vaults and said: "Why am I on the wrong side of this door?"' Finally, she achieves her will when she herself lies on the altar-tomb, at Stonehenge—'now I am at home'. She is, in effigy, a sacrifice on the tomb of the D'Urbervilles. In this way Hardy manages to get into the final scene a force which has been gathering momentum throughout the novel.

The character of the heroine, the profound sense of landscape, the interlocking pattern of symbol and image—these all contribute to give the novel its eventual unity, but within that enclosing rim there are severe stresses and strains.

They proceed from varying levels of imaginative realization.

'Tess of the D'Urbervilles' (1891)

At the heart of the novel is the ballad world. When Tess returns from a day in the fields after her tragic encounter with Alec, 'her female companions sang songs . . . they could not refrain from mischievously throwing in a few verses of the ballad about the maid who went to the merry green wood and came back a changed state'. That is the world—the maid, the seducer and the true lover. It is primal in form and content. More exactly, it is the world of an extinct noble family, with its sinister legend of a mysterious coach. Tess mistakes it for her wedding coach, and she imagines she hears it again when Alec walks back into her life. There are the three forlorn milkmaids at the Dairy; the rose given to Tess by Alec, which later pricks her so that 'steeped in fancies and prefigurative superstitions, she thought this an illomen'; her mother consults *The Compleat Fortune Teller*, which has to be removed from the house at night; when Angel and Tess drive off for their honeymoon a cock crows, and it is the middle of the afternoon; when a dairyman tells a story it is about a bull chasing a man until, finally overcome by his playing of Christmas music, it falls to its knees and the man makes his escape; as Tess contemplates her wedding gown, 'there came into her head the ballad of the mystic robe, "That never would become that wife/That had once done amiss." . . . Suppose this robe should betray her by changing colour, as her robe had betrayed Queen Guenever.' When Alec meets her again he makes her swear over a strange stone pillar that she will never tempt him again. He departs, and she hears the pillar is a thing of ill-omen put up by the relations of a man who was hung. At the end of her tether, oppressed by her work and by Alec, she begins to learn, in the wan hope of Angel's return, the ballads that he liked, 'the simple, silly words of the songs resounding in painful mockery of the heart of the singer'. This primal world of love and grief, of omen and song, forms the centre of the novel, its densest presentation of what James called 'felt life'. Tess belongs to it entirely, and like all ballad heroines she is fundamentally changeless.

When we consider Alec D'Urberville, we move into a world different from this one, but the shift still lies completely within Hardy's power of dramatic presentment. It has been frequently urged against Alec that he is simply a stock-in-trade figure from Victorian melodrama. He is certainly a stock figure, but only because he belongs to a stock world; he is the eternal tempter. He describes himself to Tess as 'the old Other One who can tempt you in the disguise of an inferior animal'. To a large degree he is simply the anonymous villain of the ballad. He is dressed and cut for the part, 'moustarchers', a fashionable tweed suit, a gay walking-cane, and idiom to match ('Well, my Beauty...'). Here Hardy is establishing an historical perspective. The rural ballad world now comes to be seen more specifically as an agricultural community beginning to disintegrate under the threats of industrialism, the Changeless giving way to the Changeful. We are reminded in this connection of his remark that 'if the world stood still at a felicitous moment there would be no sadness in it'. Alec is an embodiment of the Change.

Outsiders, assuming an old family name to which they have no right, the Stoke-D'Urbervilles settle in Wessex. For them 'everything looked like money'—houses, animals, people. They brought with them power without responsibility. Across the old ways of life cracks are beginning to run. A horse is killed and a family is brought to the edge of ruin; agricultural machinery is turning workfolk into labourers; scarcity of work is forcing annual migrations. And, literally cutting its way through the countryside, is the ever-extending railway. Sometimes the old and the new world are vividly juxtaposed: 'There was the hissing of a train, which drew up almost silently on the wet rails, and the milk was swung can by can into the truck. The light of the engine flashed for a second upon Tess Durbeyfield's figure, motionless under the great holly tree. No object could have looked more foreign to the gleaming cranks and wheels than this unsophisticated girl, with the round bare arms, the rainy face and hair... the print gown of no date or fashion, the cotton bonnet drooping on her brow.' But soon even the foreign objects are to disappear and the world of 'gleaming cranks and wheels' is to take over. That world is Alec's. Present at the station with Tess, however, is another person, Angel Clare, and

'Tess of the D'Urbervilles' (1891)

he is really a stranger to both the worlds so vividly evoked here. He exists in the realm of philosophic speculation—and it is this which provides a top-dressing to the novel.

Just as Alec is lightly connected to the ballad world of Tess, but really 'lives' (in so far as he lives at all) in the new capitalist world, so Angel is lightly connected with that world of Alec's— 'He did not milk cows because he was obliged to milk cows, but because he was learning to be a rich and prosperous dairyman, landowner, agriculturalist, and breeder of cattle'—but his real element is that of the Free-Thinkers' Hall. In either case he is a world away from Tess, too far for differences to become conflicts, and effective communication peters out in the vacancy between. In a novel less fiercely conceived such a dramatic crack, reaching practically to the centre, would have been fatal.

In the thin air in which Angel lives there is only debate, and languid debate at that. We notice primarily the ambiguous presentation of 'Nature'. To say this is not to take Hardy to task for his defects as a philosopher, but to suggest that he juggles with the word 'nature' in a way damaging to his artistic purpose. At times the protest would appear to be against the human condition as such; this is surely the force of Tess's most uncharacteristic reflection that the world is 'a blighted star'. When the three milkmaids fall in love with Angel Clare, Hardy observes that 'they writhed feverishly under the oppressiveness of an emotion thrust on them by cruel Nature's law—an emotion which they had neither expected nor desired'. This then is how things would appear to be, and, setting aside questions as to the legitimacy of calling something 'blighted' or 'cruel' if it is its nature to be so, and the futility of complaint against things being what they are, we can turn to Hardy's other, and more frequent, use of the word 'nature'. This relies for its effect precisely on the possibility of change; as they are, things are healthy, the blight is social custom and attitude. It is on this axle that the abstractly formulated 'defence' of Tess turns: 'Walking among the sleeping birds in the hedges, watching the skipping rabbits on a moonlit warren, or standing under a pheasant-laden bough, she looked upon herself as a figure of Guilt intruding in the haunts of Innocence. But all the while she was making a distinction where there was no difference. Feeling herself in antagonism she was quite in accord. She had been made to break an accepted social law, but no law known to the environment in which she fancied herself such an anomaly.' Innocence ... Guilt, such is the kind of juxtaposition between the natural and the social environment; if men looked into their hearts things could be very different. This somewhat Rousseauistic view of nature contrasts strangely with the determinist one, which Hardy runs alongside it. In a 'blighted' world distinctions like this echo hollowly: 'The impressionable peasant leads a larger, fuller, more dramatic life than the pachydermatous king.' On Tess's relations with Alec, we have this: 'But for the world's opinion those experiences would have been a liberal education.' 'Opinion', 'education', the reference constantly points to the possibility, at least, of change and enlightenment. In exploring and assessing Tess's situation, Hardy is continually using a double standard. His immediate defence is by way of beneficent Nature: 'She was ashamed of herself for her gloom of the night, based on nothing more tangible than a sense of condemnation under an arbitrary law of society, which had no foundation in Nature.' But then, when Hardy is taking a remoter view, the tragedy is inherent in Nature's 'cruel law'—in the way things are. To take the force of one point, we have to forget the other; there is contradiction here, not complexity. On the other hand, the small measure in which this confusion, which is central to the theme of the novel, really decreases its artistic compulsion, suggests how effectively the latter is protected against the raids of philosophic speculation.

This ambivalence is related to the weakness in presentation of Angel Clare in the tale. The thinness of this aspect of the novel is due to Hardy's failure to integrate his 'thought' into his art. This is revealed in a variety of ways.

At one point, in the person of Clare, he himself makes this accusation of imaginative failure at those who fail to appreciate and understand the rural world. He can afford to do this with impressive authority: 'The conventional farm-folk of Clare's

'Tess of the D'Urbervilles' (1891)

imagination—personified in the newspaper press by the pitiable dummy known as Hodge—were obliterated after a few days residence. At close quarters no Hodge was to be seen.' 'Hodge', however, in *Tess*, has merely shifted house and is to be found in Emminster Vicarage and its environs. Here, for instance, Hardy juxtaposes caricature and portrait and appeals for judgment: 'Miss Mercy Chant . . . was great at Antinomianism and Bible Classes, and was plainly going to hold a class now. Clare's mind flew to the impassioned, summer-steeped heathens in the Var Vale. . . .' At such moments, Hardy seems not so much to have his thumb in the scale, as his whole right arm. How lightly Hardy the artist is engaged with this material is suggested by a conversation like this, where imaginative tact seems to desert him completely. Angel has just returned to the Vicarage, having left Tess:

> 'But where's your wife, dear Angel?' cried his mother, 'how you surprise us.'
> 'She is at her mother's—temporarily. I have come home in a hurry because I have decided to go to Brazil.'
> 'Brazil! Why, they are all Roman Catholics there surely!'
> 'Are they? I hadn't thought of that.'

Given such a passage for identification, one would feel confident in assigning it to one of the satires of Mr. Evelyn Waugh. When Hardy attempts to discuss ideas, there is no imaginative resonance in their presentation. They stand out with awkward boldness, and we feel the typeface ought to change. Angel's brother, a clergyman, is speaking to him:

> 'But I do entreat you to endeavour to keep as much as possible in touch with moral ideals. Farming, of course, means roughing it externally, but high thinking may go with plain living, nevertheless.'
> 'Of course it may,' said Angel. 'Was it not proved nineteen hundred years ago—if I may trespass on your domain a little? Why should you think, Felix, that I am likely to drop my high thinking and my moral ideals?'
> 'Well, I fancied, from the tone of your letters and our conversation —it may be fancy only—that you were somehow losing intellectual grasp. Hasn't it struck you, Cuthbert?'
> 'Now Felix,' said Angel drily, 'we are very good friends, you know;

each of us treading our allotted circles; but if it comes to intellectual grasp, I think you, as a confirmed dogmatist, had better leave mine alone, and enquire what has become of yours.'

This hit-or-miss attempt at conversational 'polish' is self-conscious and clumsy; there is no imaginative grasp here, only a gesture towards a notion of what 'intellectual conversation' sounds like. It may be that Hardy is exposing the pretensions of Felix, but Angel's replies are of a similar kind. And Angel, however wraith-like dramatically, Hardy advances as 'an advanced and well-meaning young man, a sample product of the last five and twenty years'. We have only to think of some of the poems of Arnold or some passages from George Eliot to see his inadequacy as an imaginative representative of 'this strange disease of modern life'.

If *Tess* has a centre capable of formulation in abstract terms, then such a statement is found in Clare's reflections on 'the old appraisements of morality. He thought they wanted adjusting. Who was the moral man? Still more pertinently, who was the moral woman? The beauty and ugliness of a character lay not only in its achievements, but in its aims and impulses; its true history lay not among things done, but among things willed.' This is a forceful passage, making the point succinctly and without rhetorical flourish. Hardy is here feeling his way towards a criticism of 'behaviour' as an adequate moral register—'not things done, but things willed'. In James this criticism is vastly extended and subtilized, and the way is prepared for the characteristic twentieth-century novel, which takes as axiomatic the moral supremacy of 'things willed'. The citadel defended by the Victorian novelist was 'innocence', and 'innocence' can be seen most clearly in behaviour; the citadel defended by the modern novelist has shifted to 'integrity' and here we are more naturally at home in the psychological world of motive and intention. Abstractly Hardy could see the shifting strategy, but in practice he occupied the old position.

The citadel was 'innocence'—this leads us back to the point from which we started, the idea of the 'pure woman', who occupies the centre of the novel. This centrality exists not because

'Tess of the D'Urbervilles' (1891)

Hardy, in Angel's reflections, has *said* so; it is sustained because it has been imaginatively created by the art of the novelist. We are led back from the abstract to the concrete, from the philosophical gloss to the living scene. To try and enforce this I want to conclude by examining a particular episode, which seems to have all that is strong in the novel behind it, which brings to a sharp focus what I have said about the ballad world and its steady disintegration, and, above all, illuminates its centre, the 'pure woman', as seen and understood by the author.

It is the threshing-scene at Flintcomb-Ash. As the farm workers arrive in the dawn light, they find the field already occupied by two machines, a threshing-machine and an engine which drives it. In control is the engineman who has been hired for the day: 'He was in the agricultural world, but not of it. . . . He spoke in a strange northern accent; his thoughts being turned inward upon himself, his eye on his iron charge, hardly perceiving the scenes around him and caring for them not at all; holding only strictly necessary intercourse with the natives. . . . The long strap which ran from the driving-wheel of his engine to the red thresher under the rick was the sole tie-line between agriculture and him.' To his workers he is nameless, being referred to simply as 'the engineer'. Work begins and Tess, accompanied at times by her two milkmaid friends, finds herself engaged on the platform of the threshing-machine. Inexorably the wheels spin, the drum turns and work continues, with Tess feeling increasingly shaken and faint. The older men recall the days when threshing was done with flails on the oak barn-floor. Work continues, positions are changed; but because she is quick and efficient the farmer keeps Tess on the platform.

Conversation is drowned by the noise of the engine and Tess fails to notice the arrival, behind the rick, of a man in a fashionable tweed suit, 'twirling a gay walking-cane'. It is Alec D'Urberville. He has cast off the last of his scruples about his preaching, has resumed his ordinary clothes, and is now totally intent on winning Tess back again. Quietly and inevitably the metaphorical implications extend and darken. The shaking platform of the machine merges into the hammering of the new temptation about to beset Tess; behind the nameless engineman, there is Alec, the Seducer, seen again in his true clothes: 'I am the old Other One come to tempt you . . .'; but the realistic surface of the scene remains undisturbed.

Dinner-time comes. The machine is left and the workers withdraw to the edge of the field to eat. Tess, who has now seen Alec and recognized 'the old, jaunty, slap-dash guise' for what it is, decides to remain up on the platform. Alec crosses over to her and argument begins: explanations, pleadings, followed by stubborn refusals. Mockingly, Alec the ex-preacher quotes the prophet Hosea to her: 'And she will follow after the lover, but she shall not overtake him . . . then shall she say, I will go to return to my first husband; for then was it better with me than now.' This quotation reflects an earlier one, when Mr. Clare, mindful of Tess, reads to Angel and his household, from the book of Proverbs: 'Who can find a virtuous woman? for her price is far above rubies.' It is this quotation which the scene is concerned to make real and endorse. Alec continues his persuasion remorselessly:

'Tess, my trap is waiting just under the hill . . . you have been the cause of my back-sliding . . . you should be willing to share it, and leave that mule you call your husband for ever.' One of her leather gloves, which she had taken off to eat her skimmer-cake, lay in her lap, and without the slightest warning she passionately swung the glove by the gauntlet directly in his face. It was heavy and thick as a warrior's, and it struck him flat on the mouth. Fancy might have regarded the act as the recrudescence of a trick in which her armed progenitors were not unpractised. Alec fiercely started up from his reclining position. A scarlet oozing had appeared where her blow had alighted, and in a moment the blood began drooping from his mouth upon the straw. But he soon controlled himself, calmly drew his handkerchief from his pocket, and mopped his bleeding lips. . . . 'Now, punish me,' she said, 'I shall not cry out. Once a victim, always a victim—that's the law.'

Her protest to Alec suddenly becomes a physical protest; honour is threatened, she seizes her only weapon, and the gauntlet is literally thrown. The straw is stained with blood and two themes are fused, Alec's threat to Tess, and the machine's threat to the community to which she belongs. In the fusion each theme

'Tess of the D'Urbervilles' (1891)

is strengthened by the other, so that behind Tess's resistance we feel the desperate resistance of a community, a fall here is far more than a personal fall; and on the other hand the resistance of the community to the machine is personalized in the antagonism between Tess and Alec, so that what is at stake is expressed as a matter of persons and not a matter of abstractions. If we look at the scene from the personal side we find magnification, from the communal side, concentration. Whichever way we look we find at the centre a person, and that person, Hardy makes clear, is for him a 'pure woman', and it is in social terms that her quality is defined and defended.

The scene closes with fateful calm. Alec and the machine become even more closely identified. He steps across to her, talking of his ultimate mastery, and takes hold of her 'so that she shook in his grasp'. He then goes down from the platform. The workers reassemble: 'Then the threshing-machine started afresh; and amid the renewed rustle of the straw, Tess resumed her position as one in a dream, untying sheaf after sheaf in endless succession.' By now the scene has acquired such resonance that this picture, in its bleakness and sense of fatality, lies transparently over another, that of the Future which Tess is to have. Already implicit in the blood on the straw lying at her feet is the blood on the ceiling which 'had the appearance of a gigantic ace of hearts'. The cards are already stacked; only the trump card remains for the gods to play.

In Jamesian terms the whole scene is superbly 'done'. The whole pattern of the book is caught up and magnified, without the support of a philosophic 'gloss'. Every detail contributes precisely, giving just so much emphasis and no more—the stark field, the machine, the nameless engineman, the twirling cane, the shaking platform, the biblical quotations, the thrown gauntlet, the blood on the straw—to form an irresistibly powerful unity.

Criticism ought to be able not only to analyse the meaning of a book, but to convey something of what it feels like to read it. Whatever reservations analysis may suggest about *Tess*, a reader's general impression is one of deeply 'felt life'. And it is precisely this that discussion of the threshing-scene brings home. To talk of symbolism here would be patently clumsy. One requires a more impressionistic, elusive language, something that would lay bare the fact that in this chapter we are watching an artist who is often uneven hitting the very top of his form, so that every touch and movement is as swift as it is unerring. And in the last analysis what does come through is the force of Hardy's sub-title—'a pure woman' seen and presented within a social framework. Hardy may talk of 'things willed' but here everything is externally 'done', the gauntlet is visibly thrown. The individual physically confronts her antagonist. But the way is beginning to be clear for 'things willed' to find their imaginative expression in art, for the contest between corruption and innocence to take place not in a field, but within the human heart itself. For this we have to leave Hardy and enter the world of Henry James.

6

The Novel of Moral Consciousness: 'The Awkward Age' (1899)

> That virtue, therefore, which is but a youngling in the contemplation of evil and knows not the utmost that vice promises to her followers, and rejects it, is but a blank virtue, not a pure.
>
> MILTON, *Areopagitica*

[i]

To come to *The Awkward Age* fresh from a reading of *Tess of the D'Urbervilles* is to understand sharply what Hardy meant when he remarked that 'James's subjects are those one could be interested in at moments when there is nothing larger to think of.' The key word is 'larger'; everywhere in *Tess* we are made aware that immensely serious and important issues are being contemplated, and, even when the novel is at its weakest, we feel the personal compulsion and overwhelming sincerity behind it. But with *The Awkward Age* the case seems very different. The great following out of an individual life, not only at a crucial period in English social and economic history, but against a background of cosmic speculation, is replaced by a long series of drawing-room conversations, barely distinguishable in their content, and conducted by individuals who appear to have no existence outside their conversational virtuosity. Furthermore, when we come to the conversation itself, there is nothing 'large' about it. If we describe it as dealing with personal relationships, we seem to dignify it unduly, when that description is thought of in connection with, say, the novels of Mr. E. M. Forster. The conversations would appear to be more accurately described as extraordinarily refined, sophisticated and excessively articulate gossip.

If we turn to the critics, these impressions are unlikely to be seriously disturbed. The book has not attracted the best critics of James, except in a passing reference, and the little criticism that does exist falls into two kinds. There are those who have responded to the 'content' of the novel, and their opinion is roughly that of Hardy's reaction to James's work as a whole. Edmund Wilson is a convenient representative of this kind of criticism: 'One is dismayed,' he writes, 'in reading James's comments on *The Awkward Age*, which he seems to have considered highly successful, to realize that he is unaware of the elements in the book which, in spite of the technical virtuosity displayed in it, make it unpleasant and irritating.... They combine a lifeless trickery of logic with the ambiguous subjectivity of a nightmare.' And the other kind of critic has responded primarily to the 'form'—Wilson's 'technical virtuosity'—and here the praise has been lavish. Percy Lubbock in *The Craft of Fiction* examines *The Awkward Age* as the novel of 'pure drama', remarking about its conversational method that 'the beauty of its resolute consistency is of course a value in itself'.

What is interesting is that criticism of the novel should have fallen, with almost diagrammatic neatness, into the classical division of 'form' and 'content'. A division of this kind is one which allows little hope of reconciliation. The advocates of 'content' see in the admirers of the novel a frivolous aestheticism; the advocates of 'form', on the other hand, see in the detractors only an exhibition of insensibility. This is depressing criticism, because it makes no attempt to understand the novel as an entity, but simply uses it as an occasion for the critic to appear in shirt sleeves or velvet jacket. It precludes any sustained attempt to examine the *relationship* between form and content, and so obscures the recognition that it is precisely here that the relevant literary judgment has to be made. If the novel is trivial

'The Awkward Age' (1899)

it is not because the 'subject' is not 'large', but because the attitude towards the subject is trivial; if the form is a triumph that is because the subject has found complete expression. Hardy's criticism of James is not literary but philosophical; Lubbock's praise, that of a practitioner. And relevant novel criticism must be narrower than the first and wider than the second. That intense awareness of 'form' can be as distorting as summary descriptions of 'content' is suggested by Lubbock's reference to 'the charmed circle of Mrs. Brookenham and her wonderful crew', when, demonstrably, the burden of the book is to reveal to the reader the depth of its depravity and sterility.

Behind these critical distortions and giving, as it were, an authority to them is James's Preface to the novel, written for the New York edition of 1908. The autobiographical and technical preoccupations of the Preface would be less disturbing if one could feel that James thought he was offering a partial account, a more or less technical note, on the novel. But there is nothing to suggest this in the Preface, and we have here the beginning of that critical dichotomy which I have been describing. James discusses the technical interest that *The Awkward Age* had for him in a way that makes us recall his remark to Howells: 'I find our art, all the while, more difficult of practice, and want, with that, to do it in a more and more difficult way; it being really, at bottom, only difficulty that interests me.' Lubbock can certainly point to James's Preface as warranting his interest in the 'form' of the novel. And James would also appear to endorse the opinions of those who find the content trivial. The 'prime propulsive force' he describes in this way—'the difference made in certain friendly houses and for certain flourishing mothers by the sometimes dreaded, often delayed, but never fully arrested coming to the forefront of some vague slip of a daughter'. The 'innocence' and 'corruption' with which the novel deals are smoothed out in the Preface into the difficulties of parental tact in sophisticated metropolitan society: 'One could count them on one's fingers (an abundant allowance), the liberal firesides beyond the wide glow of which, in a comparative dimness, female adolescence hovered and waited. The wide glow was bright, was favourable to 'real' talk, to play of mind, to an explicit interest in life, a due demonstration of the interest by persons qualified to feel it: all of which meant frankness and ease, the perfection, almost, as it were, of intercourse, and a tone as far as possible removed from that of the nursery and schoolroom. . . . The charm was in the freedom menaced by the inevitable irruption of the ingenuous mind; whereby, if the freedom should be sacrificed, what would truly *become* of the charm?' 'Freedom' and 'charm' would hardly appear adequate descriptions of the depth and desperation of the conflict, but, lest we should think that James was momentarily describing a minor interest of the novel, he concludes the paragraph with authoritative directness:

The Awkward Age is precisely a study of one of those curtailed or extended periods of tension and apprehension, an account of the manner in which the resented interference with ancient liberties came to be in a particular instance dealt with.

It is difficult to avoid calling this anything other than a distorted account, and a distortion, with its emphasis on 'charm' and 'ancient liberties', ill-calculated to remove the forebodings of those who already, with Van Doren, see James as 'the laureate of leisure'.

This then is the kind of critical position that someone who feels the novel to be extremely impressive finds himself facing. Let it be admitted straightaway that the novel is a difficult one, and as Graham Greene once remarked of James's work: 'The beauty of the books is very like the beauty of Turner's late pictures: they are all air and light: you have to look a long while into their glow before you discern the most tenuous outline of their subjects.' But sustained attention is handsomely repaid. It is encouraging to find that Dr. Leavis would endorse the assertion. His comments on *The Awkward Age*, brief as they are, are all the more interesting because they occur in an essay which is largely an attack on James's later novels, on the grounds that 'in the technical elaboration . . . he had lost his full sense of life and let his moral taste slip into abeyance'. This is precisely the kind of objection which lies behind a great deal of the hostile criticism of *The Awkward Age*, and when a critic with Leavis's

'The Awkward Age' (1899)

intense moral preoccupations turns aside from his argument, and not only carefully exempts this novel from his strictures, but goes on to place it with James's masterpieces, it is time to pause and re-examine the current critical orthodoxy of a technical triumph concealing triviality of material.

[ii]

With this critical reaction as a background I want to turn to a descriptive analysis of the novel itself. And then, in a final section, to go on and draw out the moral implications and assumptions of *The Awkward Age* by way of reference to Hardy and the French 'realists'.

It is perhaps useful to preface the analysis with a brief outline of the main plot:

Nanda Brookenham, a girl of seventeen, is not yet considered of a suitable age to join the social circle in which her parents, particularly her mother, delight. Reproached, however, by one of her friends, Mr. Mitchett, for keeping her daughter so 'apart', Mrs. Brookenham's attitude alters and Nanda is admitted to 'the set'. She becomes 'a modern daughter', appearing on every social occasion, generally acclimatizing herself in this society of 'free' talk—intellectual, witty, malicious, covertly scandalous in deed as well as word. Vanderbank, a particular friend of Mrs. Brookenham, has for a long time been an admirer of Nanda's, while she, in her turn, has been openly in love with him. Watching this relationship with considerable satisfaction is an elderly gentleman, Mr. Longdon, who years previously had been a great admirer of Nanda's grandmother. In Vanderbank Mr. Longdon sees a means of saving Nanda from the rather corrupt and corrupting social 'set' which surrounds her. In consequence, he tells Vanderbank that on her wedding day he will greatly increase Nanda's dowry. Mrs. Brookenham hears this from Vanderbank with mixed feelings: satisfaction at her daughter's increased value as a marriageable investment, anxiety that this enhanced value may involve her in the loss of Vanderbank's company. For different reasons Vanderbank himself is hesitant. There is the feeling that, however generously intended, Mr. Longdon's offer really constitutes a bribe; that acceptance will mean the loss of his present social freedom; above all, growing doubts as to whether or not Nanda has become corrupted by the circle in which she now moves so freely. Mrs. Brookenham observes these hesitations, and realizing that by now Mr. Longdon is so devoted to Nanda's welfare that, even if Vanderbank does not propose to her, he himself will look after her, she decides to exploit Vanderbank's doubts and so keep him for herself. At a party, given by one of her daughter's friends, Mrs. Brookenham sees an opportunity for publicly discrediting Nanda, and so confirming Vanderbank's doubts about her 'innocence'. For a while the repercussions are such that the circle appears to have been broken. Vanderbank, however, returns, but his visit, after a momentary hesitation, is confined to Mrs. Brookenham. Everything is now over between himself and Nanda. Only Mr. Longdon can rescue her from the isolation of her parents' house and, when visiting her again, he successfully renews his long-proffered invitation to her to leave the Brookenhams and come to stay with him.

As the whole novel 'works' by indirection and implication, such an outline can only suggest the order in which events happen; it can do nothing to indicate their significance. As one of my principal contentions is that the form the novel takes is intimately connected with its meaning, I have tried to enforce this most strongly by letting my analysis follow the actual unfolding of the novel, rather than by doing it 'aerially' and organizing it round dominant themes.

The novel is divided into nine books, each book being given as title the name of the character that James wants us to watch at that particular stage. An exception is the first book, which has as its title 'Lady Julia'—Nanda's grandmother, a woman who died many years before the novel opens. She is there because she is the immediate cause of Mr. Longdon's reintroduction and interest in her daughter's social circle, but more importantly it is Mr. Longdon's devotion to Lady Julia which is a crucial part of the judgment the novel is seeking to make. It serves Mr. Longdon well in enabling him—and the reader too—to assess the 'corrupt' members of the circle, but it is an idealizing blur when Longdon himself tries to see the 'innocent'. His growth in the novel is precisely to see past Lady Julia, to see in fact Nanda, not as a wonderful replica of her grandmother, but as a person living in her own right and demanding that kind of acceptance. And it is Nanda who gives her name to the final book. In Longdon's shift from Lady Julia to Nanda we see projected the shadow of

'The Awkward Age' (1899)

the movement which directs the novel—the insight which is capable of distinguishing 'a blank virtue from a pure'. Vanderbank, who can't distinguish the 'innocence' of Nanda from the 'innocence' of Aggie, remains, for all his talk of the modern world, with Lady Julia, in the past. At the end of the novel, when Vanderbank has finally rejected her, Nanda remarks to Longdon:

> 'Everything's different from what it used to be.'
> 'Yes, everything, he returned with an air of final *indoctrination* (my italics). That's what he ought to have recognized.'
> 'As *you* have?' Nanda was once more—and completely now—enthroned in high justice. 'Oh, he's more old-fashioned than you.'
> 'Much more,' said Mr. Longdon with a queer face.

Remembering where things are to end, we can turn back to the beginning of the novel, and feel the ironical edge more sharply.

The first book is really a prologue to the novel. Taken up with a long conversation between Vanderbank and Longdon, it is establishing the basic pattern of the book, the social circle of Mrs. Brookenham, represented by Vanderbank, trying to take into itself this elderly gentleman, who belongs to an earlier generation. The foundations of the novel are laid with stylized exactitude. We have 'modern life' described, and Mrs. Brookenham's circle as part of that life:

> London doesn't love the latent or the lurking, has neither time, nor taste, nor sense for anything less discernible than the red flag in front of the steam roller. It wants cash over the counter and letters ten feet high.

The tone of Van's description is one of amused self-criticism, and is calculated to impress the 'outsider' rather than permit genuine questioning. Twice Longdon manages a question, once when he asks about the possibility of friendship in such a society. Van replies that he has never believed in its existence in big societies: 'It's a plant that takes time and space and air . . . London's society . . . is an elbowing, pushing, perspiring, chattering mob.' The second occasion is more crucial. Van is talking of Nanda and the necessity of early marriage in such a society:

'Ah, certainly,' Longdon replied with a certain stiffness, 'but not as if she had been pushed down the chimney. All in good time.' Vanderbank turned the tables on him. 'What do you call good time?' 'Why, time to make herself loved.'

In a world of cleverness and brilliance, Longdon asks about friendship and love, and, in so doing, reveals an integrity and depth which are conspicuously absent in the world he is hearing described. Longdon's role is made quite clear at the beginning. 'I've accepted', he remarks, 'this queer view of the doom of coming back.' And later, we have this; 'He had indeed no presence, *but he had somehow an effect* (my italics). He might almost have been a priest . . .'. Vanderbank perceives Longdon's pastoral role, and makes his appeal: 'Don't abandon me. See what can be done with me. Perhaps I'm after all a case. I shall at any rate cling to you.' And more generally: 'You see we don't in the least know where we are. We're lost—and you find us.' This is a true perception, but it never becomes realized, because at the heart of Van is a deathly egotism which is kept preserved in the balm of his articulateness. It is through this that we are made aware that Van is completely part of the society he appears to be criticizing. The self-critical sentiment is nullified by the tone of its expression—'it strikes you that right and left, probably, we keep giving each other away. Well, I dare say we do . . . '. And this brings me to the point which the first book establishes with unmistakable clarity, the *point* of the dialogue form. The moral judgment is built into the articulateness of the characters. Vanderbank's failure is that he has become frozen within his own vocabulary; the words are all there but he has become numb to the concepts that inform them. And it is to the question of language that the first book finally directs us:

'Just tell me as a kindness. *Do* we talk——?'
'Too freely?' Mr. Longdon with his clear eyes untouched by time speculatively murmured.
'Too outrageously. I want the truth. . . . You were really shocked?'
His visitor at this smiled, but the smile somehow made the face graver. 'I think I was rather frightened. Good night.'

'The Awkward Age' (1899)

And in that exchange the first move of the drama is made. Van miscalculates his auditor; hoping for a *succès de scandale*—'You were really shocked?'—he has provoked 'fear'. And Longdon's fear arises from his perception that Van is moving in a circle where words seem to exist *apart from* values. What kind of corruption does this lead to? What kind of threat to 'innocence'—to the two girls, Aggie and Nanda, whose photographs Van has shown to Longdon? These are the questions that are to be taken up in the second book, but the first has established the approach, an approach whereby the technique of the novel is to be not only the means of its telling, but its subject also.

In the opening book James has presented the judge of his fiction; in the second book we are shown, with some precision, the nature of what is to be judged. Here we have disclosed to the reader Mrs. Brookenham's 'circle'. The method of narration is oblique, so that as the novel progresses we are not so much conscious of obtaining more information, as of seeing further into the meaning of what we have. The effect is similar to that of building up a picture by overlaying one transparent page on another. It would be tedious to illustrate this in all its detail, so I will direct my analysis towards two points in particular—the pervasive presence and pressure of economic factors, and the way in which these enter into and shape personal relationships.

The second book opens with a conversation between Mrs. Brookenham and Harold, her son, of which money is the subject. Harold has removed £5 from his mother's desk, and, with a perverted honesty, has stayed to tell her so. She cannot afford the luxury of moral condemnation, because he needs the money to finance a parasitic visit to friends, which she has arranged:

'Don't you think your children are good enough, mummy dear? At any rate, it's as plain as possible that if you don't keep us at home you must keep us in other places. One can't live anywhere for nothing. . . .'

That last sentiment reverberates throughout the novel. When

The Novel of Moral Consciousness:

Mr. Brookenham appears he takes up the question of Harold's borrowing money to pay gambling debts. Mrs. Brookenham carefully assumes indignation, an indignation which shades into a no less careful speculation: 'I want Mr. Longdon to be kind to Harold and I can't help thinking he will.' The implication needs no underlining.

This presentation of Harold's financial unscrupulousness is much more than the portrayal of a scapegrace son. It moves outwards to include the whole 'circle'. Of the Brookenham family Vanderbank remarks to Mr. Longdon: 'One doesn't quite know what they live on.' It is this which prompts Mrs. Brookenham to see in Longdon a great tap source of income: 'I want Mr. Longdon to be kind to Harold', and more important: 'He must be kind to Nanda.' Vanderbank, though a deputy chairman of a company, is described by the Duchess as having 'nothing but a poor official salary'. And Mitchett, though 'the son of a shoemaker and superlatively hideous', is preyed upon by them all because of his wealth. In this society the line from financial to moral bankruptcy is a direct one. People become 'property' and what cannot be bought is not worth having:

> Beauty in London, staring, glaring, obvious, knock-down beauty, as plain as a poster on a wall, an advertisement of soap or whiskey, something that speaks to the crowd and crosses the footlights, fetches such a price in the market that the absence of it, for a woman with a girl to marry, inspires endless terrors. . . . London doesn't love the latent or the lurking, has neither time nor taste, nor sense for anything less discernible than the red rag in front of the steam roller. It wants cash over the counter. . . .

The kind of conjunction that exists between the economic and the human could hardly be made more explicit. With this kind of pressure behind it to treat people as things, so that they become material for manipulation, the movement the novel takes is towards the creation of a completely externalized world—'London doesn't love the latent or the lurking'. And so we come back, by another route, to the external *form* of the novel, the series of dialogues where the very articulateness of the characters carries within it its own moral judgment. With these remarks in

'The Awkward Age' (1899)

mind we can turn to the first scene where they are actually dramatized—the long conversation in Book II between Mrs. Brookenham and the Duchess.

After a brief reference to Harold's departure, conversation turns to the Duchess's niece, little Aggie, who is at present attending 'Mr. Garlick's class in Light Modern Literature'. Being told in answer to her query that Mrs. Brookenham's daughter, Nanda, is staying at Tishy Grendon's, the Duchess quickly makes plain her opinion that the company of an unhappily married woman is no place for a young girl—it is a far cry from Mr. Garlick's class. Here, presented in the guise of a concern for education, we have the central value of the novel, innocence, discussed for the first time. And from the outset we have it discussed from alternative points of view. The Duchess reflects on her niece's Italian background:

'It would have been good enough for my child, as I call her—my dear husband called her *his*—if, not losing her parents, she had remained in her own country. She would have been brought up there under an anxious eye—that's the great point; privately, carefully, tenderly, and with what she was *not* to learn—till the proper time—looked after quite as much as the rest. I can only go on with her in that spirit....'

Mrs. Brookenham's retort is not delayed:

'My daughter, at any rate, is just my daughter—thank heaven, and one of a good English bunch; she's not the unique niece of my dead Italian husband, nor doubtless either, in spite of her excellent birth, of a lineage, like Aggie's, so very tremendous. I've my life to lead and she's part of it. Sugar?' She wound up on a still softer note as she handed the cup of tea.

'Protection and ignorance' against 'exposure and knowledge': this would appear to be the issue which is being acidly debated, but this concern for moral values is quite specious when we realize that the debate is simply about the most effective strategy to obtain a rich husband. 'Education', 'Innocence,' 'Experience'— these are all so many counters in the game. The Duchess speaks with malicious indulgence: 'I've not so much as thought of Mr. Mitchett—who, rich as he may be, is the son of a shoemaker and superlatively hideous—for a reason I don't at all mind telling you. Don't be outraged if I say that I've for a long time hoped you yourself would find the right use for him.' The moral concern flakes off to reveal the values of the market. But the process is to become increasingly crude: 'Why isn't it plain as a pikestaff that the thing to do with Nanda is simply to marry her —and to marry her soon?'... 'I don't say at all that I should sniff at poor Mitchy. We must take what we can get and I shall be the first to take it. You can't have everything for ninepence.... He takes, moreover, his ease in talk, but that ... is much a matter of whom he talks with. And after marriage what does it signify? He has forty thousand a year.'

It is this kind of background we have to keep in mind when, later, the Duchess returns to the party, this time accompanied by Little Aggie, 'as slight and white, as delicately lovely, as a gathered garden lily'. The Duchess adds to the air of oppressive innocence: 'Aggie and I are simple stranger-folk; there's a great deal we don't understand.' But this kind of ignorance—previously adduced with reference to Aggie's education—is now resonant with irony. Part of the Duchess's allusion is to the presence in the room of Lady Fanny, Petherton's sister, and her husband's mistress, Mrs. Donner. Any feeling of tension has been removed by the observation, made by the 'knowledgeable few', that Lady Fanny has no animosity towards Mrs. Donner, as the illicit relationship provides her with a ready-made excuse to cover her own infidelities. Previously, Mitchett, encouraged by Mrs. Brookenham, has challenged the Duchess to explain her remark about Nanda's being 'damaged and depraved'. Evading the direct question, the Duchess proceeds to speculate on the extent of Lady Fanny's knowledge of her husband's liaison with Mrs. Donner, and then with quiet effectiveness inserts Nanda's opinion:

Mr. Mitchett visibly wondered. 'But how should Nanda know—?' 'Anything about the matter? How should she *not* know everything? You've not, I suppose, lost sight of the fact that this lady and Mrs. Grendon are sisters.... What I touched on to her mother was the peculiar range of aspects and interests she's compelled to cultivate by

'The Awkward Age' (1899)

the special intimacies that Mrs. Brook permits her. There they are—and that's all I said. Judge them for yourself.'
And so the second book reaches its climax in Nanda's knowledge, working towards it by way of revealing the kind of corruption that prevails in the Brookenham circle, where the accent of the moralist disguises the values of the auctioneer. As the party grows in number, the illicit relationships are increasingly hinted at—the Duchess and Petherton, Vanderbank and Mrs. Brookenham, Mrs. Donner and Mr. Cashmore. And now we are brought to face Nanda's involvement. Mrs. Brookenham had remarked to the Duchess of Nanda: 'I've my life to lead, she's part of it'; we are now led to ask: does being a part mean being infected with its values? By the end of Book II that question and its implications have been fully stated; the rest of the novel is devoted to its exploration.

Nanda up to this point has simply been talked about, now she is directly introduced, and introduced to Longdon. Her involvement with the Brookenham circle, metaphorically suggested in her 'knowledge' of its scandals, is not quite literal. Explaining her unaccompanied arrival at Van's rooms, Nanda says: 'Mother didn't come, because she wants me now, as she says, more to share her own life. . . . She's throwing me out into the world.' The moment of Nanda's direct involvement is also, however, the moment of her introduction to Longdon. Earlier, Mitchett has reminded us again of his role: 'We want just what I'm sure you'll bring us—a fresh eye, an outside mind.' Unquestionably this is what Longdon does bring, a clarity of moral vision, but the clarity increases with his familiarity with the circle on the one hand and with Nanda on the other. At this point Longdon is too simply aware of her 'innocence'; she brings too disturbingly to life his devotion to the past: 'It's the most extraordinary thing in the world. I'm too absurd to be upset . . . but if you had known Lady Julia you would understand. It's *she* again, as I first knew her, to the life.' If Longdon's response is too etherialized at this stage, Nanda's is direct and unequivocal: 'I'm glad to be like anyone the thought of whom

The Novel of Moral Consciousness:

makes you so good. You *are* good . . . I see already how I shall feel it.' It is in that response and the fact that she is now 'a part' of Mrs. Brookenham's life that we have the tension of the novel.

For the length of Book IV Nanda is removed and our view of Mrs. Brookenham's circle is deepened. In structure it is akin to Book II, opening with a question of money, this time Harold sponging on one of his visitors, Mr. Cashmore; and orchestrating this more subtly with Mrs. Brookenham's increasing interest in Longdon as something more than a charming memento of her childhood days:

'Isn't he rather rich?' She allowed the question all its effect of abruptness. Vanderbank looked round at her. 'I haven't the least idea.' 'Not after becoming so intimate? It's usually with people the very first thing I get my impression of. . . . With his small expenses all these years, his savings must be immense. And how could he have proposed to mamma unless he originally had money?'

In Mrs. Brookenham's assertion that Nanda is going to be *made* 'the proper grandchild for mamma' we have an unwittingly ironical comment on Longdon's already seeing in Nanda an absolute re-creation of Lady Julia, and thus marking his own limitation. People as property, people as something to manipulate—the two themes reappear, helping us to define the corruption of the 'circle'. Innocence is laid under a double threat, and immorality is continually presented in a dual way.

It is there in scandal and gossip and illicit relationships, the kind of thing that Nanda is ostensibly being 'protected' from. Mr. Cashmore presents a danger of this kind when he announces to Mrs. Brookenham his liking for Nanda, having just abandoned his last mistress:

'If you don't believe Mrs. Donner is dust and ashes to me, you do little justice to your daughter.'
'Do you wish to break it to me that you're in love with *her*?'
He hesitated, but only as if to give weight to his reply.
'Awfully. I can't tell you how I like her.'

The circle are quite aware of this kind of corruption, so that, when Cashmore asks what Nanda is exposed to, Vanderbank

'The Awkward Age' (1899)

can reply with complete equanimity: 'She's exposed to you, it would seem, my dear fellow.' But a much subtler kind of immorality is revealed in the book, and this is the conversion of people to things, a process made possible by using 'a language which has been morally anaesthetized. A case in point is Mrs. Brookenham's praise of Lady Fanny to her husband, Lady Fanny whose appeal to the circle seems largely because of her calm, instinctive amorality:

> 'Fanny's *not* "bad"; she's magnificently good—in the sense of being generous and simple and true. . . . She's a great silver statue.'

What Mrs. Brookenham would appear to intend is a defence of 'simple nature'; and not only does Fanny's behaviour make nonsense of her being 'magnificently good', but the image Mrs. Brookenham uses, the 'silver statue', is revealing in a way she hardly intends. As a product of art it plays against the natural vitality she is praising, and furthermore it is a *thing*, a connoisseur's piece, in precisely the way that Lady Fanny is for the group. 'She's the ornament of our circle', Mrs. Brookenham later tells Vanderbank, and her fascination consists in the possibility of her elopement: 'She will, she won't—she won't, she will! It's the excitement, every day, of plucking the daisy over.' The attitude to Lady Fanny presents a very obvious illustration of the real corruption present in the Brookenham world, but it is wholly characteristic, and it is this which constitutes a much more serious threat to Nanda's 'innocence' than the more external aspects of immorality with which she is surrounded. The fourth book closes, like the second, with a reported action of Nanda's—this time an increasing intimacy with Tishy Grendon —which suggests, formally at least, her increasing absorption in the role of 'the modern daughter'. But a distant signal has been flashed to a watchful eye, and Mr. Longdon 'appeared to have caught from Nanda's message an obscure agitation'.

Up to this point in the novel James has been largely concerned with establishing three themes—the nature of the corruption of Mrs. Brookenham's circle, the integration of Nanda with that circle, and the presentation of Mr. Longdon as 'a fresh eye, an outside mind'. But with Book V finer discriminations begin to be made with regard both to the 'corruption' and the 'innocence' involved. In one direction we begin to distinguish more precisely between Mitchett, Vanderbank and Mrs. Brookenham, and in the other between Nanda and little Aggie. Our increasing ability to distinguish is Mr. Longdon's also.

For the first time the action moves out of doors. Mitchett has rented a house for the summer and invited the 'circle'. Nanda wanders alone in the garden and meets Van who has just arrived. The scene which follows gives us, for the first time, this crucial relationship. Once again we are made aware of the babble of words and never so much as when it is being denied: 'Because we're such jolly good friends we really needn't so much as speak at all? Yes, Thank goodness—thank goodness.' When Nanda tries to cut through this self-conscious ease, she breaks out: 'Happy relations don't matter. I always think of you with fear.' But this shock attempt to strike a real emotional response runs aground as Van turns it into 'a curiosity'. Again it is in terms of language that we hear that Longdon is still learning about Nanda, when she remarks to Van that he is still puzzled by 'the extraordinary difference between my speech and my grandmother's'. But Nanda's intuition about Longdon's importance for her is certain: 'I'm about as good as I can be—and about as bad. If Mr. Longdon can't make me different, nobody can.' And her hope lies in her self-criticism and her understanding of silence: 'Between his patience and my egotism anything is possible. It isn't his talking—it's his listening.' This kind of self-criticism is radically different from Van's, and reveals the difference between a genuine humility awkwardly expressed and a profound egotism enclosed in empty gallantry.

It is self-criticism which characterizes Longdon's conversation when he comes out to join Nanda. For the first time he checks himself from using the past as a simple criterion of excellence, remarking that he is a Rip Van Winkle who has slept half a century. But this increasing awareness of his own simplicity in no way modifies the soundness and authority of his judgments. Talking about Mitchett's renting of the house he deplores the

'The Awkward Age' (1899)

way homes are taken over by strangers to make quick profits for their owners, and when he turns to Nanda saying, 'I want to show you what life *can* give. Not, of course, of this sort of thing,' he is not proposing a visit to his own home as an idyllic retreat, to be contrasted with the bustle of the 'rented house', but as a promise of a life more richly lived, because it cares for its surroundings and doesn't try merely to use them. Once again, it is an attitude to property which is made to reveal human values. And it is this attitude which James uses to provide the first clue about Mitchett, who, though in the Brookenham circle, is by no means of it. Nanda makes this plain to Longdon, 'Mitchy doesn't care . . . for himself. I mean for his money. For anything anyone may think. . . .' From this moment Longdon senses in Mitchett an ally, but, when Nanda emphatically denies that she would ever marry him, he sees sadly that such an ally will only be able to help him obliquely. He voices his regret: 'Well, that doesn't make me wish it any less.' And Nanda's reply is all too prophetic: 'It's lovely of you to wish it, but I shall be one of the people who don't. I shall be at the end one of those who haven't.' It is in the bleak mood induced by this that Longdon meets the Duchess, and in the conversation that follows, the centre of interest switches away from the 'corruption' of the circle to the 'innocence' of Nanda. Again, comparison and discrimination are the instruments, and Nanda's innocence is played off against Aggie's:

> On little Aggie's slate the figures were yet to be written; which sufficiently accounted for the difference of the two surfaces. Both the girls struck him as lambs with the great shambles of life in their future; but while one, with its neck in a pink ribbon, had no consciousness but that of being fed from the hand with the small sweet biscuit of unobjectionable knowledge, the other struggled with instincts and forebodings, with the suspicion of its doom and the far-borne scent, in the flowery fields, of blood.

The distinction could hardly be more explicitly made. The point is Milton's: 'That virtue, therefore, which is but a youngling in the contemplation of evil, and knows not the utmost that vice promises to her followers, and rejects it, is but a blank virtue, not a pure.' That Aggie's was 'a blank virtue' there was little doubt—'on (her) slate the figures were yet to be written'—but could Nanda's be said to be 'pure'? If the slate becomes too heavily scored what value has it then? It is with these anxieties in his mind that Longdon, to his amazement, hears the Duchess pick up his earlier thoughts and boldly restate them: 'Nanda, my dear man, should marry the very first moment. . . . And I want for Nanda simply the man she herself wants . . . Vanderbank. . . .' Inevitably, the point is sharpened with an economic factor: 'You can make him propose . . . you can settle something on her that will make her a *parti*. . . . Poor Edward, you know, won't give her a penny.' Without the bonus, what incentive can there be? Lucidly, Longdon sees the proposal for what it is—'the idea you're so good as to put before me is to bribe him to take her'. Unshaken, the Duchess pursues her course, referring to Longdon's devotion to Lady Julia, his no less touching devotion to her granddaughter, and then with a brutal frankness: ' "Nanda's fairly sick—as sick as a little cat—with her passion." The oddity of the image could draw from him no natural sound.' But he acknowledges the basic truth of the observation. Warning him that opposition will come from Mrs. Brookenham, because she wants Van for herself, the Duchess leaves him.

This scene is the turning point in the novel, catching up all that has gone before—Longdon's growing awareness of Nanda and the nature of her mother's circle, her relationship with Vanderbank and with Mitchett, the kind of innocence she has compared with Aggie's, the realization that only marriage will give her the necessary control over her circumstances—and it offers now, through the Duchess's proposal, an effective mode of action. The economic key has been placed in his hands and Longdon decides to use it. It is the effect of this decision on the 'circle' that constitutes the material of the second half of the novel.

What is interesting in the next scene, where Longdon puts the proposal to Van, is the new confidence his action has given him. Up to now he has been the listener, the rather bewildered spectator, but now he grows in authority and sets the pace. Longdon's rise is the 'circle's' decline, and the 'talk' appears noticeably

'The Awkward Age' (1899)

more hollow. When Longdon, for instance, makes his proposal to Van, he goes on:

'Of course, what it superficially has the air of is my offering to pay for taking a certain step. It's open to you to be grand and proud—to wrap yourself in your majesty and ask if I suppose you bribeable. I haven't spoken without thought of that.'

But Van's reply is too self-consciously conciliatory, too 'modern':

'Yes... but it isn't as if you proposed to me, is it? anything dreadful. If one cares for a girl one's deucedly glad she has money. The more of anything good she has the better, I assure you.'

Any embarrassment there is in the scene is now Van's and not Longdon's. The inner unease reflects itself at once in the 'talk'. Repeatedly, Van has insisted on the freedom of the talk in the Brookenham circle, but now, in reply to Longdon's question about Mrs. Brookenham's interest in him, Van sounds merely evasive and trivial:

'We call everything—anything. The meaning of it, if you and I put it so, is—well, a modern shade.'
'You must deal then yourself,' said Mr. Longdon, 'with your modern shades.'

The crisp moral dismissal is revealing of them both.

This change-over in the rhythm of the novel is strengthened in Book VI. The circle, which delighted in feeling themselves the object of Mr. Longdon's wondering gaze, now begin to look at *him*, and, in doing so, constantly miscalculate and bring about internal friction. In the first half of the novel the 'modern' values had been criticized mainly by Longdon's questions and misunderstandings; now that Longdon has acted, the group is simply left to expose itself. Appropriately, it is money which has caused the critical shift. An increasing self-exposure of the Brookenham circle is the subject of Books VI, VII, and VIII.

In Book VI Mrs. Brookenham sees in Longdon her 'daughter's security'. But she is now becoming remote from the real situation and Van realizes this. 'We keep him in touch with old memories', she says and Van replies sharply, 'I do so like your phrases.' And it is precisely this kind of interchange—the talk becoming aware of itself as just that—that marks the beginning of the destruction of 'the temple of analysis' in Mrs. Brookenham's drawing-room. Van tells her of Longdon's proposal and that he is his 'candidate' for Nanda. Imperturbably, she remarks: 'In so far as they count on you, they count, my dear Van, on a blank.' Shocked, he now —ironically—praises her acumen. At this point Mitchett arrives and immediately, quiveringly, one might almost say, Mrs. Brookenham passes the news on to him. Van feels the scarcely concealed barb and takes up the familiar theme, but orchestrated in a very different way:

> 'What *is* splendid, as we call it, is the extraordinary freedom and good humour of our intercourse and the fact that we do care—so independently of our personal interests, with so little selfishness or other vulgarity, to get at the idea of things. The beautiful specimen Mrs. Brook has just given me of that was what made me break out to you about her when you came in.'

Nothing that Longdon has said or implied had been so devastating. Toiling in a world of words which have lost their meaning, Van tries angrily to escape:

> 'What are we playing with, after all, but the idea of Nanda's happiness?'
> 'Oh, I'm not playing!' Mrs. Brook declared with a little rattle of emotion.
> 'She's not playing,' Mr. Mitchett gravely confirmed it.

The tonal variation on 'playing' suggests how thoroughly the trap of language has been sprung.

Nanda comes into the conversation, and there is a double edge to the contribution of all three; the defensive but defaming note struck by Mrs. Brookenham, the bitter-sweet note of Mitchett, the lover who cannot be accepted, and Van, alternating bluff assurance with anxious query. Once again Mitchett marks himself out as refusing to share the circle's preoccupation with persons as things capable of being labelled, and defending Nanda he says: 'When I like the individual, I'm not afraid of the type. She knows too much—I don't say; but she doesn't know, after all, a millionth part of what I do.' If Nanda is corrupted, they are

'The Awkward Age' (1899)

all, he argues, in their various ways, to blame. It is left to Mrs. Brookenham, however, to make explicit the connection between this possible corruption and the particular vice to which she has been exposed:

'And yet to think that after all it has been mere *talk*!' Something in her tone again made her hearers laugh out; so it was still with the air of good humour that Vanderbank rejoined: 'Mere, mere, mere. But it's exactly the "mere" that has made us range so wide.' Mrs. Brook's intelligence abounded. *'You mean we haven't had the excuse of passion?'* (my italics).

The insight is central to the meaning of the whole book.

After this analysis by linguistic exposure, the scene concludes with a reminder of the practical form it takes. Nanda has returned from a visit to Mr. Longdon to find her mother alone. She is questioned about his attitude towards her, about the possibility of his adopting her, and in the following exchange 'innocence' and 'corruption' are carefully juxtaposed. Nanda says:

'Oh, the great advantage, I feel, is doing something for *him*.' Nanda's companion, at this, hesitated afresh. 'But doesn't that, my dear, put the extravagance of your surrender to him on rather an odd footing? Charity, love, begins at home and *if it's a question of merely giving* (my italics), you've objects for your bounty without going so far.' 'Why, I thought you wanted me to be so nice to him!'

Between Nanda's 'him' and Mrs. Brookenham's 'object' we have the measure of the moral gulf between them. And from the cool, lucid surprise of the final remark we can be sure that on one side of the gulf there is 'not a blank virtue, but a pure'.

This almost casual conversation prepares the way for a much more intense and sustained look at the question: 'What is Nanda?' which provides the subject of Book VII. For Van, urged on by Longdon's proposal, this becomes the obsessive question. What kind of knowledge is it that she has? This is the dominant note of their second meeting:

'Don't I know everything?'
'Do you? I should rather ask,' the young man gaily enough replied.

The Novel of Moral Consciousness:

'Why should I not? How should I not? You know what I know . . . I remember you once telling me I must take things in at my pores.'

Van must be left in no doubt as to the extent of her exposure; what this means is left for him to decide. Is knowledge synonymous with endorsement? The question is imperative and again Van postpones it and escapes into *bonhomie*.

The analysis moves forward swiftly and with delicate precision when Nanda seeks to advance Aggie's merits to Mitchett: 'Now the beauty of Aggie is that she knows nothing—but absolutely, utterly: not the least little tittle of anything. . . . Ah! say what you will—it *is* the way we ought to be.' And here, unwittingly, Nanda does reveal her weakness—but it emerges not as a failure of knowledge but a failure of self-knowledge. She makes two errors, both of which, formally considered, are errors of the Brookenham circle. She mistakes a 'blank virtue' for a 'pure', and, in proposing to Mitchy that he marry Aggie, she is attempting to manipulate persons. But in both cases, her motives transform her errors; unlike the 'circle', who continually seek to dehumanize people, Nanda, in praising Aggie and proposing a marriage, is seeking to enrich human lives, by delivering Aggie from the Duchess and Mitchett from Petherton 'who preys on you'. Nevertheless, James shows us here that Nanda's innocence is still not free of naïvety; he succeeds in circumscribing her virtue, without, in any way, lessening it.

Just as earlier Longdon, presented with one of the 'corrupting' interests of the Brookenham circle, the reduction of behaviour to economic necessity, had accepted it and turned it to his own use, and grew immensely in understanding, so now Mitchett accepts Nanda's 'manipulation' and grows likewise. In a scene in which he tells Van that he is going to marry Aggie, he reveals Van's own limitations with increasing clarity. The conversation turns to Nanda, and whether she is aware of Longdon's proposed 'settlement', whether he will offer her anything as compensation, if his offer should not be taken up; as one issue develops into another it becomes clear that Van is preparing his escape. Finally, he bursts into this:

'The Awkward Age' (1899)

'... She knows everything ... everything, everything.'
'Everything, everything.' Mitchy got up.
'She told me so herself yesterday,' said Van.
'And she told *me* so today.'

The words are the same but the meanings quite dissimilar. For Van to 'know' is to become corrupt; and it *is* this, because he dehumanizes. The corollary to seeing people as plastic material for economic pressure is to see them as 'blank virtue' passively exposed to 'corruption'. Nanda had once remarked to Van: 'I remember you telling me that I must take in things at my pores.' He now re-emphasizes this to Mitchett, 'everything ... in London is in the air she breathes—so the longer she's in it the more she'll know.' As in the case of economic manipulation, the specifically human attribute of the will is ignored. The double corruption of the Brookenham circle is revealed as basically one. Virtue can be bought, providing it is sold in a glass case. Faced with making a choice which cuts behind appearance, which seeks to understand rather than to observe, Van retreats and 'the extraordinary freedom of our intercourse' contracts into a preference for ignorance. It is little Aggie who really wins the day:

'Ah, but your choice....'
'Is such a different sort of thing?' Mitchy, for the half-hour in the ambiguous dusk, had never looked more droll.

The irony is totally missed, and Vanderbank, as he blows out the candles, is completely unaware of his self-exposure and the thoughts that preoccupy Mitchy as he stands 'in darkness, face to face with the vague, quiet garden'.

Throughout Books VI and VII the consequences of Longdon's proposed settlement on Nanda have been explored, but the exploration has been conducted in various segments of the 'circle', Vanderbank, Mitchett, Mrs. Brookenham. Individual reactions are now clear; what is needed is a complete assembly, for the full meaning to be brought out. This provides the substance of Book IX, the party at Tishy Grendon's, held to celebrate the departure of Mitchett and his wife, Aggie, before they travel abroad.

The Novel of Moral Consciousness:

It begins almost casually with Vanderbank arriving early and finding himself the first guest. He is joined by Nanda and Harold. The conversation turns to Longdon, and Harold becomes a magnifying mirror in which Van sees his own moral position. Glaringly, he lights up the conjunction between exploitation and the defence of innocence; with reference to Nanda's relationship with Longdon we have this:

'You are nice, old woman . . . and one can still feel for the flower of your youth, something of the wonderful "reverence" that we were all brought up on . . . I'll be hanged if he shall have her for nothing.'

And the accompanying attitude to this is:

'London . . . is quite awful for girls and any big house in the country is much worse. . . . I know some places, where, if I had any girls, I'd see 'em shot before I'd take 'em.'

The crudity of attitude is such that Van draws back in disgust, but it is a withdrawal which brings with it a moment of self-insight: 'I feel I must figure to Harold very much as Mr. Longdon figures to me.' But the moment doesn't last, and Van doesn't understand the implications of his self-criticism, when the time comes to act. As long as Harold is there, his vision of ruthless egoism is sharp—he glimpses in Nanda the same kind of detachment that she sees in Mitchy—but the party grows larger, Harold joins Lady Fanny, and the vision dims. And before the evening is over his view of innocence is to be indistinguishable from Harold's—and the Duchess's.

On her arrival she seizes Longdon and, with a fulsome compliment, describes, with unwitting accuracy, a true situation: 'How can I help it, if I see your hand in everything that has happened since the so interesting talk I had with you last summer at Mertle,'—since, in fact, her suggestion to Longdon about Nanda's settlement. As in the earlier conversation, she warns him of Mrs. Brookenham's hostility. The force of this warning is made clear when the Duchess and Mrs. Brookenham confront each other in a scene which recalls their encounter at the beginning of the novel. It is the last time Mrs. Brookenham takes the centre of the stage, and now it is a baited, angry woman, no longer looking outwards and trying to 'use' Longdon, but turning inwards and ready to destroy her own circle, rather than continue to occupy the peripheral position into which circumstances have forced her. Her first blow rebounds, crushingly, against her. She appeals to Longdon, on behalf of Edward and herself, for the return of Nanda—'we yet have our natural feelings'. Edward appears, is questioned by the Duchess, and provides a lethal commentary on their 'natural feelings':

'Want her, Jane? We wouldn't take *her*.' As if knowing quite what he was about, he looked at his wife only after he had spoken.

The moral execution of the Brookenhams, by each other, marks the beginning of the death of the 'circle'. What follows is the way this fatality spreads out to include the others.

Mrs. Brookenham, who is completely unaware of what has happened, says to Mitchy, whose marital party has turned into a wake: 'Direct your energies as much as possible, please, against our uncanny chill.' It is the advice which he heeds. Dramatically the door is locked and the circle is left to destroy itself. The means presents itself. An obscene book is being playfully fought over by Petherton and Aggie. Aggie, yielding, ruefully explains: 'From the moment one has a person's nails, almost his teeth, in one's flesh——' As one person after another is involved in this book—Van's property and bearing his name, it was lent by him to Mrs. Brookenham, and from there taken to Tishy Grendon's by Nanda who read and condemned it—the effect is that of a flame running along the fuse to the explosive at the end. The explosion occurs when Mrs. Brookenham compels Nanda to admit that she has read the book. Characteristically, it is the *reading* not the judgment that is considered decisive in establishing Nanda's corruption; in other words, behaviour isolated from the will which gives it *human* meaning. It is Van's book and that point is left for Aggie to make with a withering, if unconscious, irony: 'It was just seeing Mr. Van's hand ... that made me think one was free....' But it is precisely this kind of freedom that the 'free' society cannot afford; Aggie is forcibly torn from the book she is fighting for, and her 'innocence' is vindicated. That in a

The Novel of Moral Consciousness:

scene in which Harold is revealed as exploiting Lady Fanny, the Duchess and Petherton treat Mitchy's marriage with complete cynicism, and the Brookenhams virtually disown Nanda, the single point of corruption should be adjudged Nanda's reading Vanderbank's book, indicates the completeness of James's criticism of 'pure behaviour' as a moral criterion. It is to this that the worship of 'the blank virtue, not the pure' has led. The guilty have accused themselves; a judge, even as onlooker, is superfluous: 'Mr. Longdon had by this time ceremoniously approached Tishy, "good night".'

The rest of the novel is an epilogue, the settling of dust after destruction. As Vanderbank says to Mrs. Brookenham: 'You pulled us down—just closing with each of the great columns in its turn—as Samson pulled down the temple!' The positive action is Longdon's return and the vindication of Nanda. To say that she is rescued would be untrue, except in the most superficial sense of her physical removal by Longdon from the Brookenham world. The tragic truth would seem to lie in her mother's description: 'She's as bleak as a chimney-top when the fire's out.' The circle is now, quite literally, broken; Mrs. Brookenham sits in her room downstairs receiving visitors, but not guests; Nanda does likewise in her room upstairs. And the visitors come—Vanderbank, Mitchett, Longdon—first to one room and then to the other, establishing their final relationships with the respective occupants. The social circle has broken to be replaced by another, a moral one, which seeks to respect the human person and talks the language of sincerity. Nanda is at its centre, a centre which has been almost negatively created by the precision with which the bounding line of corruption has been drawn. With her are Longdon and Mitchett, who, in their various ways, have come to learn the meaning of innocence.

In this final section James creates a mood of weariness. The great opposite poles have been established, the corruption of ruthless egotism on one side, showing itself as the need for possession and ignoring the distinction between the human and the material, and on the other side innocence, showing itself primarily as detachment and truly accepting things as they are.

'The Awkward Age' (1899)

Longdon has come to accept Nanda for what she is and not as an extension of Lady Julia; Mitchett, Aggie, for Nanda's sake; Nanda, a future with Longdon, though her heart is with Vanderbank: ' "Oh, I don't know how to say it." She fairly coloured with the attempt. "One must let the sense of all that I speak of—well, all come. One must rather like it. I don't know —but I suppose one must rather grovel." '

Mitchett, looking at his dark future with Aggie, can say to Nanda:

'... what does stretch before me is the happy prospect of my feeling that I have found in you a friend, with whom so utterly and unreservedly I can always go to the bottom of things. The luxury, you see, of *our freedom* (my italics) to look facts in the face, is one of which I promise you, I mean to fully avail myself.'

For him and for Nanda language has at last become possible, because the saying and the believing are one. It is a theme caught up for the last time in the conversation between Nanda and Longdon, when, discussing Vanderbank's final rejection of her and his motives for refusing the settlement, Nanda goes on:

'You've admitted as much when we've talked——'
'Oh, but when *have* we talked?' he sharply interrupted.
This time he had challenged her so straight that it was her own look that strayed. 'When?'
'When.'
She hesitated. 'When *haven't* we?'
'Well, you may have; if that's what you call talking—never saying a word.'

It is a remark which reverbates back through the novel, making hollow conversation after conversation, exposing them finally as simulacra of the hollow values they sought to describe and make prevail. The true value, innocence, was to be found only in the hidden—'London doesn't love the latent or the lurking'—in the uncertain question, and finally, in this most excessively articulate of novels, in 'never saying a word'.

The Novel of Moral Consciousness:

[iii]

A descriptive analysis, such as I have attempted, cannot of course turn a bad novel into a good one. It can only try to bring out as clearly as possible what the novel seems to be about, and consequently to make possible a more relevant criticism and a more informed appreciation. It would be disingenuous to claim that an analysis, however objective, does not imply a judgment, but my main effort has been directed towards the dissipation of certain kinds of reaction to the novel which make genuine recognition of 'the way it works' somewhat uncommon. These reactions—that the novel is trivial in theme or a masterpiece of technical virtuosity—I have described in the opening section of this essay. Having gone on to examine their validity in the detailed context of the novel itself, I want to conclude by enlarging the perspective and setting them in the light of the contrast James's work provides with Zola's and Hardy's.

James greatly admired the work of Zola, but he felt that when it succeeded it was in spite, rather than because of, the literary principles which governed French realist fiction. Exclusively absorbed with 'the surface of life', they denied, or at least took no interest in the spirit of man. Consequently we find him writing of Flaubert that 'his imagination was so fine that we take some time to become conscious that almost none of it is moral or even human'. Nevertheless he was not unaware of particular achievements:

This profuse development of external perceptions—those of the appearance, the sound, the taste, the material presence and pressure of things, will at any rate, I think, not be denied to be the master sign of the novel in France. . . . They carry into the whole business of looking, seeing, hearing, smelling, into all kinds of tactile sensibility and into noting, analysing and expressing the results of these acts, a seriousness much greater than that of any other people.

But 'when they lay their hands on the spirit of man they cease to become expert'. James, however, would also assert that his description of sensible reality was, for his own purpose, quite as

'The Awkward Age' (1899)

true as anything of Zola's; and indeed in a letter he makes precisely the 'realist' point: 'I must at any rate mention that I had in view a certain special social (highly 'modern' and *actual* [my italics]) London group and type.' The difference was entirely one of scale and material, and if Zola had chosen to portray adequately this 'London group and type' this is the kind of novel he would have *had* to write. What 'happens' in this world is social meetings and conversation, and the novelist whose declared business was 'looking, seeing and hearing' would have had to record that as fully and exactly as possible. James chose this highly sophisticated and limited world in which to set his novels, because it permitted him the maximum exploration of consciousness consonant with the preservation of external credibility.

James's point is really that the weakness of the novelists of Zola's school was that they were not realistic enough, that, in identifying 'the facts of life' with observable realities, they were guilty of a spiritual evasion as distorting as anything they themselves complained of. To this, of course, the realists might have replied that this criticism only held if one accepted the 'inner'-'outer' dichotomy which James constantly appealed to; that for them there was only one reality, and in so far as the 'spirit of man' could be apprehended apart from the surface it was a deception. The same defence would certainly not have been made by Hardy; but, like the French novelists, though from a rather different point of view, James found him too lacking in 'realism'.

Writing to Stevenson in February 1893, James, commenting on his correspondent's hostile criticism of Tess, remarked:

> I grant you Hardy with all my heart and even with a certain quantity of my boot toe. I am meek and ashamed where the public clatter is deafening—so I bowed my head and let *Tess of the D's* pass. But oh, yes, dear Louis, she is vile. The pretence of sexuality is only equalled by the absence of it, and the abomination of the language by the author's reputation for style. There are indeed some pretty smells and sights and sounds. But you have better ones in Polynesia.

The Novel of Moral Consciousness:

It may at first seem odd that the author of *The Awkward Age* should bring a charge of sexual evasiveness against the author of a book which aroused more public hostility than any comparable work of its time—curious and unjust. But this would be to misunderstand James's position. He, no less than Hardy, felt the pressure of Victorian 'taste' on the novelist, but he argued that sex was a dominant factor in life in a way that the Victorian novelists ignored rather than concealed. By this he meant not the portrayal of physical passion, but the effects it had on the human personality. James would argue that adultery lay at the centre of *The Portrait of a Lady* and *The Wings of a Dove* as surely as at the centre of *Tess*. But for him it was not the act itself that was of consequence—so that he was never involved in difficulties of censorship—but the *effect* of the act, on Isabel Archer in the one case, and on Milly Theale in the other. Hence his criticism of *Tess*—'the pretence of sexuality is only equalled by the absence of it'. The concern is simply with an act and not with what the act means.

His attack on *Tess* would appear to have much in common with his attack on the Italian realist D'Annunzio, for whom 'sexual passion . . . insists on remaining . . . *only* the act of the moment, beginning and ending in itself. . . . Shut out from the rest of life it has no more dignity than . . . the boots and shoes in the corridors of promiscuous hotels'. But presumably this is to make exactly Hardy's point about *Tess*: her relationship with Alec was precisely only 'the act of the moment', and her tragedy was that she was made to suffer for it for the rest of her life. Alec's effect on her, as a person, was nil, and consequently Hardy would have agreed that as far as this part of the book was concerned there was a 'pretence of sexuality', and moreover that that effect was deliberate and sustained. If we turn, however, to Tess's relationship with Clare, the situation is very different. Indeed here we find Hardy trying rather uncomfortably to turn our attention *away* from the sexuality he has so palpably created. It is a pleasant irony to consider the following passage and bear James's criticism in mind. One sunny afternoon at the farm Clare surprises Tess, who has been sleeping:

'The Awkward Age' (1899)

> She had not heard him enter and hardly realized his presence there. She was yawning and he saw the red interior of her mouth as if it had been a snake's. She had stretched one arm so high above her coiled-up cable of hair that he could see its satin delicacy above her sunburn; her face flushed with sleep and her eyelids hung heavy over their pupils. The brimfulness of her nature breathed from her.

Hardy then continues in this way:

> It was the moment when a woman's soul is more incarnate than a any other time; when the most spiritual beauty bespeaks itself flesh; and sex takes the outside place in the presentation.

It is difficult to see Hardy writing that last phrase without watching him glance in the direction of his reading public, and yet, in a sense, it is true that the sexuality of the passage is very much a matter of external description. And certainly in this sense James is right in seeing the whole creation of Tess as being done from an 'outside place'. When it comes to criticism of the novel, to artistic self-awareness, there can be no doubt that James had forgotten more than Hardy ever learnt, but in practice this has not the importance that might be imagined. The passage I have quoted is an example of heavy and ill-calculated comment such as James would never have been guilty of, and yet it does surprisingly little damage to the presentation of the description that precedes it. When James fails the penalties are much higher. At the centre of *The Awkward Age* lies the character of Nanda, but our experience of her is much more as a study of Innocence than as an innocent person. We never really become engaged with her in the way that we ought to if the novel is to have its full effect. Two important remarks, made at very different points in the novel, indicate this remoteness. On one occasion we find the Duchess remarking to Mr. Longdon that Nanda is 'fairly sick— as sick as a little cat—with her passion', and, while this is effective in revealing the Duchess, we cannot help feeling, at the same time, that we are never close enough to Nanda for remarks like this one to have much meaning. Similarly, when later in the novel Mrs. Brookenham says of her that 'she's as bleak as a chimney-top when the fire's out' we are at a loss to know how to take it. Certainly it is a remark which would match the tragic pathos of the closing chapters, but Mrs. Brookenham is the last person we would rely on for an unvarnished truth. Clearly it is important that we should know Nanda's state of mind at the end of the novel; yet James, with all his skill, leaves us uncomfortably in the dark.

Nevertheless it would be perverse not to admit that one of the great differences between the two novelists lies in James's remarkable ability to recognize and bring out the importance of 'things willed' behind 'things done', and there is certainly one occasion in *Tess* when Hardy would have benefited by a lesson from the master. I refer to his uncertainty about preparing us for Clare's reaction to Tess's confession. In his treatment of their love affair in Var Vale Hardy seems continually caught in two minds about the presentation of Clare's love for Tess, so that we are never quite sure whether a slightly ominous note is being struck, or whether it is simply lyrical intensification. For instance, in the early days of their courtship, we find them meeting in 'the spectral half-compounded aqueous light of the dawn', and this leads naturally to:

It was then . . . that she impressed him most deeply. She was no longer the milkmaid, but a visionary essence of woman—a whole sex condensed into one typical form. He called her Artemis, Demeter and other fanciful names half-teasingly, which she did not like because she did not understand them.

Here Hardy would appear to be conveying with perfect tact and success the fatally idealizing element in Clare's love, whereby he sees Tess less as a person, than as a goddess. He has built her into a mythology; and when he is made to realize that she has a human 'past' he is forced to see her anew. Only in this way can we understand his later retorts to Tess after the confession: ' "You were one person: now you are another?" "I repeat, the woman I have been loving is not you." "But who?" "Another woman in your shape." ' But when we look at Tess's love for Clare, which is clearly intended to be free of this kind of idealization, we find Hardy remarking: 'She loved him passionately . . . he was god-like in her eyes.' Hardy seems to lack here the ability to make the necessary emotional distinc-

'The Awkward Age' (1899)

tions while maintaining the lyrical intensity of the whole episode. His brush is not fine enough for this kind of shading.

In the last stage of the novel, however, it is the very thickness of his brush which works to his advantage, and saves the 'purity' of his heroine when a more subtle novelist would have felt that he was in danger of severely compromising her. When Tess returns to Alec to live with him at Sandbourne, Hardy explains it away in simple narrative terms: 'I wrote to you and you did not come! He kept on saying you would never come any more and that I was a foolish woman. He was very kind to me and to mother and to all of us after father's death.' While these are understandable reasons any novelist who was more aware of the 'atmosphere of the mind' than Hardy would feel that, between being suddenly and reluctantly seduced by Alec and going to live as his mistress, a moral line has been crossed, and that an explanation is needed if the moral status of the heroine is not to be impugned. But by this time Hardy has managed so successfully to impose on the reader the kind of story he wants to tell, a story profoundly concerned with the remorseless drive of 'things done', that we accept the externality of the explanation as a necessary commonplace, without realizing that a moral crux has been neatly side-stepped.

James's criticism of Tess may look trivial enough, even when it is seen in relation to his more comprehensive critique of the French realists. Fundamentally, however, James is attacking a moral criterion which has been unchallenged in the bulk of fiction up to his time, the criterion of 'behaviour', and substituting for it another, the criterion of 'moral consciousness'. This is to put it much too simply, but if the two criteria are not antithetical they certainly represent decisively different ways of regarding human actions. In *Tess* we sense Hardy's notional sympathy with the transition, 'the beauty or ugliness of a character lay not only in its achievements, but in its aims and impulses; the true history lay, not among things done, but among things willed'. He was unable to see, however, the implications this shift had for the novelist's conception of his art. James's achievement was not only to have something to say, in

Hardy's phrase, about 'the appraisement of morality', but to be able to provide a form perfectly adapted to its new expression.

Debating with Walter Besant on the nature of the novel, James had written:

> Experience is never limited and it is never complete; it is an immense sensibility, a kind of huge spider-web of the finest silken threads suspended in the chamber of consciousness, and catching every airborne particle in its tissue. It is the very atmosphere of the mind. . . .

The Awkward Age records the fine point of balance between 'behaviour' and 'consciousness', between Victorian 'innocence' and modern 'integrity'. A particular concern of the nineteenth century still has power to provide a serious novelist with a subject, but the eyes through which he sees it are modern. *The Awkward Age* bridges a moral and artistic chasm between the two centuries, and the title is apposite in a way hardly intended by the author. With this in mind it seems appropriate to conclude this essay with a remark of a contemporary novelist who is an artistic descendant of James—Graham Greene; and it is a remark particularly relevant to the emphases of this study:

> The long care which James gave to the technique of his art was all a gain for vividness, and the kind of ivory tower he inhabited admitted life more truthfully than a hatter's castle. His rules were not cramping; they had as their object the liberation of his genius, and the extent of his liberation is best seen when we compare him to his great contemporary, Thomas Hardy. Hardy wrote as he pleased, just as any popular novelist does, quite unaware of the particular problems of his art, and yet it is Hardy who gives the impression of being cramped, of being forced into melodramatic laocoon attitudes, so that we begin to appreciate his novels only for the passages where the poet subdues the novelist. In James the poet and the novelist are inseparable.[1]

We do not need to agree with Greene's estimate of the relative merits of Hardy and James to realize that with this accent we are in the middle of the twentieth century, looking back on the origins of modern fiction.

[1] *The Lost Childhood*, p. 50.

7

Grace and Morality: 'Thérèse Desqueyroux' (1927); 'The End of the Affair' (1951)

> 'Immorality?' he asked, with the slightly false note we can't avoid with such a word. 'That's never a problem,' Father Crompton replied.
>
> *The End of the Affair* (Bk. V: Ch. VI)

[i]

With the death of James the religious sense was lost to the English novel, and with the religious sense went the importance of the human act. It was as if the world of fiction had lost a dimension: the characters of such distinguished writers as Mrs. Virginia Woolf and Mr. E. M. Forster wandered like cardboard symbols through a world that was paper-thin. Even in one of the most materialistic of our great novelists —in Trollope—we are aware of another world against which the actions of the characters are thrown into relief. The ungainly clergyman picking his black-booted way through the mud, handling so awkwardly his umbrella, speaking of his miserable income and stumbling through a proposal of marriage, exists in a way that Mrs. Woolf's Mrs. Ramsay never does, because we are aware that he exists not only to the woman he is addressing but also in God's eye.

It is in this way that Graham Greene begins an essay on his distinguished contemporary, François Mauriac. He goes on to suggest that Mauriac's first claim on the attention of the English reader is that he belongs with the great traditional novelists, in that he restores this religious sense to the novel. That Greene would like a similar claim to be made about himself is obvious enough.

Grace and Morality:

Setting aside the justice or otherwise of this claim, what must strike the reader as unusual is Greene's contention that 'the religious sense'—and his own work makes it abundantly clear how he understands this—has always been a mark of the traditional *English* novel. That novel, whether we regard it as descending mainly from Fielding or from Richardson, has been dominantly ethical in preoccupation, and has found expression more often in action than in disposition. In this reference to Trollope's 'ungainly clergyman', Greene would seem to be agreeing with this, but the whole burden of his work, and, with a different turn of the screw, of Mauriac's too, is to reveal a disjunction between the moral and the religious, and, correlative with this, the constant deception of appearance. Considering Mauriac's *La Pharisienne*, Greene remarks, 'We are saved or damned by our thoughts, not by our actions.' And that belief, with all its implications for the practice of the novelist's art, may lie at the centre of his work, but hardly at the centre of what we understand by the 'traditional' extroverted English novel. What I wish to examine in this chapter is precisely those implications for the novelist's art, as they arise from a clash between thought and action, between faith and morals. In the present section I want to sketch briefly the Greene-Mauriac 'world' as it might be deduced from their fiction, and then go on to consider its embodiment in two particular novels, Greene's *The End of the Affair* and Mauriac's *Thérèse Desqueyroux*.

At the heart of the world Greene and Mauriac have created in their fiction is the existence of grace; it is this which gives shape and meaning to their universe. For Greene, 'the world is all of a piece . . . it is engaged in the same subterranean struggle . . . there is no peace anywhere where there is life; but there are . . . quiet and active sectors of the line'. This is the nature of life, abstractly expressed. Concretely, Greene expresses it in terms of certain clearly defined *locales*. There is Mexico, the Godless and abandoned state; there is 'the sinless, empty, graceless chromium world' of Stockholm, Vienna, Havana; there is bombed London, 'the world we lived in could not have ended in any other way'; there is West Africa—why, Scobie wonders, do I like the place?

'Thérèse Desqueyroux' (1927); 'The End of the Affair' (1951)

Is it because here human nature hasn't had time to disguise itself? Nobody here could ever talk about a heaven on earth. Heaven remained rigidly in its proper place on the other side of death, and on this side flourished the injustices, the cruelties, the meannesses, that elsewhere people so cleverly hushed up. Here you could love human beings nearly as God loved them, knowing the worst.

Though Greene varies his settings perhaps more than any other contemporary novelist, they are all images of a world 'implicated', in Newman's words, 'in some terrible aboriginal calamity'. For Mauriac too, the 'aboriginal calamity' is no less continually present and landscape is for him also a decisive factor in its expression. Unlike Greene, however, he locates it in a single, constantly repeated setting—the desolate Landes region near Bordeaux. It is in the stifling heat of this arid, sandy region, where the sun pours down like 'molten metal' and the dry wind blows through pines, that cruelty, lust and murder take root and turn to a monstrous growth.

This is 'the world', and it is hardly surprising that Greene and Mauriac should regard its inhabitants with awe and horror. Andrews, the coward in *The Man Within*, tells of 'a terror of life, of going on soiling himself and repenting and soiling himself again'. And it is with this 'terror of life' in the background that Greene and Mauriac populate their world. This is the world which has been completely ruined by Original Sin, in which man cannot do anything to save himself without the direct intervention of the grace of God. This implies that man cannot work for his salvation, and that his ultimate fate is predestined. Against this sombre background, Greene's characters assemble. Basically speaking, they are divided into three groups, those who accept the world, those who reject and are rejected by it, and those who are bewildered and abandoned. In the first group we have contentment made possible by egoism; we have Ida Arnold who 'didn't believe in heaven or hell. . . . Let Papists treat death with flippancy; life wasn't so important perhaps to them as what came after; but to her, death was the end of everything'; we have Pyle who 'was determined to do good . . . not to any individual person but to a country, a continent, a world'; we have Mr. Hands whose 'old tired grey face had peculiar nobility. For nearly seventy years he had been believing in human nature against every evidence—it hadn't been good for his promotion in the bank. He was a Liberal, he thought men could govern themselves if they were left alone to it, that wealth did not corrupt and that statesmen loved their country.'

'Belief in human nature', however, can contain an explosive content for those who cannot share this belief. 'I'm a stickler where right's concerned,' says Ida as she ruthlessly hunts Pinkie down. No quarter is given to those for whom this world is a prelude to the next. Exiled, hunted, betrayed, the sinners and the saints—Pinkie, the Priest, Scobie, Sarah, Harry Lime—play out, with endless variations, their role in the archetypal betrayal and suffering of Christ. In this they are caught up in the authentic drama of life, and this drama is, for Greene, essentially a melodrama. In the last analysis, 'life' can be expressed most accurately in the simplified lines of a cartoon. Between the pursuers and the pursued there exists another group, bewildered bystanders. There is Mr. Tench, unable to leave Mexico, and Arthur Rowe, who has to reassemble painfully the pieces of his life, puzzling over the discovery of human cruelty: 'Is life really like this? . . . I thought life was much simpler and grander. . . . I was brought up on stories of Captain Scott writing his last letters home, Oates walking out into the blizzard. . . . It's as if one had been sent on a journey with the wrong map.'

For Mauriac, the characters are, in some ways, grouped even more simply: 'I am a metaphysician who works in the concrete. Thanks to a certain gift of atmosphere, I try to make perceptible, tangible and odorous the Catholic universe of evil. I make incarnate that sinner of whom the theologians give an abstract idea.' The sinner lies at the centre of Mauriac's work, however variously imagined—Thérèse, Brigitte Pian, Gabriel Grandère, Maria Cross. Opposed to the sinner, and playing the part of those who in Greene's world 'believe in human nature', are the great landlord bourgeois families, whose material complacency barely covers their avarice and cruelty when their interests are

'Thérèse Desqueyroux' (1927); *'The End of the Affair'* (1951)

threatened. 'The family is not a thing we joke about,' Bernard tells his wife Thérèse, and we are made to realize the lengths to which such 'propriety' will go.

After 'the world' and 'the inhabitants', we have the way they behave. Constantly, in Greene and Mauriac, we find stressed the deception of appearances and the devaluation of 'action'. This, of course, is simply an extension of the reading of life as basically corrupt and corrupting, save for the intervention of grace. Greene summarizes it in this way: 'The little duke is dead and betrayed and forgotten: we cannot recognize the villain and we suspect the hero and the world is a small, cramped place.'

Two things have to be said about the pervasive presence of paradox and near-paradox in these novels. In so far as they deal with Christian themes, we have to remember that Christianity itself is centred in paradox—'the Word became Flesh'; 'he who shall lose his life shall save it'; 'to him that hath shall be given, and from him that hath not shall be taken away even that which he hath'—and, consequently, novels dealing with Christian experience will express, in some way, this paradoxical centre. In the case of Greene and Mauriac, however, this element of paradox is intensified by the particular colouring their Christianity takes, a colouring which it would not be inaccurate to describe as Jansenist. It is necessary to use this description with care, because by it we are trying to describe a certain cast of mind, rather than subscription to a doctrinal position. The overwhelming emphasis on grace entails a devaluation of human action, *particularly* those actions which proceed from individual virtue. This undercutting of the moral order is so persistent and deep that the opposite of vice is seen to be not virtue, but faith. Only with 'faith' can we really be insured against our corrosive egoism. A brief illustration of the way in which the moral order comes under fire is a conversation in Greene's play *The Living Room* between the priest and his sister Helen, who is making a 'moral judgment' about her niece's seducer:

JAMES: Don't blame him. Blame our dead goodness. Holy books, holy pictures, a subscription to the Altar Society. Do you think if she

Grace and Morality:

had come into a house where there was love, she wouldn't have hesitated, thought twice, talked to us——

HELEN: And why didn't she?

JAMES: Because there was fear, not love in this house. If we had asked her for a sacrifice, what would we have offered? Pious platitudes.

HELEN: Speak for yourself, James.

JAMES: I do. Goodness that sits and talks piously and decays all the time.

HELEN: He seduced her.

JAMES: It's a silly word, but what if he did? God sometimes diverts the act, but the pious talk He seems to leave like the tares, useless.

Ostensibly, Greene is criticizing a classification of an action being considered synonymous with a judgment of it, but in his eagerness to press the point home—'It's a silly word, but what if he did?'—he gives the impression that moral judgment is irrelevant anyway. He seems to invoke moral book-keeping on a double-entry system—'action' and 'talk'—and, while this might be a salutary pastoral reminder in life, it has curious repercussions for art.

To place Greene's remark 'We are saved or damned by our thoughts, not by our actions' beside George Eliot's 'Our deeds determine us, as much as we determine our deeds; and until we know what has been or will be the peculiar combination of outward with inward facts, which constitute a man's critical actions, it will be better not to think ourselves wise about his character', suggests the extent of shift in fiction of the balance and criteria of moral judgment. Our interest in the shift must be in the way in which the art is affected.

I began this chapter with a quotation by Greene on the work of Mauriac; and the sympathy and similarity which exists between their work can be suggested by citing from Mauriac a quotation on the work of Greene which both aptly summarizes what has been said and provides a general point of reference for the detailed analyses which follow. Introducing *The Power and the Glory* to French readers Mauriac describes the 'universe' of the novel in this way:

There is the corruption of nature and there is the omnipotence of Grace; there is the misery of man, who is nothing even in evil, and that

'Thérèse Desqueyroux' (1927); 'The End of the Affair' (1951)
mysterious love which takes possession of him at the very bottom of his ridiculous misery and ludicrous shame to make of him a saint and martyr.

With *The End of the Affair* and *Thérèse Desqueyroux* to direct our inquiry we can go on to ask what kind of implications this kind of world has for the writing of fiction. How does the presence of grace, the 'religious sense', affect the traditional moral judgment? Has it, in fact, restored a dimension to the novel and an importance to the human act which has been lost since the death of James?

[ii]

Of all Graham Greene's novels *The End of the Affair* is most likely to get summary justice. The reason lies, quite simply, in the apparent directness and explicitness with which the religious theme has been presented. In consequence, literary criticism tends to melt much too rapidly in the heat of extra-literary convictions.

For the reader who shares Greene's religious views, the theological contentions in *The End of the Affair* will tend to loom too large in his perspective. He may, for instance, welcome the novel as an intelligent and sensitive discussion of problems which are of great importance to him and be pleased that these questions are being given such persuasive publicity. Another kind of Catholic reader may be irritated precisely by the fact that publicity is being given to views which he considers, if not actually heretical, at least severely mistaken in emphasis. Both readers are guilty of the same confusion of thought. They fail to distinguish between theology and theology-in-fiction, between 'views' and 'the use of views' as artistic material. For both readers this failure has its consolation. If orthodoxy in fiction is unlikely to make for religious conversions, heterodoxy, similarly presented, is unlikely to disturb the faith of the believer. The influence of fiction is more elusive than the believer tends to think, though it would be rash to assume that it is less penetrating.

The reader who does not share the religious views behind

Grace and Morality:

The End of the Affair will tend to depreciate their significance. He will see them perhaps as a gratuitous addition to an otherwise satisfactory work; he will argue that the novel is finally 'closed' to him because he finds it philosophically or theologically unacceptable; he may go further and argue that the introduction of the divine into imaginative literature is an unwarrantable extension of the province of art. In doing so, he would forget Dante, Marlowe and Dostoevsky. He would forget, too, that however alien the miraculous is to his own thought and experience, it has clearly not been alien to a great number of the human race; and there certainly seems no intrinsic reason why such experience, genuinely felt, should be prohibited from art. Again there is the basic failure to distinguish between theology and theology-in-fiction. Where a certain kind of Catholic reader sees in Greene an apologia for his faith, a certain kind of sceptic sees an indictment of his. But fortunately Greene has written a novel and not a theological discourse, and it is this which makes the hypothetical reactions I have been describing largely irrelevant, and allows the whole matter to be taken further.

When this has been said it is no less important to stress that relevant discussion of *The End of the Affair* does not imply that the critic 'drops' his beliefs. This charade would be as undesirable as it would be unnecessary. Rather we have to find a way of talking about a religious novel which does not rely for its cogency upon our own beliefs, not because these should be neutralized, but because they should hardly be brought into play. There is a sense in which *all* discussion is eventually theological or philosophical, but clearly this does not render invalid the discussion which leads us to that terminus. Literary criticism, in so far as it remains that, only takes place between intermediate stations.

We can begin by setting down briefly the plot of *The End of the Affair*:

> Bendrix, a middle-aged novelist, and Sarah, the wife of a Senior Civil Servant, are lovers. Their 'affair', lasting through most of the war, runs an uneven, passionate and unscrupulous course, largely owing to the tormented jealousy and bitterness of Bendrix. It is brought to an

'Thérèse Desqueyroux' (1927); 'The End of the Affair' (1951)

abrupt end during an air raid. Bendrix is knocked unconscious under a door. After a few minutes he recovers, goes upstairs, and finds Sarah on her knees praying. She leaves the house and he doesn't see her again. All his attempts to get in contact with her fail. Eighteen months later Bendrix accidentally meets Sarah's husband, Henry. He invites Bendrix for a drink, and tells him that he is worried by Sarah's frequent absences from home. He is thinking of engaging a private inquiry agent. Bendrix urges Henry to allow him to make the engagement. Unknown to Henry he does so, and proceeds to get reports on Sarah's movements and to obtain her private journal. Reading the journal he learns that during the air raid, Sarah, believing Bendrix to be dead, had made a bargain with God promising that she would give Bendrix up if He would restore him to life. She tries, in vain, various ways of forgetting him. She visits a rationalist preacher, hoping that he will convince her to break her bargain. But his arguments only feed her faith. Her love for Bendrix continues as strongly as ever, and, in the closing entries of her journal, she begs God for peace. Deeply moved by this account Bendrix attempts to see her, but she avoids him, even going out into the rain although she is unwell. A week goes by, and then Bendrix receives a telephone call from Henry to say that Sarah is dead. After her death, and through her intervention, the private detective's little boy is cured of appendicitis and the rationalist preacher of a strawberry mark. Invited by Henry, Bendrix goes to share his house, his jealousy and hatred of Sarah's lover unabated by the fact that his rival was not human but divine.

This bald recital of events is more than usually inadequate because the novel is told from the point of view of Bendrix, whose bitter and distorted view of events gives an extraordinary impression of emotional immediacy; it also makes it difficult for the reader to assess them objectively. This problem, of course, always arises when the narrator's point of view and the author's are not identified.

Allowing for this, however, we might—given this summary of the plot—presume that this was a novel, basically, about adultery and remorse. Whatever else Sarah is, she is a 'fallen woman'; on that state of moral guilt she turns her back with extraordinary determination and agony of mind, and returns to her husband. Greene, we might go on to conclude, has provided us in this novel with an endorsement of Hardy's contention in *Tess of the D'Urbervilles*: 'Who was the moral woman? The beauty and ugliness of a character lay not only in its achievements, but in its aims and impulses; its true history lay not among things done, but among things willed.' If Sarah triumphs in anything it would seem precisely to be in her will to give up Bendrix. And thus the moral order is affirmed and restored. All this would be a reasonable inference from the account of the plot, but it plays false to our experiences of reading the novel.

The End of the Affair only has the appearance of a moral story, just as it has the appearance of a detective story. There is what looks like adultery and what looks like remorse. But these are false clues leading to a false conclusion, just as the detective by dusting the door bells tracks down Sarah's visits to the rationalist preacher and concludes the mystery is solved. 'Adultery' and 'remorse' like 'the private detective' and 'the unknown man' are stock-properties of a certain kind of plot which Greene takes over to explore a theme connected neither with morality nor detection. The theme is, quite simply, grace, and although it raises no moral problems for Bendrix or for Sarah, it certainly raises a critical one for the reader of the novel.

Always present in Greene's earlier religious novels, the problem of grace becomes fully explicit only with *The End of the Affair*. In *Brighton Rock* and *The Power and the Glory* Greene makes reference to the 'appalling strangeness of the mercy of God'; in *The End of the Affair* it becomes his *subject*. The transition is crucial. The reader of the earlier novels takes in the reference to grace as a meaningful one, it indicates a direction which he is asked to observe rather than explore, in the manner of an arrow in the margin of a map indicating proximate places. In *The End of the Affair* the reader is presented with a different kind of map. The arrows are reversed in direction, pointing towards the central section which has been left blank. In one map the arrows serve to give a context to an area already defined; in the other they plot the limits of the known. With the central section blank, the relation of the other sections to each other becomes problematical. Whichever road we take we are confronted with the unknown. And the reason is not far to seek. At

'Thérèse Desqueyroux' (1927); *'The End of the Affair'* (1951)

the centre of *The End of the Affair*, we have Christ present in the world, supernatural grace in the presence of the natural order, and to trace out this spiritual cartography one would need to be God. And if we should presume to speculate we have St. Paul's reminder, 'How incomprehensible are His judgments, and how unsearchable His ways! For who hath known the mind of the Lord? Or who hath been His counsellor.' M. Sartre has provided a gloss on this for the novelist: 'In the sight of God, who penetrates through appearances without coming to a halt in them, there is no novel, no art, since art lives by appearance. God is not an artist. . . .' For the same reason He can never be directly included in a work of fiction, but in *The End of the Affair* the degree of directness is such as to make Him virtually a 'character'. If the purpose of art is to reveal an order in life, by imposing an order on it, God cannot be imposed on in this way. If this is the picture in general terms, we have to go on to ask what kind of effect this 'unknowable', and necessarily unknowable, centre has on the actual working out of the novel.

'You seem to have a very strange set of values,' Father Crompton remarks to Bendrix, and, though it is clear what he means, the same remark made to Sarah would be much more illuminating. Complex and tormented as he is, Bendrix is a natural inhabitant of a pagan, materialist world, sharing its values, its assumptions: 'If two people loved, they slept together; it was a mathematical formula, tested and proved by "human experience".' It is a wholly characteristic remark of Bendrix, arrogant, sardonic, amoral. But Sarah's character defies this kind of summary. 'She was good, Bendrix. People talk but she was good.' Henry's remark is not at variance with the reader's experience, and yet, when we begin to ponder the nature of her 'goodness', we wonder just why this should be so.

Consider the contrasting attitudes of Bendrix and Sarah towards 'the affair' itself. Consumed with jealousy whenever Sarah is absent, the only happiness Bendrix knows is when he actually possesses her, and even then it is interrupted by accusation and bitterness. Sarah, looking back on the affair, observes: 'We were sometimes so happy and never in our lives have we known more unhappiness. It's as if we were working together on the same statue, cutting it out of each other's misery.' The misery proceeds, however, from different causes. In Bendrix's case it is because of the inherent precariousness of the whole affair; in Sarah's, it is Bendrix's own unhappiness which causes hers. She accepts the affair in a way that he never does and Bendrix gives us the reason: 'She had no doubts. The moment only mattered. . . . I never lose the consciousness of time; to me, the present is never here . . . it is always last year or next week.' We are meant to take this as indicating a special quality in Sarah, but it seems to me the point is ambiguously present. If there is generosity and trust in Sarah's immersion in the moment, there is also the reason why the affair never grows, never becomes a relationship, drawing on memory, confident in hope. And it is this that Bendrix is seeking, however blindly and selfishly. At the heart of Sarah's warmth there is something which Greene seeks to persuade us is divinity, but its features uncomfortably resemble inhumanity.

It is this tense ambiguity which serves to explain the odd note which sounds so often in Sarah and Bendrix's exchanges. We have it here, for instance:

> It angered me that she didn't make any claim. 'You may be right. I'm only saying I want you to be happy. I hate your being unhappy. I don't mind anything you do that makes you happy.'
> 'You just want an excuse. If I sleep with somebody else you feel you can do the same—any time.'
> 'That's neither here nor there. I want you to be happy that's all.'
> 'You'd make my bed for me?'
> 'Perhaps.'

Here the tide appears to be moving strongly in one direction, but there is a powerful undercurrent moving against it. The overt intention is to show Sarah's virtually superhuman selflessness, but there is an undertone which reveals a curious amoral indifference. The altitude from which Greene's observation is made is so great that all the distinctive features are lost in the general blur.

The same thing happens, disastrously, in the scene where

'Thérèse Desqueyroux' (1927); 'The End of the Affair' (1951)

Henry, who is ill, has unwittingly interrupted Sarah and Bendrix's love-making. He leaves and Bendrix remarks to Sarah:

'Do you mind?' She shook her head. I don't really know what I meant—I think I had an idea that the sight of Henry might have aroused remorse, but she had a wonderful way of eliminating remorse. Unlike the rest of us she was unhaunted by guilt. In her view when a thing was done, it was done: remorse died with the act. She would have thought it unreasonable of Henry, if he had caught us, to be angry for more than a moment. Catholics are always said to be freed in the confessional from the mortmain of the past—certainly in that respect you could have called her a born Catholic, although she believed in God as little as I did. Or so I thought then and wonder now.

The ambiguity of this is so considerable that it becomes ironic. That it should become so suggests how far Greene is prepared to go in establishing 'virtue' independent of morality. The declared intention of the passage would seem again to be that Sarah's love is so complete and overwhelming that it obliterates all other considerations. But, if that is the surface of the passage, it covers anomalies and confusions. It is left to Bendrix, the amoral seducer, to raise the moral question, although he quickly realizes its irrelevance to Sarah. She had 'a wonderful way of eliminating remorse', which is coming close to saying that she is without conscience. We can see that a result of Sarah's 'life in the moment' is that any form of moral appraisal is rendered null and void; an act is simply what it is, having neither history nor consequence. From this point of view, 'anger' on Henry's part at his wife's seduction is 'unreasonable'. The palpable unreality of this is such that we feel the justice of Bendrix's earlier remark to Sarah, 'you simply haven't caught up yet on ordinary human emotions'.

It is not always easy to distinguish Bendrix speaking from Greene speaking through him and the reference to Catholics would seem to be the latter. In that case it is difficult to understand the misrepresentation. Only sorrow for sin can free Catholics from 'the mortmain of the past', and the confessional is there as a formal means to this end. If it is Bendrix speaking in a tone of sardonic criticism, then his perception of Sarah being 'unhaunted by guilt', and her seeming to be 'a born Catholic', loses considerably in force. Whatever emerges from this confused and confusing passage, one thing is clear, that the quality Greene is trying to isolate in Sarah has not merely nothing to do with morality, but seems actively opposed to it.

If the reason for these strange ambiguities and distortions is that Greene is trying to mirror in human love the absolute selflessness of the divine, what happens when the emphasis shifts and Sarah addresses not Bendrix but God? Greene's purpose is to show us that her love was all of a piece, whether the object was Bendrix or God. A passage like this is carefully interchangeable:

> She had no doubts. The moment only mattered. Eternity is said not to be an extension of time, but an absence of time, and sometimes it seemed to me that her abandonment touched that strange mathematical point of endlessness, a point with no width, occupying no space.

It is not difficult to convert that 'point' of Bendrix's into God. And years later Bendrix reads a torn page from her journal, unaware that it is addressed to God:

> I have no need to write to you or talk to you, you know everything before I can speak, but when one loves, one feels the need to use the same old ways one has always used. I know I am only beginning to love, but already I want to abandon everything, everybody but you. . . .

We are meant to pick up and note the consistent attitudes—the same trust, the same generosity of spirit, the same abandonment. This is true even in the smaller details of the book. Bendrix says of Sarah: 'All I noticed about her that first time was her beauty and her happiness and her way of touching people with her hands as though she loved them.' And then later we have her cure of Parkis' little boy, '. . . . he told the doctor it was Mrs. Miles who came and took away the pain—touching him on the right side of the stomach,' and Smythe's facial disfigurement which she cured with a kiss.

We might say that the whole of her 'affair' with Bendrix was in essence the same as her subsequent 'affair' with God. But having said this one must be immediately aware of its near meaninglessness. God cannot be apprehended as a person, and to

'Thérèse Desqueyroux' (1927); 'The End of the Affair' (1951)
convey the transition by shuffling names and saying 'one feels the need to use the same old ways one has always used' is hopelessly inadequate.

Bendrix, speaking in the accents of Greene, remarks in a general way:

> The sense of unhappiness is so much easier to convey than that of happiness. In misery we seem aware of our own existence, even though it may be in a form of monstrous egotism: this pain of mine is individual, this nerve that winces belongs to me and no other. But happiness annihilates us: we lose our identity.

This is an interesting passage because it shows Greene stating what looks like a difficulty of communication, but is in fact a philosophical conviction. It is with God, in the aspect of the suffering Christ, that Sarah seeks to identify herself. But to say this is not to say that we can only apprehend the pain of God. When Smythe says bitterly to Sarah of his disfigurement, 'Why should I love a God who gives a child this?' she comments: 'I shut my eyes and put my mouth against the mark. I felt sick for a moment because I fear deformity, and he sat quiet and let me kiss him and I thought I am kissing pain and pain belongs to you *as happiness never does* (my italics). I love you in your pain. I could almost taste metal and salt in the skin and I thought how good You are. You might have killed us with happiness, but You let us be with You in pain.' The trouble with this is that we are in danger of projecting our own pain and calling it the pain of Christ, of building Him in the image of our own unhappiness. Instead of moving outwards towards God, we are assuming Him into our own world, so that he becomes simply another factor in our torments of abandonment, jealousy and loyalty. For Bendrix, Sarah's action is hysteria and her belief is of a kind which would not enable her to contest that description. The upshot of this presentation of Sarah—a presentation emphatic in its stress on disposition rather than act, on the moment rather than duration, on faith rather than morals—is to tend to make Sarah, in her relations with Bendrix, 'selfless' to the point of inhumanity, and, in her relations with God, self-projected to the point of delusion.

Grace and Morality:

The fact that the reader feels the portrait of Sarah is more flatteringly lit than this is due largely to the way in which he is persuaded to concur in a particular view of reason and a particular view of faith. 'Reason' is most obviously present in the character of Smythe, the rationalist preacher. Critics have remarked on the injustice of Greene's presentation and how he has deliberately given Smythe a crudity of outlook which suggests he is afraid to present the anti-Christian position with proper seriousness and cogency. This protest is only partially valid. Greene is hostile to religious argument, and the attack he mounts, in the person of Smythe, is not so much on the inadequacies of rationalist argument as on the irrelevance of reason to faith. And Smythe's self-defeating rationalism hammers the point home. Too fiercely, however, because the crudity of Smythe's views, however explicable in 'life', suggests in fiction that Greene is unwilling to expose Sarah to a mind more subtly sceptical. The ultimate result might well be the same, but the *effect of the process* on the reader would be very different. Greene would reveal that Sarah's faith had been more rigorously tested, and, when it triumphed, its presence would carry a greater reality. In life it is only the triumph that matters, in art it is more the manner of the triumph, even in matters of faith. Here, mirrored in a detail, is the central difficulty of the novel. In Henry, Greene might have taken an opportunity to vary the quality of the sceptic's outlook, but his accents are exactly those of Smythe:

'Materialism isn't only an attitude for the poor. . . . Some of the best brains have been materialist, Pascal, Newman. So subtle in some directions; so crudely superstitious in others. One day we may know why: it may be a glandular deficiency.'

And, lest the point should not have been taken, we have it made again, this time with conscious irony. Sarah wonders:

'Have I some glandular deficiency that I am so uninterested in the really important unsuperstitious things and causes—like the Charity Commission and the index of living and better calories for the working class?'

But the devaluation of reason is all-pervasive and extends be-

'*Thérèse Desqueyroux*' (*1927*); '*The End of the Affair*' (*1951*)

yond the non-believers. The priest tells Henry and Bendrix about Sarah's intention of becoming a Catholic:

> 'Is that enough to make her one?'
> Father Crompton produced a formula. He laid it down like a bank note. 'We recognize the baptism of desire.'

This is not merely a description of Bendrix's reaction, there is the same quiver of hostility here to debate and explanation as there is in the presentation of the rationalist preacher's polemic.

The clue to this attitude lies in Greene's own experience. 'And so faith came to one,' he writes in the autobiographical *The Lawless Roads*, 'shapelessly without dogma, a presence above a croquet lawn. . . .' Inexplicable, fortuitous, unavoidable, incalulable, this is Greene's presentation of the arrival of belief. The hand of God is too close for us to understand the kind of gesture it makes.[1] In *The End of the Affair* this attitude is conveyed by two repeated images. The first is of infection. In her last letter to Bendrix, Sarah writes:

> I believe there's a God—I believe the whole bag of tricks, there's nothing I don't believe, they could subdivide the Trinity into a dozen parts and I'd believe. They could dig up records. . . . I've caught belief like a disease.

And Sarah's mother talking of her child's baptism says:

> 'I always had a wish that it would "take" like vaccination.'

Later, Bendrix hears Henry repeat the idea:

> 'It's an extraordinary coincidence isn't it? Baptized at two years old, and then beginning to go back to what you can't even remember. . . . It's like an infection.'

The emphasis of this reiterated image is on the passivity of the individual, the incapacity to resist or encourage this inexplicable event. Related to this is another image, that of drowning, which underlines the same attitude. Sarah compares herself to a lost ship,

---

[1] Mauriac is quite explicit about this difficulty: 'Whenever a novelist has tried to re-create the way of grace, with all its struggles and its ultimate victory, he has left an impression of arbitrariness and mis-representation . . . God is inimitable and he escapes the novelist's grasp' (*Dieu et Mammon*).

with the water rising, and the air thick with mist. Bendrix, shaken in his scepticism by her miraculous intervention in the lives of others, says: 'I felt like a swimmer who has overpassed his strength and knows the tide is stronger than himself, but if I drowned, I was going to hold Henry up to the last moment.' Spiritual determinism could hardly go further. Sarah is pursued by the love of Christ as surely as Tess by the implacable President of the Immortals. Greene's outlook in *The End of the Affair* finds an admirable gloss in Mauriac's *La Pharisienne*:

> People do not change. At my age one can have no illusions on that point: but they do quite often turn back to what they once were and show again those very characteristics which they have striven tirelessly through a whole life-time to suppress. This does not mean that they necessarily end by succumbing to what is worst in themselves. God is very often the good temptation to which many human beings in the long run yield.

By isolating 'reason' and 'faith' in this way I have of course given them a prominence which they do not have in the novel. But they are crucial in helping to shape the reader's response to Sarah—and to her Bargain with God.

It is in this central act that the details of her presentation come sharply into focus, so that we are moved into accepting something which, viewed through a less extraordinary lens than that which Greene has employed, would have been quite incomprehensible. The kind of scepticism which has to be overcome is suggested by Smythe's remark, '. . . leave God out of this. It's just a question of your lover and your husband. Don't confuse the thing with phantoms.' But given Sarah as she has been presented, we realize that neither Smythe's reasons, nor anyone else's, would move her. If she makes the Bargain, there is also a sense in which the Bargain is made for her.

To begin with it is an affair which belongs purely to 'the Moment', and she enters into it with the same complex abandonment as she has entered into her 'Moments' with Bendrix. Demanding of God 'Make me believe', she has to meet her spiritual liabilities in full, because any kind of hesitation, any kind of reasoned doubt, is alien to her. Her decision is insulated

'Thérèse Desqueyroux' (1927); *'The End of the Affair'* (1951)

against every reason. There are psychological reasons for breaking her bargain, but if she labels her action 'hysterical', her experience tells her she is wrong. Such an 'explanation' is only there to protect her from the burden of mystery. On the other hand, there are moral reasons, such as loyalty to Henry, which she might draw on to enable her to maintain her bargain. But a moral appraisal, like a psychological solution, is irrelevant to her. If she didn't feel 'guilt' before with Bendrix, she certainly doesn't feel 'innocent' without him. Any moral aura which surrounds the bargain is an illusion. It is the promise itself, not the nature of the promise, which is the imperative. It is obvious that with Sarah's bargain we are in the suburbs of Illuminism, where 'reason' is taken as synonymous with pride. Whatever prompted and sustained Sarah's pact with God, one thing is abundantly clear: that is that, on its own definition, it can never be shown—only stated.

At this point description of the religious background of the novel begins to shade into literary judgment about its value. Religious orthodoxy, after all, is not synonymous with artistic merit. And in this particular case there seems an intimate connection between its religious emphases and what we must regard as its literary failings. It is important to make clear exactly what kind of point is being made here. There is no *a priori* reason why successful novels should not be written about the life of grace, about saints and sinners. But their success will depend on their power of communicating their drama in human terms; in art there is no other perspective. This assertion is not humanist, but human.

An illustration may clarify the point. In Dostoevsky's *Crime and Punishment* the murderer Raskolnikov excitedly urges a girl who loves him to read him the Bible:

'Why? You are not a believer, are you? . . .' she whispered softly, gasping a little.
'Read! I want you to!' he insisted. 'You used to read to Lizaveta!'
Sonya opened the book and found the place. Her hands shook, her voice failed. Twice she tried to begin, but could not utter the first word.

Grace and Morality:

'Now a certain man was sick, named Lazarus of Bethany . . .' she pronounced at last, with an effort, but after two or three words her voice broke like an over-strained violin string. Her breath caught and her heart laboured.

Raskolnikov had understood why Sonya could not make herself read to him, and the more he understood, the more roughly and irritably he insisted. He knew very well how difficult it was for her to expose and betray all that was *her own*. He understood that those feelings in fact constituted her real long-standing *secret*, cherished perhaps since her girlhood, in the midst of her family, with an unhappy father, a stepmother crazed by grief, and hungry children, in an atmosphere of hideous shrieks and reproaches. At the same time he now knew and knew for certain that although she was troubled and feared something terrible if she were to read now, yet she had a tormenting desire to read, and read for *him* to hear, and read *now*, 'whatever might happen afterwards'. . . .

It is difficult to convey the atmosphere of a novel briefly, but even in this extract we feel in the presence of a powerful complex of emotions which are given their particular tension by religious faith. And we are made to feel this through and with Raskolnikov. However mysterious and inexplicable Sonya's faith, it finds expression in human terms. In Greene's own work this has been true. In *The Power and the Glory* we are shown, in the working out of a human conflict, something of what goes into the making of a saint. But in *The End of the Affair* Greene would seem to have taken the fundamental mysteriousness of sanctity not simply as the theme, but as directing its manner of expression also.

To see the implications of this artistic dilemma, it is worth quoting the conclusion of the *Times Literary Supplement* review of the novel:

The common-sense point of view is surely that whatever the inward marks of sanctity, the overruling outward one is that in some way the candidate's life should be more than ordinarily edifying. Is a married woman who gives up her lover for the love of God a saint? As Ibsen's Nora says in almost the opposite context: 'Thousands of women have done so.'

The bluff, sardonic note of this is useful because it reveals, in an obvious way, the critic held fast in the same sort of trap as the novelist. There is confusion, basically, between 'art' and 'life'. If we think of *The End of the Affair* as an autobiographical work, the critic's objections weaken. The life of Mary Magdalen was not to the outward eye 'more than ordinarily edifying', and, when this criticism was in fact made, it met with a stinging rebuke. There is no real difficulty in believing that a married woman who gives up her lover for the love of God could be practising heroic virtue; martyrdom is not limited by its visibility. If, however, *The End of the Affair* is considered not as a spiritual autobiography, but as a novel, then the objections appear rather differently, though the difference has certainly nothing to do with 'the common sense point of view'. In life, we are continually warned against rashness of judgment, because all the evidence can never be available to us. In art, *all* that has been created of the fictional world is available to us. Fictional characters must speak to the reader in the same way as the psalmist speaks to God: 'Thou searchest out my path and my lying down, and art acquainted with all my ways. For there is not a word in my tongue, but lo, O Lord, thou knowest it altogether.' The reader's judgment can, then, be authoritative in fiction, in a way in which it never can be in life. In life we have to accept the adequacy of statement as the clue to the reality of experience, in art we can demand demonstration. Consequently, from the *literary* point of view we must agree that 'inward marks of sanctity' must be revealed outwardly. Otherwise, the writer is sawing through the plank which supports him.

Earlier in this essay I suggested that Sarah leaves the reader with an impression of her 'goodness'. Literary examination suggests the difficulty of supporting this. The reason for this contradiction should now be becoming plain. In responding to Sarah's 'goodness' we are unwittingly going 'outside' the fictional character and substituting in her place an 'historical' one. The tone of the book is such that we deceive ourselves into reading Sarah's journal as though it was St. Augustine's *Confessions*. We mistake statement for creation. This reaches its extreme point in the question of the miracles. In life, miracles are claimed to testify to a reality other than themselves, in fiction

Grace and Morality:

they can only testify to the reality which has made them occur. One part of the fictional world is being made to allege the inexpressible reality of another. And to try to do this is to confuse the whole nature of fiction.

Although this kind of criticism is strictly literary, and is not shaped by philosophical or theological assumptions, it has nevertheless religious implications. If Greene in *The End of the Affair* has become involved in a situation which exceeds the novelist's province, this is not because of his ambitious theme, but because of the particular way he has laid his religious emphases. An incarnational, sacramental view of Christianity leads to the disclosure of the divine *within* the essential imperfections of the human, but in Greene's view the divine offers a stark alternative to the total corruption of the human. Only grace can bridge the gap—and the action of grace as Greene seems to present it is fortuitous, inexplicable and ultimately unknowable. Literary criticism can have nothing to say on the validity of these views, except in so far as they touch on literature. Greene's view has been present in all his religious novels, giving them their taut, vivid and dramatic outline. If these views disturb us in *The End of the Affair* in a way they do not in the earlier novels, this is because he has taken down the melodramatic scaffolding and directly revealed the beliefs themselves. Seen in this way they seem inimical to the public ordering and the public demonstration which successful fiction requires. In the character of Sarah Greene has created someone whose goodness can be understood only in extra-fictional terms. Within the novel we can point only to moral categories, and these are set aside as irrelevant. Sarah is the 'fallen woman' for whom 'guilt' and 'innocence' are meaningless terms.

In deadening the moral nerve of the novel Greene has made its whole movement, however vivid and compelling in detail, finally unknowable. Unknowable in the way that human beings are, and fictional characters are not. A report on *The End of the Affair* would conclude not that the art was too remote from life, but rather that there was a failure to distinguish between them.

'Thérèse Desqueyroux' (1927); 'The End of the Affair' (1951)

[iii]

In *The End of the Affair* we have detection without crime, in *Thérèse Desqueyroux* crime without detection; but in each case the paradox supports an attitude common to both novels. It enables the same devaluation of human action, the same dichotomy between motive and behaviour. To see the two novels from the angle of plot—the angle where 'action' dominates the scene—is to see range upon range of paradox.

Sarah deceives her husband but she remains loyal to him; she gives up her lover but her love for him increases; Henry, the wronged husband, declares his 'guilt' in marrying his wife. Thérèse attempts to poison her husband to rid herself of her own inner dishonesty. Her husband perjures himself and ensures the miscarriage of justice; in this way his family honour is preserved. To talk about the two novels in these terms is, of course, to distort them. Quite clearly, there is a sense in which Sarah and Thérèse are innocent victims and a sense in which Henry and Bernard are guilty judges, and these senses are part of our understanding of the novel. But there is point in laying bare the paradoxes in this way because they reveal both the idiosyncrasy and the consistency of the Greene-Mauriac world. This can be further illustrated by going on to consider other features of the two novels. Both Thérèse and Sarah are 'guilty' women, but such a 'judgment' is the distinguishing mark of the malicious or the obtuse. Neither character chooses to act, rather they are driven by a force apparently beyond their control—one to sanctity, and the other 'to react against the power she exercises to poison and corrupt the lives of those around her'. If the course they follow is predetermined, they strive to understand the pattern in retrospect. Six years after 'the end of the affair', Bendrix tries to piece together its history and meaning; the case over and acquittal given, Thérèse, lying back in the train, reflects on her life and tries to see the point which may move Bernard to forgiveness. In both cases an action is probed to discover its 'real' meaning—Sarah leaving Bendrix, Thérèse poisoning

Bernard. The further the probing extends, the more the 'action' fades into a whole pattern of incident, and decision is revealed as illusion. Bendrix says: 'A story has no beginning or end: arbitrarily one chooses that moment of experience from which to look back or from which to look ahead. I say "one chooses" . . . but do I in fact *choose* that black wet January night on the Common in 1946. . . .' Thérèse, working out her 'explanation' to Bernard, reflects: ' "I shall have to begin from the beginning. . . ." But what is the beginning where our actions are concerned? Our destiny, once we try to isolate it, is like those plants which we can never dig up with all their roots intact. Would she find it necessary to go back to her childhood? But even our childhood is, in a sense, an end, a completion.' This impossibility of finding a point of responsible decision leads us to the main problem that *Thérèse Desqueyroux* must pose for the critic, namely to determine the moral reality of the conflict it seeks to describe and explore.

In February 1939, M. Sartre wrote a long essay entitled *M. Mauriac et la Liberté*. In it he examined Mauriac's conception of freedom and pointed his argument with an analysis of *La Fin de la Nuit*, the novel in which Mauriac deals with the later life of Thérèse. The argument is equally relevant to *Thérèse Desqueyroux* and it provides one with a useful approach to the morality of the novel, to the 'innocence' and the 'guilt' with which it deals.

Sartre argues that the vitality of the novel depends upon the freedom of its characters. Only in this way can they be said to 'live'. Maintaining that the Christian writer, with his emphasis on free-will, ought to be in a good position to create 'the living character', Sartre proceeds to an examination of Thérèse. The progress of his argument is not as direct as it might be, but, though one is occasionally faced with gnomic remarks about Time and Liberty, the drift emerges clearly and convincingly enough: 'It is a fixed law, independent of Thérèse's will, that governs her acts as soon as they escape from her, and that leads them all, even the best-intentioned of them, to unhappy consequences. . . . What is it, after all, but the expression of that

'Thérèse Desqueyroux' (1927); 'The End of the Affair' (1951)

other spell, Original Sin? I therefore grant that M. Mauriac is in earnest when he speaks of destiny as a Christian. But when he speaks as a novelist, I can no longer follow him.' The distinction is crucial and lies at the heart of Sartre's argument; and though a great deal of the remainder of the essay is taken up with discussing Mauriac's shifting viewpoint with regard to Thérèse, it is an illustration, not an addition to the argument. The problem lies in the conflict between Mauriac's intention—'She took form in my mind as an example of that power, granted to all human beings—no matter how much they seem to be the slaves of a hostile fate—of saying "No" to the law which beats them down'—and the spiritual determinacy implied in his actual presentation. From the point of view of the presentation to believe in such a power is a disastrous form of self-deception. The conflict is clear enough but it has a complexity to which Sartre's argument fails to do justice.

Ostensibly, *Thérèse Desqueyroux* proposes a struggle between the rich landed bourgeoisie and an independent spirit trying to establish itself in opposition to the material satisfaction with which it is enveloped. Mauriac's hatred for the landed families is a watermark showing through all his fiction. This novel is no exception. Pride in physical possessions, pride in the family name, and, issuing out of this, a terrible complacency and righteousness which is ruthless to any opposition, it is this which arouses Mauriac's withering contempt. 'The spirit of the family', Thérèse reflects about her husband, 'inspires his every action, making it impossible for him to hesitate even for a moment. Always, in every circumstance, he knows what must be done in the interests of the family.' It is a reflection which Bernard himself endorses: 'I am not considering myself in this matter. For the moment I am out of the picture. The only thing I am worrying about is the family. For the honour of the family I consented to cheat justice. . . . For the sake of the family the world must suppose we are in complete harmony.' The preservation of appearance as opposed to the claims of reality, the weight of custom against the living spirit of a particular situation—this is the Declaration which Bernard seeks to uphold. The maintenance of possessions gives way to their worship, and everything that Bernard touches turns to spiritual dross. Touring Europe we see 'Bernard of the vacant gaze—Bernard for ever worried lest the numbers on the pictures did not correspond with those in his Baedeker'; and later we have, 'Bernard ... who was never satisfied until he had labelled, ranged and set aside each separate emotion ...'; ultimately, 'he remained imprisoned in his own pleasure like one of those charming pigs whom it is so amusing to watch through the railings rooting about delightedly in their own sty.' The situation is abundantly clear, and the nature of Thérèse's tragedy would seem to be obvious.

Mauriac, however, is anxious to extend the tragedy beyond the personal. Thus, Thérèse's world is expressed in terms of a cage. We find Thérèse lying back in the darkness of a railway carriage, as it proceeds through thick fog, reflecting on her past life. As she broods on her marriage the same note is struck again and again: 'She had entered the cage like a sleep-walker ... she was like a transported criminal ... anxious only to see the Convict Island where she would have to spend the rest of her life, she stared before her seeing in imagination the cage with its innumerable bars ... a cage full of eyes and ears, in which she would have to spend the whole of her life.' Supplementing the image of the cage we have this: 'she was like a trapped animal that hears the pack drawing close and lies exhausted after a gruelling chase.' The prisoner, the trapped animal, the cage—this is the emotional pattern of the book as it centres on Thérèse and its vividness and insistence deflect us from inquiring about the nature of the prison. It seems sufficient that it should exist. To put the point more precisely: we experience in reading the novel a great feeling of the injustice that has been committed, but the ultimate cause of the injustice is by no means clear. From one point of view it would appear to be the ruthless pride of Bernard and his family, but from another point of view this pride would seem simply a particular expression of the vicious and corrupt nature of Life itself. If 'Life' is being indicted, then the pervasive image of the 'trap' is disingenuous. Presumably, we only talk of a trap or cage when we

'Thérèse Desqueyroux' (1927); 'The End of the Affair' (1951)

have known another kind of condition; if *la condition humaine* is like this, then however much we are distressed and crushed by it, it is false to image it in a way which depends for its poignancy on the possibility, at least, of change. In *Thérèse Desqueyroux* Mauriac seems uncertain where he wants his emphasis to fall. If he allows his Jansenist tendencies full scope, seeing in a graceless world the necessity and violence of evil, then *all* the characters simply fulfil the destiny to which they have been called. They are like actors reading a prepared script. And, in consequence, Bernard's responsibility for his behaviour is diminished. If, however, Mauriac gives full stress to this, he makes Thérèse's tragedy a personal one, something which arises from the particular circumstances in which she finds herself. But for Mauriac, Thérèse 'belongs to that class of human beings . . . for whom night can end only when life itself ends.' In other words, he sees her primarily not as Bernard's victim but as Life's.

This ambivalence in Mauriac's attitude shows itself in several ways. When Mauriac talks of Bernard being 'imprisoned' in his pleasure this is obviously meant to be understood quite differently from Thérèse being 'imprisoned' in her suffering. Conversely, we have full assent given to the freedom and responsibility of Bernard in marrying Thérèse and his subsequent treatment of her, but the 'freedom' of Thérèse in accepting him and then trying to destroy him is muted in such a way that we hardly recognize it at all. When we look in the direction of Bernard we are invited to see 'responsibility', when we look in the direction of Thérèse, 'fate'. In consequence, the novel becomes a curiously bifocal one. Writing of Bernard, Mauriac describes him in terms of moral condemnation, and his cruelty, pride, calculation, all take a separate, sharp, underlining. 'Your business is to listen', Bernard tells Thérèse, 'to receive my orders, to abide by my irrevocable decision.' And we feel that the viciousness of this lies precisely in his *ability* to make this kind of decision. There is no encompassing irony here, indicating the fatuity of any man's thinking he can make an 'irrevocable decision'. But this 'freedom' is denied to Thérèse. When *she* acts it is 'in obedience to some profound, some inexorable law of her being. . . . Useless to look for any other reason than that 'they are they and I am I. . . .' When questioned by Bernard for her motive in trying to poison him she says: 'I was the victim of a terrible duty. Yes, honestly, I had the feeling that it was a duty.' Mauriac's intention is plain here. It is partly the strategic necessity of underplaying Thérèse's moral guilt, of not alienating our sympathy, but more profoundly it is the character of Thérèse herself which haunts Mauriac's imagination, a woman without grace mutely protesting against the corruption of the world. With her Mauriac's Jansenist view is completely uncovered, and in his preface to the novel he longs that grace should have been given to her to turn her heart towards God. Bernard and his family do not constitute a particular tragedy for Thérèse, they are simply the agents that Life has chosen to accomplish her downfall—'they are they and I am I.'

It is this double vision of the world in *Thérèse Desqueyroux* that makes the question of freedom a more complex business than M. Sartre suggests in his essay. When Thérèse, reflecting on her crime, says: 'How do those who act *know* the crimes they are committing? . . . I *didn't* know, I never wanted to do that with which I am charged. I don't know what I did want', she is not intended to be expressing the confusion of a particular individual but stating a general human dilemma regarding 'responsibility' for action. We seem to obey mysterious impulses. We feel it to be 'our duty', 'our destiny'. In a sense, this is the underworld of grace and indeed it is precisely this suggestion that Bernard mockingly puts to her when she fails to give any adequate account for her attempted murder, 'so the idea came to you on the spur of the moment, did it?—almost like a visitation of grace.' We are meant to react against this irony, but Mauriac has created Thérèse in such a way that Bernard *cannot but* be baffled by her 'explanation'. Whatever else he may be, Mauriac has decreed that Bernard lives in the world of moral choice; he is not driven, he elects to drive, and a world in which these conditions do not obtain is incomprehensible to him. So we get the curious paradox emerging from the novel of a character in a determinist world pleading for a chance, for for-

'Thérèse Desqueyroux' (1927); 'The End of the Affair' (1951)

giveness, and a character in a world of free choice made incapable of understanding such a plea. It is not a mutually profitable dialogue.

In the novel Mauriac uses one scheme of moral reference with regard to Bernard and quite another with regard to Thérèse. It is the construction of the novel, not the constitution of the characters, which makes communication between them impossible. Mauriac not Bernard has cut the wires with Thérèse. We feel this strongly in the final angry exchange when Bernard seeks to find Thérèse's motive in attempting to poison him:

'For heaven's sake, do try, once and for all, to tell me what it was you wanted. The truth of the matter is that you can't.'
'What I wanted? It would be a great deal easier to tell you what I didn't want. I didn't want to be for ever playing a part, to go through a series of movements, to continue speaking words that were not my own. . . .'

Here we have the 'guilty act' seen at last by Thérèse and defended in terms of integrity; wrong behaviour vindicated by admirable intention. This, of course, is Thérèse defending herself, not Mauriac defending her—but the poignancy of the book depends largely upon our accepting this, the discounting of behaviour in the light of the claim of an 'inner truth' to be obeyed. We are obviously moving here into the extra-moral world, the world of Sarah Miles in *The End of the Affair*. Sarah is responsive to grace in a way that Thérèse is not, but if one is a saint, the other is a sinner. They are the positives and negatives of the same film. And the basic artistic conflict that ensues is the same in both novels. The moral order has been disrupted in favour of the order of grace, and however 'true' this may be in life, in art it can only lead to confusion and ultimate incoherence. Of necessity, we have to be *told* about the 'inexorable law' to which Thérèse responds, we can never be *shown* what it is. The conclusion is M. Sartre's: 'I . . . grant that M. Mauriac is in earnest when he speaks of destiny as a Christian. But when he speaks as a novelist I can no longer follow him.' He can no longer follow him because Mauriac has led him to a site where the public and moral order on which the novelist must build has been removed, and in its place has been set the order of grace clearly perceptible only to the eye of faith.

I want to conclude this chapter with an illustration which shows most fully the kind of dichotomy present in the novel, and the kind of pressure that lies behind it. As in *The End of the Affair*, sex lies, if not at the heart of the story, at least near enough to make the distinction trivial. I say 'sex' advisedly, rather than love, because in both novels there is a raw, isolating insistence on physical detail. In spite of the fact that the relationship between Bendrix and Sarah is one that is desired and the relationship between Bernard and Thérèse one that is hated, this dominant impression is common to both. It is not difficult to see why. The sexual act is the flashpoint of the Jansenist world. Here 'two are made one flesh' and the corruption of the world is sounded to its very depths. In Greene's first novel, *The Man Within*, written in 1929, the note is touched which is to reverberate throughout all his work. Andrews is walking along a street at night and hears voices:

> He passed on. Two voices speaking softly in a doorway made him pause. He could not see the speakers. 'Come tonight.' 'Shall I? I oughtn't to.' 'I love you, love you, love you.' Andrews, to his own surprise, smote the wall against which he stood with his fist and said aloud with a crazy fury, 'You damned lechers. . . .'

'To his own surprise' reveals the author's sudden intrusion. But this note is omnipresent in Greene's work. In *Brighton Rock* there are Pinkie's appalled memories of the parental ritual at Nelson Place; in *The Power and the Glory* it is the priest's memory of his adultery and the illegitimate child that shakes him with lonely misery; in *The Heart of the Matter* Scobie only achieves a relationship with his wife and mistress when they have been transformed into objects of pity; in *The End of the Affair* the case appears to be different, in that for the first time a sexual relationship does not seem to bring destruction with it; but the screw has been given another twist, and it is only when the relationship is over that positive re-creation can begin. In all of Greene's novels love marks the entry of pain. Sex for him is the leper's bell, repugnant and welcome, announcing the true condition of

'*Thérèse Desqueyroux*' (1927); '*The End of the Affair*' (1951)

the world in which we live. We remember the prison cell in *The Power and the Glory*, 'The place was very like the world: overcrowded with lust and crime and unhappy love; it stank to high heaven. . . .'

In Mauriac the case is similar, though the obsession is less obtrusively present. In *Le Fleuve de Feu* we have the following:

> It was the delicious and desperate moment when two beings, though still making a pretence of resistance, know that they are lost. The abyss had not yet swallowed up their entwined limbs, but they were leaning so far out over its depths that they were sure that henceforth no power in earth or in heaven could snatch them back.

Commenting on this passage, Mr. Martin Turnell writes: 'The tone is undeniably equivocal. It is also characteristic. What gives Mauriac's work its distinctive flavour, its extraordinary seductiveness, is precisely the mixture of sorrow and fascination that we find here. . . . It is not a simple antithesis between sacred and profane love, between spirit and flesh. The fascination and the revulsion are inseparable; the pleasure is immense, but it is always a poisoned pleasure and the poison, the sense of doom, in a perverse way heightens the pleasure.'[1] The observation seems to me just and apt. In *Thérèse* this predilection is masked to some extent by the fact that Thérèse's reactions to Bernard may seem to belong *in propria persona* and be explicable in terms of the psychology of character. In the sexual act Thérèse can be imaged most powerfully as victim, and Bernard as insensible destroyer. But admitting this, it is not difficult to feel a certain overloading: 'The gloomy battle would be broken off and Bernard, retracing his steps, would, as it were, stand back and see me there, like a dead body thrown up on the shore, my teeth clenched, my body cold to his touch.' If, however, we are still inclined to take this simply as Thérèse's reactions to Bernard's callous insensitivity, the Foreword to the novel reveals Mauriac's emphasis directly: 'People who "wear their hearts upon their sleeves" have no story for me to tell, but I know the secrets of the hearts that are deep buried in, and mingled with, the filth of the flesh.' This is illuminating in that it suggests that Thérèse's

[1] *The Art of French Fiction*, p. 309.

sexual reactions to Bernard are not so much the consequence of a particular unhappy relationship as an expression of life's inherent corruption. The whole drama of an independent spirit striving to free itself from the coil of family pride and material complacency is, in reality, not about freedom but about doom, a Jansenist's gloss on the meaning of life.

As in our discussion of *The End of the Affair* the literary critic can have nothing to say about this gloss *as such*, but he can point to it as the cause of the artistic weakness of the novel, in that it tempts the author into making fiction do something which lies outside its province. In *The End of the Affair* the moral order was superseded, in *Thérèse* it is present, but confused by being brought into conflict with the order of grace; both novels mark the place where fiction ends and faith begins. Greene and Mauriac, in their attempts to restore 'the religious sense' to the novel, have forgotten the limitations of fiction pointed out by Newman, considering this very question of 'Christian literature'. His words provide a fitting conclusion to this chapter:

> ... literature is to man in some sort what autobiography is to the individual; it is his Life and Remains. Moreover, he is this sentient, intelligent, creative and operative being, quite independent of any extraordinary aid from Heaven, or any definite religious belief; and *as such*, as he is in himself, does Literature represent him; it is the Life and Remains of the *natural* man, innocent or guilty.

'Catholic novelists,' Greene once wrote in a letter to Elizabeth Bowen, 'should take Newman as their patron. No one understood their problem better....' It would seem that some of 'the patron's' advice, at least, has gone unheeded by his admirer.

8

The Novel as Prophecy:
'Lady Chatterley's Lover' (1928)

> In the novel ... you can develop an instinct for life, if you will, instead of a theory of right and wrong, good and bad.
>
> D. H. LAWRENCE

[i]

'The essential function of art is moral,' Lawrence wrote in an essay on Whitman, 'not aesthetic, nor decorative, not pastime and recreation. But moral.' It is a remark which has been widely quoted and echoed in the literary criticism of the last thirty years. What, however, has been noticeably less publicized is the sentences which follow it: 'But a passionate, implicit morality, not didactic. A morality which changes the blood rather than the mind. Change the blood first. The mind follows later, in the wake.' 'A morality which changes the blood' should be sufficient to warn us that Lawrence's conception of the moral function of art was not quite as transparent in meaning as it is often made to appear.

This passage, with its simple assertion and dark qualification, reflects, in a small way, the whole conflict and uncertainty that arise when we come to look at the relationship of the moral to the story in Lawrence's work. In the early novels this relationship is obviously present, but it remains in the background; in *Lady Chatterley's Lover* it is the very subject with which the

The Novel as Prophecy: 'Lady Chatterley's Lover' (1928)

novelist is concerned. Thus, we are not surprised to find in this novel one of the most famous descriptions of the purpose of the Novel as a literary form. And Lawrence uses Clifford's writing of short stories as a way of making a moral point about him, just as he later defines Mrs. Bolton's gossip by saying that it was 'Mrs. Gaskell, and George Eliot, and Miss Mitford all rolled into one'. *Lady Chatterley's Lover* is very much a novel which is concerned, implicitly at least, with the status of the Novel—a status which is described in Lawrence's remark that it is 'necessary for us now'. What is interesting about a claim like this is not its justice or otherwise, but its unusualness. Of no other novel in this book, for instance, could we imagine such a claim being made—though some are heavily social and didactic in drive—and if it had been made it would have seemed foolish. Consequently, it is not surprising to find that a novel for which such claims are made readily lends itself to a moral defence, should it be needed. Equally clearly, it is vulnerable to moral attack, because if a novel which asserts that 'it is necessary for us now' is found not to be so, it is more than likely to be found 'dangerous'. The artist who contends for a socially therapeutic function exposes himself to the risk, at least, of being accused of quackery.

In *Lady Chatterley's Lover* we find, carried to an extreme, positions which are present in all of Lawrence's work, positions, moreover, which are largely responsible for his swift rise in prestige during the last ten years or so. To begin with, there is the importance with which he invests the medium of the novel, 'it can help us to live as nothing else can.' In a period when literary critics have seen themselves increasingly as custodians of a humane culture against the encroachments of mass civilization, so that the study of literature can become an educational touchstone in a more far-reaching way than it has ever been before, Lawrence's claims for the novel bring assurance and inspiration. The only art he is concerned with begins with a small letter, and it ministers dedicatedly to his vision of life, which is both diagnostic and prophetic. In the general contemporary breakdown of communal purpose, a personal vision, expressed with the

The Novel as Prophecy: 'Lady Chatterley's Lover' (1928)

conviction and power which Lawrence had at his command, comes to be valued for its own sake. Integrity of purpose provides its own justification.

Given this kind of purpose and vision, it is inevitable that the form of the novel will undergo radical changes. But there will be nothing doctrinaire, 'experimental' about such changes, and, if his novels look different from the traditional nineteenth-century novel, the impulse for such a revolution is moral rather than aesthetic. It is within this perspective that we notice 'character' giving way to 'consciousness' in his work, narrative outline being replaced by symbol and theme, conclusions being subordinate to explorations. These were highly congenial shifts for a critical age which had learnt that in art 'there is always another story, there is more than meets the eye', and had inquired, with irony, how many children had Lady Macbeth? If Lawrence's novels were much to our taste in reading fiction, they were no less well suited to our talking and writing about it. The way, for instance, in which they suddenly concentrate themselves into brief scenes of overwhelming immediacy was particularly rewarding to that kind of detailed, local analysis of verbal texture which is such a marked feature of our critical practice. And if his work rewarded us where our critical methods are strongest, it did not disturb us where these methods are weakest. 'Conclusions', in Lawrence, are very much a matter veiled and obscure, but we have absorbed so thoroughly the implications of Mr. Eliot's dictum—'when we consider poetry, it is as poetry we must consider it, and not as another thing'—that we are extremely reluctant to pursue a literary discussion beyond the bounds of formal analysis, even while recognizing the arbitrary nature of that boundary. 'Another hand ... another paper' is the invariable drift of our concluding paragraphs. If this has been an age remarkable both for the quality and the quantity of its literary criticism, it has found in the work of Lawrence notable reassurance and stimulus. Indeed, it seems to me likely that, when future literary historians come to look back on the present period, they will see the legal vindication of *Lady Chatterley's Lover* marking not so much a stage in 'literary freedom', as the

The Novel as Prophecy: 'Lady Chatterley's Lover' (1928)

high-watermark and triumph of a particular phase of literary criticism. There is, however, as the phrase 'literary freedom' suggests, another side to this story.

The fact that *Lady Chatterley's Lover* can raise such an issue as 'freedom of expression' points to the deep disturbance that the novel has always provoked in a great number of readers. If the legal expression of this disturbance is, from the literary point of view, naïve and crude, this should not be allowed to obscure the fact that it is connected with other reactions, which are certainly not naïve or crude. Lawrence may have regarded the novel as 'the bright book of life', but the novelist, he felt, had to have inside him, 'something vicious, old Adamish, incompatible to the ordinary man'. And so we find, throughout Lawrence's work, intense affirmations arising out of no less intense negations. 'Life' is affirmed when the conventional moral pattern is exposed for the deathly thing it is; the self emerges properly only when notions of personality have been abandoned; the vitality of his particular episodes overwhelms because it breaks down that contemplative response, that aesthetic distance, which we usually associate with successful art. Thus it becomes a commonplace to say that in reading Lawrence we find ourselves constantly thrown into a state of violent endorsement or violent rejection. In *Lady Chatterley's Lover* there are intense affirmations of the importance of creativity, and the reader who responds to them will make his account of the novel a matter of illustrating clearly its overt seriousness of purpose, its relevance for 'our time'; and he will endorse this by pointing to its liberating honesty in its treatment of sexual relationships, its diagnosis of and opposition to the acquisitive spirit of the age, its tender, perhaps lyrical descriptions of human love and the natural life of the wood. He will probably choose, as an epigraph for his account, Lawrence's statement of purpose:

> ... I always labour at the same thing, to make the sex relation valid and precious, instead of shameful. And this novel is the furthest I've gone. To me it is beautiful and tender as the naked self....'

Those, however, who see in *Lady Chatterley* the pressure of nihilism will maintain that it is a novel which attacks the dignity

The Novel as Prophecy: 'Lady Chatterley's Lover' (1928)

and responsibility of the person, that it proclaims the infallibility of feelings, and that it turns sex into a psychotheology for the elect. The epigraph chosen here is likely to record the mood present in Mellors's remark:

'I feel the colonies aren't far enough. The moon wouldn't be far enough, because there you could look back and see the earth, dirty, beastly, unsavoury among all the stars: made foul by men.'

'Reverence', 'disgust'—the attitudes behind these passages can lead the reader, in his turn, into expressions of high moral approval and vehement moral condemnation. A close examination of the novel may help to show the reason for these antithetical views and allow a judgment between them; what it will certainly show is that this is a kind of opposition which makes *Lady Chatterley's Lover* the most curious moral 'case' in the whole range of English fiction.

[ii]

'Ours is essentially a tragic age,' the novel begins, but 'we've got to live, no matter how many skies have fallen.' In that statement and counter-statement the novel takes its shape and meaning; it is concerned on the one hand to analyse and present us with the 'tragedy', and on the other to reveal the 'life' that must oppose it.

Lawrence embodies this in a tale which has the severe outlines of fable. 'Once upon a time . . .', the narrative simplicity of *Lady Chatterley's Lover* is of that kind, and it would be a mistaken perspective which concentrated on complexity of plot. All that needs to be said, at this level, can be tersely said. There is the marriage in the last year of the First World War of Connie Reid with Clifford Chatterley, heir to a large estate in the Midlands. A year later Clifford succeeds to the estate, but he has been fatally crippled and made impotent by the war. He learns to adapt himself to his new life, inviting house parties of his friends and writing short stories which soon become fashionably successful. Connie, increasingly lonely and cut off from her husband's world, takes as a lover one of the young writers

The Novel as Prophecy: 'Lady Chatterley's Lover' (1928)

who visit their home. It is very much an affair of the moment and her sense of loneliness deepens. Only by walking in the estate which surrounds the house is she able to find a sense of peace and satisfaction, particularly by watching the gamekeeper Mellors at work building coops for the pheasants and feeding the chickens. Her intimacy with him grows and they become lovers. Clifford has now revived his early interests in engineering and he is intent on restoring industrial prosperity to the area. The gulf between him and his wife is now virtually complete. Connie's family invite her to Venice for a holiday, knowing that she will use the opportunity it offers to tell Clifford that she is going to have a child and that she wishes a divorce. For a time, Mellors's name is kept out of the affair, but local scandal takes over and his relationship with Connie becomes public news. Clifford, infuriated, refuses Connie a divorce; she leaves him and goes to stay with her family until such time as she can rejoin Mellors, whose divorce against his own unfaithful wife is pending.

Clearly the narrative as such is not one that commands much interest; there is very little progression of incident and what there is seems forced on the novelist. It is only in the last three chapters that anything resembling plot comes into being, and there it has an apologetic and makeshift air. The novel is driven not by developing incident but rather by the friction of antitheses. It is the constantly repeated antitheses of setting and character that constitute the power-centres of the book, each being vitally connected to the other.

Lady Chatterley's Lover is rooted in a deep sense of region, at once intensely localized, a precise part of the Nottinghamshire-Derbyshire border, and intensely stylized. Connie goes for a drive by car, and the local villages pass by, Tevershall, Stacks Gate, Shipley, the car crosses the railway lines as they curve north to Sheffield, and then turns sharply west to Matlock. It is a region of great houses falling into decay, Nonconformist chapels, miners' cottages, new council estates, corner-end shops, and then, suddenly, long rolling woods which end abruptly on the slag heaps of a colliery. As Connie makes her journey we can

The Novel as Prophecy: 'Lady Chatterley's Lover' (1928)

make it too, gazetteer in hand. But there is another way of regarding this setting, a way in which all particularities fade and we are left looking at a gaunt stage-setting for a morality play. Instead of the traditionally opposed entrances of Heaven and Hell, we have, on the right, the fretted silhouette of a great wood, and on the left, the pyramid outline of the colliery slag heap, and the shadows of both darken the façade of the great house which is placed in the centre of the stage. Continually, we have the double awareness of the setting, realism is shot through with symbolism and vice versa. As Connie and Mellors walk through the wood at night, they see, shining through the leaves, the winking lights of the colliery; as the sun comes up it is the pit hooters which break their sleep. When Connie looks at the clouds at night she sees them streaked with red from the blast furnaces, and she notices that the main path which runs through the wood is gravelled with the refuse of the pit-bank, so that, when it rains, it turns a dull pink. Everywhere this contrast is present and it is absolute. Even when Connie moves about the house she can hear 'the rattle-rattle of the screens at the pit, the puff of the winding engine, the click-click of shunting trucks and the hoarse little whistle of the colliery locomotive. Tevershall pit-bank was burning, had been burning for years and it would cost thousands to put out. So it had to burn. And when the wind was that way, which was often, the house was full of the stench of this sulphurous combustion of the earth's excrement. But even on windless days the air always smelt of something under-earth; sulphur, iron, coal or acid. And even on the Christmas roses the smuts settled persistently, incredible, like black manna from the skies of doom.' 'Black manna from the skies of doom . . .', the disfiguring of the earth coming as a warning from the gods, the physical scene intimating a spiritual doom. One antithesis discloses another, setting gives way to character.

We have observed the machine that is outside the wood, dominating the horizon, colouring the night skies, echoing through the house; but, more deadly, we have the machine inside the park. It is a Sunday morning, pear and plum are in

The Novel as Prophecy: 'Lady Chatterley's Lover' (1928)

blossom, and the sound of shunting trucks has been replaced by church bells. Connie has taken Clifford out in his motorized chair, 'quiet and complacent, Clifford sat at the wheel of adventure. . . .' And then, as they are returning, the chair jerks to a halt and stops. Clifford shouts for Mellors to help and 'they waited among the mashed flowers under a sky softly curdling with cloud.' He arrives but is unable to find the fault. Clifford runs the engine viciously, it clicks into action, he refuses Mellors's offer of help; suddenly the chair lurches and virtually falls. Mellors saves it. Again Clifford orders him to leave it. The brake jams and Clifford is now quite helpless. He abuses Mellors but eventually has to ask for his assistance. Connie helps too. 'At the top of the hill they rested and Connie was glad to let go. She had had fugitive dreams of friendship between these two men: one her husband, the other the father of her child. Now she saw the screaming absurdity of her dreams. The two males were as hostile as fire and water. They naturally exterminated one another. . . .' 'Now she saw . . .', it is the machine which has revealed the nature of her husband to her, dominant yet impotent, asserting his will over the machine, turning it into a moral support, blind to the fact that he is utterly dependent upon it, morally as well as physically. ' "Thanks so much, Mellors," said Clifford, when they were at the house door. "I must get a different sort of motor—that's all." ' Connie looks at Clifford, and then at Mellors, and sees now the kind of opposition between them; she sees that the machine can indicate a dimension of soul as well physical fact. In this, of course, we see plainly Lawrence's inheritance from a whole tradition of nineteenth-century social and political thinking. In 1829, for instance, we find Carlyle writing: 'Not the external and physical alone is now managed by machinery, but the internal and spiritual also . . . men are grown mechanical in head and in heart as well as in hand.' It is a contention which we can find as early as Blake and appearing in Cobbett, in Dickens and Matthew Arnold, in Ruskin and William Morris, and it is within that social tradition that Lawrence writes. But this scene illuminates for Connie not simply Clifford's relationship with the machine but his relation-

The Novel as Prophecy: 'Lady Chatterley's Lover' (1928)

ship with Mellors, 'the two males were as hostile as fire and water.' And it is this note which is uniquely Lawrence's, namely his presentation of character in terms of consciousness.

It is a presentation which, on the whole, is alien to change or development, consisting mainly of increasingly forceful repetitions of the datum. We will consider the critical implications of this later; for the time being we can confine ourselves to descriptive commentary. Clifford's essential datum is given to us very early in the novel: 'He was remotely interested: but like a man looking down a microscope or up a telescope. He was not in touch. He was not in actual touch with anybody. . . .' He is insulated by instruments from the world in which he lives, he sees the miners as 'labour' serving his engineering experiments; he hears of the outside world through the radio and a voice from Frankfurt or Madrid is closer to him than his wife's. When he seeks his leisure, he plays chess with his nurse throughout the night in the intimacy of his bedroom, with a terrible kind of perverted lust. The withering of his emotional and sentient life has created a vacuum which has been filled by pure mind and will. He can no longer live above the earth, 'he felt life rush into him out of the coal, out of the pit. The very stale air of the colliery was better than oxygen to him.' He can only live in an atmosphere of death and consequently, when Connie looks at him, his eyes are vacant, when she touches him, he is cold. Desperately she turns away, not so much in search of a person as in search of life itself. And it is precisely not as a person, but as a power, that she first encounters Mellors.

Walking out with Clifford in the estate she meets the new gamekeeper and is startled, 'he seemed to emerge with such a swift menace . . . like the sudden rush of a threat out of nowhere.' Throughout the novel this associated sense of mysterious power and indefinable danger is an intrinsic part of the presentation of Mellors, and clearly, however elusive this aura is to define, it is the antithesis of the 'deathliness' of Clifford. Whatever human characteristics Mellors possesses, we feel, are there to serve this 'life' that he possesses, and this life is not something that can be understood in terms of personal qualities. Mellors is

The Novel as Prophecy: 'Lady Chatterley's Lover' (1928)

like a medium who is capable of transmitting a life to others, a capacity which cannot be thought of as co-extensive with his conscious intention or individual ability. When Connie first meets Mellors she notes his isolation, 'why was he so aloof, apart?', 'a man very much alone, yet on his own', 'a pallor of isolation came over him'. But this remoteness, this isolation is very different from Clifford's—where his proceeds from hatred of life, Mellors's comes from fear of its terrible and necessary claims:

> Especially he did not want the old contact with a woman again. He feared it; for he had a big wound from old contacts. . . . His recoil from the outer world was complete; his last refuge was this wood, to hide himself there.

It is here, in the wood, that he meets Connie and their relationship begins.

> 'I thought I'd done with it all. Now I've begun again.'
> 'Begun what?'
> 'Life.'
> 'Life,' she re-echoed with a queer thrill.
> 'It's life,' he said, 'there's no keeping clear. And if you do keep clear you might almost as well die. So I've got to be broken open again. . . .,

This is an interesting conversation not only because it hints at the moral calculus Lawrence is employing, but because it suggests how that calculus works. The key lies in the concept of 'Life'. Clifford 'dies' because he tries to keep clear, which means shutting down his affective nature; Mellors 'lives' because he realizes in time the folly of such an attempt. It is in the sexual relationship that 'Life' is most fully embodied, and it is embodied there because, as Mellors says, 'sex is really only touch, the closest possible touch', and as Lawrence says elsewhere, because it is in sex that 'man comes to the limits of himself and becomes aware of something beyond him . . . aware of what surpasses him.' Both of these assertions must be borne in mind if we are to understand the centrality of sex for Lawrence, but it is important to notice their order. There is first the assertion that the fulfilment of the individual human life depends upon our capacity for intimate sensual relationship with one another, found most com-

The Novel as Prophecy: 'Lady Chatterley's Lover' (1928)

pletely in sex. And then, consequent on the first assertion, is the second: in the achievement of this relationship we come into union with the very source of Life itself. Arguing that Lawrence's preoccupations are religious rather than ethical, F. R. Leavis writes of the characters in *The Rainbow*: 'Each lover is for the other a "door"; an opening into the "unknown", by which the horizon, the space of life, is immensely expanded, and unaccepted limits that had seemed final are "transgressed".'

When we stop regarding Mellors as an example of cosmic force and look at him as an individual, we feel a steep decline in Lawrence's creative interest. Faced with the social and economic questions of the day, Mellors emerges as a disillusioned Luddite: 'I'd wipe the machines off the face of the earth and end the industrial epoch absolutely, like a black mistake. But since I can't and nobody can, I'd better hold my peace and try and live my own life.' On two occasions Connie asks what he would like to see in place of the industrial society which he opposes so bitterly, but his proposals for the Revival of Folk Culture fail to hold even her attention. Like Mellors, Lawrence has no hopes in this direction either, and the social gesture is a routine impulse. If there is hope it lies only in the individual life, and Mellors concludes by saying: 'You can't insure against the future, except by really believing in the best bit of you. So I believe in the little flame between us. For me now, it's the only thing in the world.' However desperate the hope may be, the novel ends by endorsing it. Mellors has emerged from his isolation, been broken open by the emotional and sensual claims of another person, and agreed to the responsibilities entailed, suitably symbolized by his approaching fatherhood.

Connie's development in the novel lies in her rejection of Clifford and in her acceptance of Mellors, and it should be clear by now that in saying this we are not saying that she has come to hate one person and love another, so much as that she has learnt that a man can die without ceasing to exist, and that an adult can be born into life as surely as a child can. Like Clifford, and like Mellors, Connie also is out of contact at the beginning of the story, 'an inward dread, an emptiness, an indifference to

The Novel as Prophecy: 'Lady Chatterley's Lover' (1928)

everything gradually spread in her soul.' Her condition, however, has to be distinguished from theirs—where one is detached, and the other enclosed, she is lonely. Even in her loneliness, she reacts strongly and sensitively against the world of Clifford, and the whole of the first part of the book is taken up, as far as she is concerned, with these negative reactions. There is opposition to the world of talk with which he surrounds himself, antipathy to his malicious short stories and to his olympian plans for the redirection of labour, 'she could not help feeling how little connection he had with people. The miners were, in a sense, his own men, but he saw them as objects rather than as men, parts of the pit rather than parts of life, crude raw phenomena rather than human beings along with him.' Correlated with this is his attitude towards the wood as a kind of museum of memories, 'I want this wood perfect, *untouched*, I want nobody to trespass in it' (my italics). But for Connie, the miners are human beings who have been broken by the world in which they live, and the wood is the only living thing that she knows, '... she sat down with her back to a young pine tree that swayed against her with curious life, elastic, and powerful and rising up. The erect live thing with its top in the sun.' Obviously, we see here a foreshadowing in terms of the wood of her subsequent sexual response to Mellors. The more complete her rejection of the Clifford world, the more she is made open to the life that is to come to her. She feels it first in the wood, and then, more explicitly, when she watches Mellors feeding the chickens, 'life, life, pure sparky fearless new life. For in a moment a tiny, sharp head was poking through the gold brown feathers of the hen and eyeing the Cosmos. Connie was fascinated. And at the same time never had she felt so acutely the agony of her own female forlornness.' It is in this mood of desolation that Mellors sees her, is touched, and their relationship begins. And almost immediately it finds expression in sexual terms, because all that Lawrence is concerned to do is to bring to Connie 'life' where up to now she has found 'death'. I put it this way in order to emphasize how very far from Lawrence's interest or purpose is the creation of a realistic human situation, of anything resembling what is usually

The Novel as Prophecy: 'Lady Chatterley's Lover' (1928)

understood by a 'love story'. If we argue that the progress of Connie's relationship with Mellors and his with her is lacking in credibility or in variety, we are really asking for a portrait, where the whole structure of *Lady Chatterley's Lover* has been designed to take X-ray photographs. Consequently, when we say that the sexual episodes have to be seen in the context of the whole story, we shall look in vain if we think that Lawrence is presenting them as only an element in the relationship of Connie and Mellors. They are, as everyone knows, the total relationship, but they are this not because Lawrence imagined this was how people actually lived or how they ought to live, but because Lawrence is relating a fable and a fable does not attempt to copy reality in this way. Lawrence's fable is concerned to isolate and plot the interaction of two forces, to which he gives the simple labels of 'life' and 'death'. We don't need to cavil about the labels, they are only there to suggest an archetypal opposition. The drama, however, must be a human one, because it is only in human beings that these forces exist. Given this, it is reduced to the simplest possible shape, with one character embodying death, another life, and a third the victim of one or the other. Connie resolves it by finding 'life' in her sexual relationship with Mellors. It is not happiness that she aims at, but salvation. Giving the words their full weight, we might say that the upshot of *Lady Chatterley's Lover* is that a woman learns to live her life, and we all have to learn what that means.

[iii]

Up to now I have been describing the kind of novel *Lady Chatterley's Lover* aims to be. Whether it succeeds or not is another question, but obviously it is one which is contingent upon its aim. The intention is plain, the structure of the novel should make it clear beyond dispute; but no one was more trenchant than Lawrence in warning us against accepting intention as achievement: 'Let me hear what the novel says. As for the novelist, he is usually a dribbling liar.' If the storm of controversy that has followed the publication of the novel is any indica-

The Novel as Prophecy: 'Lady Chatterley's Lover' (1928)

tion, then this novel would appear to say a great number of contradictory things. Immediately, the question must arise: why should a novel with such a markedly simple outline as *Lady Chatterley* have given rise to the kind of dispute which I described at the beginning of this chapter? Admittedly, some of the opposition arises out of, or is related to, Lawrence's employment of a number of words usually considered taboo, but it would be readily granted by both 'sides' that that is merely a symptom of a disagreement much more radical than one over the use of an offensive vocabulary. What would seem to be at stake is Lawrence's whole attitude in the novel.

I will illustrate what I mean by two quotations, which both comment on the same incident, namely, Connie's decision to leave Clifford and join Mellors. The first is as follows:

> When Connie leaves Clifford she sins against bourgeois morality—Clifford sins against organic life. Two moral systems clash and yet we recognise that phallic marriage is creative and moral, above and beyond our vision of Clifford's plight.[1]

And this is the second:

> Connie and Mellors are so plainly headed, not for tragedy, but just a dusty limbo, their fate interests us as a kind of curiosity. It is true that her youth was robbed by her husband's fate in the war. I think he was worse robbed even, with no way out, yet nobody seems to feel sorry for him. He is shown as having very dull ideas, but he is not more dull than the gamekeeper, who forgets that the lady's aristocratic husband was not born impotent, as Lawrence insists, by way of his dubious hero, all upper-class men were.[2]

What is interesting about these quotations is not simply their clash, but the way they clash, the one vibrant with approval, the other with exasperation. It is this undertone of emotion which seizes both writers and blurs their judgment. For instance, there is Mr. Spilka's high-pitched remark that 'Clifford sins against life.' What is 'organic' doing here that 'life' is not, and what is 'life' doing here that is meaningful? Life, as such, is a biological process, it only enters the realm of values in relation to human

---

[1] Mark Spilka, *The Love-Ethic of D. H. Lawrence*, Indiana, 1955, p. 197.
[2] Katherine Anne Porter, 'A Wreath for the Gamekeeper', *Encounter*, Feb., 1960, p. 77.

The Novel as Prophecy: 'Lady Chatterley's Lover' (1928)

beings. To suggest that an appeal from 'morality', however bourgeois, to 'life' is the 'clash of two systems' is to empty language of meaning. What is at issue surely is not 'life' but rival conceptions of 'the good life'. Miss Porter talks of Clifford's 'dull ideas', but it is precisely his 'bright ideas' which Lawrence sees as evil; Clifford is all mind and will. What is it that makes one critic anxious to make ethical considerations vanish, and another no less anxious that nothing else should appear? Mr. Spilka turns fiction into gospel, Miss Porter into a transcript for divorce proceedings. And the division here between the critics seems to mirror a division in the novel. Mr. Spilka conceals it by reading *Lady Chatterley's Lover* as a great symbolic novel; Miss Porter exposes it by reading it in the spirit of realist fiction. From the viewpoint of one it is deeply moving and apocalyptic, from the other tiresomely repetitive and ludicrous. I have mentioned the opinions of Mr. Spilka and Miss Porter chiefly because their attitudes are conveniently representative of the kind of criticism which *Lady Chatterley's Lover* has continually provoked. And it has provoked it not because of obscurity in the novel—we have already indicated its clarity of plot and intention—but because in the total pattern of the novel there is a fundamental ambiguity about the artistic status of the setting and the characters. If it is read as a realistic tale, then it not only presents human relationships, for the most part, from a severely exclusive point of view, but it ignores the exigencies and complexities of living in an irreversibly industrial society. If this is a symbolic tale, then the insistent realistic details—historical, geographical, industrial, sexual—short-circuit the range of meaning. But these general statements only have meaning when we see their effect in the novel. And I want to turn back, critically now, to some of the features of the novel I described earlier.

The most useful starting point here is to look again at Lawrence's presentation of character. If we assemble the various details we are given about Clifford and think of them in relation to his dramatic role, we shall find a man who is physically crippled, isolated, self-centred, devoted to the life of the mind and the worship of the machine. If we do the same for Mellors

The Novel as Prophecy: 'Lady Chatterley's Lover' (1928)

we shall find a man who has been emotionally hurt, isolated, increasingly involved in a sexual relationship, devoted to the infallibility of the feelings and to the life of the wood. In neither case will these details account for the archetypal opposition between the two characters; an opposition constantly expressed in terms of 'life' and 'death'. Indeed, looked at as 'characters', there seems little to choose between them. If we think of Connie complaining that Clifford's devotion to talk was excessive and wearisome, then she can hardly have found Mellors's distinguished by its charm and variety; if we feel Clifford enjoying his authority as an employer, we can remember Mellors enjoying his authority over his employer's wife; if Clifford seems to believe in the mystical properties of coal, Mellors sees in forget-me-nots something more than woodland flowers. Now, of course, it will be protested, and rightly, that this divorces incident from context, and confuses, perversely, modes of presentation which are sometimes realistic, sometimes symbolic. But when this protest has been heeded, the fact still remains that as *characters* Clifford and Mellors do not convey the basic antithesis which Lawrence intends. If we feel that they do, then I suggest that our impression emerges from something other than the dramatized incidents of the novel. What that 'other' is, is not difficult to locate; it lies not in the individuality of Clifford and the individuality of Mellors, but in their differing kinds of consciousness. This is a distinction which has far-ranging implications for the status of the novel as a medium of imaginative communication.

Ever since 1913, when Lawrence published *Sons and Lovers*, he had been persistently accused by critics of faulty characterization, of involving his characters in emotional conflicts in excess of the dramatic facts. Feeling was abundant, but motivation was obscure. This led, it was argued, towards anonymity of character, so we find Middleton Murry writing about *Women in Love*:

> .... we can discern no individuality whatever in the denizens of Mr. Lawrence's world. We should have thought that we should have been able to distinguish between male and female at least. But no! Remove the names, remove the sedulous catalogues of unnecessary

The Novel as Prophecy: 'Lady Chatterley's Lover' (1928)

clothing . . . and man and woman are as indistinguishable as octopods in an aquarium tank.

and Edwin Muir remarking:

> We remember the scenes in his novels; we forget the names of his men and women. We should not know any of them if we met them in the street. . . .

Lawrence replied to Muir and his answer seems a convincing one for this whole kind of criticism:

> I have lunched with Mr. Banality and I'm sure I should know him if I met him in the street. . . . Alas, that I should recognize people in the street by their noses, bonnets, or beauty. Does nothing exist beyond that which is recognizable in the streets? How does my cat recognize me in the dark? Thank God, there are more and other sorts of vision than that which Mr. Muir esteems above all others.

'There are more and other sorts of vision . . .', the claim is surely an unexceptionable one. Lawrence, benefiting, often intuitively, from the insights of psycho-analysis, is genuinely extending the province of the novelist, and today it seems difficult to deny that novels like *Sons and Lovers*, *The Rainbow* and *Women in Love* rely for their distinction largely on Lawrence's extraordinary ability to render 'other kinds of knowledge' vivid and compelling to the reader. If then we find the characterization in *Lady Chatterley's Lover* ambiguous and unsatisfactory, this is not because we are applying the kind of criteria implied by Muir, or are reluctant to accept the character presentation as valid, but because Lawrence's own presentation changed as his work went on. In the 'twenties the exploring artist in his work was yielding to the needs of the prophet, his fiction began to oscillate between autobiography and tract, and in the process 'other kinds of knowledge' tended to contract into 'the *only* kind of knowledge'. A rare ability for a certain kind of artistic creation was now being pressed to serve a gospel for salvation, and it is this which makes Lawrence's reply to Muir no longer adequate. When Ursula leaves Skrebensky in *The Rainbow* we can understand why this should have come about, though it is certainly not a break which could be accounted for in terms of the characterization employed by a nineteenth-century novelist. 'Warmth',

The Novel as Prophecy: 'Lady Chatterley's Lover' (1928)

'coldness', Lawrence has made these terms, in a multiplicity of ways, dramatically convincing for us, and he has done it because he has concentrated on getting to the truth of a relationship between two individual beings. He is not using them as a means of attacking or propagating beliefs about a kind of sexual relationship. But in *Kangaroo* and *The Plumed Serpent* and *Lady Chatterley's Lover*, we feel Lawrence's characters are neatly chiselled figures, with a sharp outline, being turned this way and that, so that they can cast their shadows most effectively on the screen of Modern Life; and it is on to *that* screen that Lawrence directs our attention.

To try and show more exactly what is implied in the distinction between 'character' and 'consciousness' in the later novels of Lawrence I want to select two passages from *Lady Chatterley's Lover* and examine our response towards them. The first is from a scene where Clifford and Connie are discussing their marriage, and Clifford goes on to reflect:

'... the occasional sexual connections ... if people don't exaggerate them ridiculously, pass like the mating of birds. And so they should. What does it matter? It's the life-long companionship that matters. It's the living together from day to day, not the sleeping together once or twice. You and I are married no matter what happens to us. We have the habit of each other. And habit, to my thinking, is more vital than any occasional excitement.'

Now clearly this passage is intended to bring home to the reader Clifford's 'deathly' consciousness. But as we read the novel we respond to this passage not as a denigration of sex, but as the words of a particular man in a particular situation, a man who has been made impotent by war, outlining the only kind of marriage that is possible for him, and, even if mistakenly, at least very understandably, making it out to be a good marriage. Lawrence has rendered Clifford incapable of enjoying a proper marriage; to go on and attack him for the perversity of his views is perversity on the part of the author. The critical point is that Lawrence is continually muting our response to a particular character, which, as a novelist, he can *dramatize*, in order to sharpen our response to a generalized consciousness,

The Novel as Prophecy: 'Lady Chatterley's Lover' (1928)

which, as a seer, he can only *announce*. To think that this kind of difficulty can be overcome by talking of Clifford's crippling being 'symbolic' of the inward death he embodies, is to underestimate considerably our response to the physical attributes of personality.

This underestimation works in the opposite way in a passage, much later in the novel, when Connie is talking to Mellors of the practical difficulties which prevent their being able to live together for some time. Mellors pauses to consider and then:

'I could wish the Cliffords and Berthas all dead,' he said.

'It's not being very tender to them,' she said.

'Tender to them? Yea, even the tenderest thing you could do for them, perhaps, would be to give them death. They can't live! They only frustrate life. Their souls are awful inside them. Death ought to be sweet to them. And I ought to be allowed to shoot them.'

'But you wouldn't do it,' she said.

'I would though! and with less qualms than I shoot a weasel. It anyhow has a prettiness and a loneliness. But they are legion. Oh, I'd shoot them.'

Connie's response here is much the same as the reader's; we are disturbed at Mellors's violence. We see a terrible autocracy here, an unchallengeable sense of righteousness, which can only think of any opposition in terms of its annihilation. And yet clearly, for Lawrence, Connie's response does not proceed from her humanity but from her uncertain faith, because the 'life' that Mellors embodies and proclaims is so overwhelmingly 'right' that even to demur at its expression is to belong to the devil's party. At this point, I want to make the simple criticism that in *Lady Chatterley* Lawrence not only gives us no dramatic key to the 'deathly' consciousness of Clifford and the 'vital' consciousness of Mellors, but that he has got himself into a position where, if the reader thinks in these terms, he misunderstands the whole position. When the earlier novels, *Sons and Lovers*, *The Rainbow*, *Women in Love*, seemed obscure and unsatisfactory, this was either because Lawrence had not been able to express completely what he wanted to say or because the reader was looking for the wrong thing. But in his last novels what he is increasingly concerned to say can no more be dramatized in terms of the novel

The Novel as Prophecy: 'Lady Chatterley's Lover' (1928)

than faith can be conveyed in logical discourse. The outlines of individual men and women fade and become incandescent with the awesome, impalpable presences of 'Life' and 'Death'. The voice of the artist has become lost in the voice of the prophet, and the burden of his message is—how shall we be saved? It is salvation by an election no less fearful and exclusive than that which haunted Bunyan himself, a salvation which will be found finally and inescapably in sex, because sex, as Lawrence remarked simply in one of his last poems, 'is a state of grace'. And without this psychotheology there can be no access to 'life'.

Having brought the argument to a point at which it might become plausible to think of *Lady Chatterley's Lover* as, in some sense, a 'religious' novel, we might briefly glance back at *The End of the Affair* and *Thérèse Desqueyroux*, and see what it has in common with those 'grace-driven' novels. At first sight, it would seem to be a great deal.

There is, to begin with, a common plot. All three novels deal with a marital conflict between a cruel or insensitive or egotistic husband and his younger, attractive, frustrated wife. Henry, Bernard and Clifford have enough in common to arouse a similar antipathy in the reader. There is their worldly success, complacently flaunted:

> There was Clifford's success ... his books brought him in a thousand pounds. His photograph appeared everywhere. There was a bust of him in one of the galleries.... He seemed the most modern of modern voices.
>
> *(Lady Chatterley's Lover)*

> Henry was successful now: in the last Birthday Honours he had received a C.B.E. for his services at the Ministry, he had been appointed Chairman of a Royal Commission; and here he was at the gala night of a British film called *The Last Siren*, pallid and pop-eyed in the flashlight. . . .
>
> *(The End of the Affair)*

And, in stark contrast to this comfortable public success, is the fear and loneliness of their respective wives. Connie wanders alone through a house 'as dreary as an unused street'; Thérèse stares through her windows at the dark pine trees and thinks

The Novel as Prophecy: 'Lady Chatterley's Lover' (1928)

they will witness 'the slow process of her suffocation'; Sarah, accompanying Henry to fashionable public functions, thinks of her life without Bendrix as 'a desert without water holes'. This bitterness and separation between husband and wife has been brought about by a number of emotional attitudes, shared by Henry and Clifford and Bernard. There is Henry dismissing the mystical fervour of Pascal as the result of 'glandular deficiency'; there is Bernard 'the most precise of men . . . never satisfied until he had labelled, ranged and set aside each separate emotion'; and Clifford, admiring Racine because in his work 'the emotions are ordered and given shape'. In the place of personal feeling there is passion for Work—Henry for the Civil Service, Bernard for his estate, Clifford for engineering—and talk, continual talk, so that Sarah listening to Henry feels as if she is 'fossilizing under the drip of conversation', and Connie hears Clifford's words as 'dead leaves crumpling up and turning to powder'. Outside the world of work and talk Henry and Bernard and Clifford have no real existence. For all three, sex is a degrading affair. When, at length, their victims try to free themselves from their marital relationship, this is presented as something, if not imperative, then inevitable; there is no question of a moral conflict, a worried conscience:

> Mellors had a sense of foreboding. No sense of wrong or sin; he was troubled by no conscience in that respect. He knew conscience was chiefly fear of society, or fear of oneself.
> *(Lady Chatterley's Lover)*

> 'Do you mind?' I asked her and she shook her head. I really didn't know what I meant—I think I had an idea that the sight of Henry might have aroused remorse. Unlike the rest of us she was unhaunted by guilt.'
> *(The End of the Affair)*

> I never felt I was being cruel—except when my hand hesitated. . . . I was the victim of a terrible duty. Yes, honestly, I had the feeling that it was a duty.
> *(Thérèse Desqueyroux)*

These three statements carry, in each case, the sympathy of the novelist, and the various novels have been constructed in such

The Novel as Prophecy: 'Lady Chatterley's Lover' (1928)

a way that the statements are calculated to enlist our sympathy too. Mellors, Thérèse, even Bendrix, the conduct of all three can be said to be vindicated, and, if their future is dark, it is due to the hostility of the world which faces them. What draws these three novels together and gives them this high degree of common detail is not merely that they are all preoccupied with showing that the basis of life is religious, in the sense that in life we encounter a power which we must respond to and which transcends the individual will, but that this religious power is often obstructed or obscured by our moral preoccupations. From this it is but a short step to seeing 'religion' and 'morality' as profoundly hostile to one another. This kind of hostility is caught in Lawrence's remark, 'You can develop an instinct for life *instead of a theory* of right and wrong, good and bad.' It is the kind of remark which should impel us to enquire more exactly about Lawrence's conception of religion, and warn us that comparisons with Greene and Mauriac will no longer help us. A remark from *Apocalypse* indicates quite clearly why: 'The Christian doctrine of love even at its best was an evasion. Even Jesus was going to reign "hereafter" when his "love" would be turned into confirmed power. This business of reigning in glory hereafter went to the root of Christianity, and is, of course, only an expression of frustrated desire to reign here and now.' The affirmation of 'an instinct for life' and the rejection of the Christian doctrine of immortality indicate sufficiently the direction of Lawrence's religious ideal, and, in so doing, guide us to the heart of *Lady Chatterley's Lover*.

'No man', Mr. Eliot once remarked rather loftily, 'would attach himself to the universe who had anything better to join himself to.' It is a remark which has a profound relevance for *Lady Chatterley's Lover*, pointing to the achievement and the tragedy of the novel. In Lawrence's attachment to the universe we have the basis of his faith, and, in the profound misanthropy of his last years, we find the force which helped him to maintain it. These two aspects are intimately related and Lawrence's deep animism emerges out of the frustration of his religious and social instincts. The concern to sense and describe a force 'behind', but

The Novel as Prophecy: 'Lady Chatterley's Lover' (1928)

inseparable from, observed realities, is everywhere present in *Lady Chatterley's Lover*. Connie looks at the miners returning from their shift, 'elemental creatures, weird and distorted, of the mineral world! They belonged to the coal, the iron, the clay as fish belong to the sea, and worms to dead wood. The anima of mineral disintegration.' If this is the animate spirit of Death, the animate spirit of Life is caught in Sex, so that not only do we encounter 'life' here, but it is an experience which enables us 'to see into the life of things'. Thus when Connie, returning from a sexual meeting with Mellors, runs through the wood, she sees 'the world as a dream; the trees in the park bulging and surging at anchor on a tide'. Sex is the anima of natural integration. And it is here, of course, in sex, that Lawrence's animist view of the cosmos chimes in with his emphasis on consciousness as opposed to character. Where love emphasizes individuality, sex conceals it; the face is hidden, speech gives way to touch. And so we find Connie thinking of Mellors, 'he was kind to the female in her, which no man had ever been. Men were very kind to the *person* she was, but rather cruel to the female, despising her or ignoring her altogether. . . . He took no notice of Constance or of Lady Chatterley; he just softly stroked her loins or her breasts.' Whatever the implication of this shift of attention for Mellors, it is considerable for the novelist, who must, by virtue of his medium, communicate through character. The kind of difficulties which this elimination of the individual presents for Lawrence are to be found in the ambiguity which surrounds his presentation of sex in the novel.

Lawrence's dilemma was a profound one; he wanted to do two things simultaneously and they warred against each other. In the first place he was intent on restoring a sacred character to sex—he would not have it vulgarized and degraded in what he considered 'the modern way'—he would reveal it again as a holy mystery. Mircea Eliade, in *Patterns of Comparative Religion*, writes: 'For the modern man sex is a physiological act, whereas for the primitive it was a sacrament, a ceremony by means of which he communicated with *the force which stood for Life itself* . . .' (my italics). It is in the light of this primitive vision

The Novel as Prophecy: 'Lady Chatterley's Lover' (1928)

that Lawrence writes. Hence his sexual descriptions are charged with the language of religion, and language which is rich in biblical association and power. This is not because Lawrence is seeking to promulgate a specific 'belief', still less is he parodying religious orthodoxy; rather he is trying to create by use of rhythm, imagery, diction, an aura of intensity and exaltation which will be recognized as religious. It is in sex, Lawrence feels, that man encounters most fully the awesome mystery of Life itself, that he comes to apprehend the Power that is in him; and at the same time it is a Power which infinitely transcends him. It is not a phallic cult but an animistic encounter which lies at the centre of Lawrence's concern with sex. For Mellors, '... she lay there crying in unconscious, inarticulate cries. The voice out of the uttermost night, the life! The man heard it beneath him with a kind of awe....' For Connie, 'out of his utter, incomprehensible stillness she felt again the slow, momentous, surging rise of the phallus again, the other power. And her heart melted out with a kind of awe....' The corollary to making sex sacred, however, is that it is also made taboo. And it was this which Lawrence persistently disregarded.

The sacred mysteries are always veiled, not because they are shameful, but because they are dangerous. But if Lawrence was bent on restoring the sacred character of sex, he was no less concerned with restoring the shameless character of sex. But the prophetic and the therapeutic make uneasy companions. It is not of course that, abstractly considered, there is conflict, but that within a common context their mode of operation must be so different as to constitute a clash. Where the concern of the first is to create a sense of mystery and rarity, the concern of the second is with clarity and normality; where one urges awe, the other urges frankness. The proper language of one is poetic; the language of the other, ethical. Consequently, the verbal and structural tactics Lawrence was employing to win battles on one front were effectively helping him to lose them on the other. It is really this kind of pull and haul which causes the uncertainty of tone in such episodes as the famous forget-me-nots scene, where the awkwardness might appear simply as an artistic con-

The Novel as Prophecy: 'Lady Chatterley's Lover' (1928)

fusion between symbolic and realistic modes of presentation. In this episode Lawrence makes his fullest assertion about the sacredness of sex; and device after device is called upon to assist him; the depersonalization of Mellors and Connie, and the explicit, but ritualistic, joining of the force of sex with the force of nature. A roughly analogous episode would be the flower episode in *The Winter's Tale*. But, unlike Shakespeare, Lawrence, having created a symbolic ambience for his religious purpose, recalls, as it were, his very different therapeutic intentions. And so this must now be a scene, literally, about two particular individuals and their specific sexual relationship. To establish this we have the stream of realistic details, the anatomical insistence, the enumerated flowers, and Connie, noticing the rain, prudently putting on rubber shoes before dashing outside naked. It is impossible to keep a picture like this in focus; if it escapes dissolving into obscenity, then it dissolves into bathos. And the clarity and honesty of the intention cannot save the scene from artistic tastelessness and moral ambiguity; the prophet and the moralist have not come to terms; because of this the scene rings false, and the effect of this falsity is of mild though unwitting prurience.

The uncertainty of Lawrence's presentation of sex in *Lady Chatterley* is not in any way a reflection of an uncertainty in his general outlook. Indeed, the reverse is the case. By the time Lawrence came to write this novel he had put far behind him the welter of ideas that we see surging behind *Women in Love*, or the elaborate variations on a theme that we find in *Kangaroo* and *The Plumed Serpent*. There is a simplicity about *Lady Chatterley* not to be found in any of these novels, but this is not the simplicity which arises from the harmony of opposites, but the simplicity obtained by the elimination of opposition. Anything that brings with it complexity must be severely circumscribed. And so we find Lawrence's best work in his last years to lie in a simple fable like *The Virgin and the Gypsy*, or a visionary gospel like *Apocalypse*, or a straight essay in polemic like *À Propos of Lady Chatterley's Lover*. Here the whole success arises from an intensity of conviction finding expression in an appropriate in-

The Novel as Prophecy: 'Lady Chatterley's Lover' (1928)

tensity of language. But unequivocal assertion is death to the novel; character and symbol cannot live in that atmosphere. And Lawrence, in writing *Lady Chatterley*, had become distrustful of character and of symbol to convey what he wanted to say; of character because it may bring complexity, of symbol because it may bring obscurity.

Earlier in this chapter I discussed Lawrence's distrust of character, but there my concern was mainly to elucidate by considering it in relation to consciousness. What I want to suggest in these final paragraphs is that Lawrence's misanthropy has now invaded his novel to such an extent that the very creation of a fictional character as distinct from a 'mouthpiece' or a 'target' is now practically beyond him. The truth of the poignant revelation in his autobiographical sketch, published in 1930, is all too clearly felt in the novel: 'I have wanted to feel truly friendly with some, at least, of my fellow men. Yet I have never quite succeeded. . . . I don't feel there is any very cordial or fundamental contact between me and society, or me and other people. There is a breach. And my contact is with something that is non-human, non-vocal.' This is the mood in which we feel that *Lady Chatterley* was written, tired, bitter, sad, and all the stress on consciousness rather than character, sex rather than love, touch rather than speech, arises directly from Lawrence's profound feeling of social alienation. 'There is a breach'—how strongly we sense this to be true in the novel! In Mellors, the direct representative of his creator, we have the man who brings love into the novel, but he talks only of hate, Swiftian in its intensity. 'I feel', he says at one moment, 'the colonies aren't far enough. The moon wouldn't be far enough, because you could look back and see the earth, dirty, beastly, unsavoury among the stars; made foul by men.' It is a remark which could be paralleled many times and it establishes a dominant mood of the novel, if only because there is nothing to suggest that these anguished cries were not endorsed by Lawrence. When we look at Clifford, we feel him to be not so much a figure of fate, as the victim of his circumstances and his author. At times, Lawrence is so anxious to support Connie's loathing that he seems to join in and jeer at

The Novel as Prophecy: 'Lady Chatterley's Lover' (1928)

his own creation, 'How extraordinary he was, bent there over the book, queer and rapacious and civilized, with broad shoulders and no real legs!' For Lawrence to permit himself that final detail is suggestive of the lack of emotional control he shows in these passages. At other times, Lawrence would seem to blame Clifford for his very *inability* to be responsible, 'Like many people, his insanity might be measured by the things he was *not* aware of; the great desert tracts in his consciousness.' Surely what we feel in the case of both Clifford and Mellors is that Lawrence has kept them so artistically impoverished that they can do little but repeat the lines he feeds to them. They exist only for that purpose. To see the truth of this, we don't need to go outside the pages of this novel. We need only turn to the person of Mrs. Bolton to feel, not a Dickensian creation or a 'round' character, but simply a fictional reality. Here Lawrence, by keeping her well clear of the main line of the novel, has allowed his imagination to create a person who will really embody what he has to say, not merely repeat it. And consequently the difference between Mrs. Bolton and the rest of the characters in the novel is an instructive one.

Lawrence, of course, is aware of this difference, but he underestimates its significance. He sees her very much in the light of someone playing a 'character part', her gossip, he tells us, was 'Mrs. Gaskell, and George Eliot, and Miss Mitford all rolled into one'; and certainly this element is there in her presentation. But there is more to her than this. She is opaque in a way rare in Lawrence, she cannot simply be looked through and classified. Thus we find her attitude to the question of social class piquantly ambivalent, and though she has a natural affinity to Clifford, she is capable of communicating the mystery of 'touch' with a poignancy which Mellors never manages. She is telling Connie about her husband being killed in a mine accident:

'. . . I kept expecting him back. Especially at nights. I kept waking up thinking: Why he's not in bed with me! It was as if my *feelings* wouldn't believe he'd gone. I just felt he'd *have* to come back and lie against me, so I could feel him with me. That was all I wanted. . . .'
'The touch of him,' said Connie.

The Novel as Prophecy: 'Lady Chatterley's Lover' (1928)

'That's it, my Lady, the touch of him! I've never got over it to this day and never shall.'

This is effective precisely because it is an individual grief, we don't feel the author 'using' it as a representative cry on behalf of the Human Condition. 'A character in a novel', Lawrence wrote, 'has got to live or it is nothing,' and it is because Lawrence doesn't feel the necessity of 'believing for' Mrs. Bolton that she becomes free to live. Free to reveal a complexity of human sympathies, free to say 'and he was a *bad* fellow and she was such a *nice* woman', without the reader being made to feel that this is the Last Judgment. This is not to say that Mrs. Bolton becomes a sympathetic figure; she is trivial, and self-centred, and malicious, but Lawrence allows her to move in a world similar to our own, she has the independence of a human being, and, when we come to judge her, it is through our eyes that we see her, not through the eyes of God. Unlike Clifford and Mellors she escapes the fate of being an idea dressed up as a person.

The profound distrust of 'character' in *Lady Chatterley* is only a symptom, though perhaps the most striking one, of Lawrence's whole distrust, by this time, of the Novel itself. He seems simply to have lost confidence in his ability to transpose his experience into the terms of fiction. In addition to writing three versions of the novel, Lawrence took up the theme and treated it in the form of a fable (*The Virgin and the Gypsy*) and in the form of a discursive essay (*À Propos of Lady Chatterley's Lover*). Taken together, the fable and the essay constitute in their ease and assurance a penetrating diagnosis of the failure of the novel. The form of the fable does not harry the writer into stating literal beliefs, nor does it overwhelm him with 'relevance' to the age; the essay, however, allows him to do precisely these things, without the necessity of illustration or imaginative transposition. At this stage of his career, Lawrence's best work is found, that is to say, in the fairy tale which becomes a vision of another life or in direct polemic. But the novel needs an artist, not a prophet, and the writing of *Lady Chatterley's Lover* required a hope, a sympathy and ultimately a humility, which Lawrence could no longer feel. It forced on him a belief in 'character'

The Novel as Prophecy: 'Lady Chatterley's Lover' (1928)

which he despised; symbolism, which he saw as an evasion. And it is out of this emotional turmoil that the novel comes, faking a hope which the writer no longer possesses. And Lawrence himself has made the necessary judgment here: 'Morality in the novel is the trembling instability of the balance. When the novelist puts his thumb in the scale to pull down the balance to his own predilection, that is immorality. The modern novel tends to become more and more immoral, as the novelist tends to press his thumb heavier and heavier in the pan. . . .' In *Lady Chatterley*, as Lawrence tries to make vision into a practicality, and cosmic scepticism into an individual condemnation, his thumb weighs so firmly in the scale that all the function of the 'balance' is lost.

The measure of Lawrence's inability to bring his fabulous and discursive material into a balanced whole is that the reader finds his criticism of the novel gradually emerging as a question, requiring an answer. He feels he must ask himself how comprehensive or generally valid is the solution which Lawrence proposes. The word 'acceptance' has a disturbing prominence in our reactions, and we feel that acceptance of the novel is intimately bound up with an acceptance of views. That questions like these should arise is of course an indication of the limitations of *Lady Chatterley's Lover*, an indication of the way in which the polemical drive has not been adequately countered by the fable. The book is challenging not as a work of art ought to be, by being disturbing, but rather by demanding agreement. In the last analysis, 'question' and 'answer' lie in wait for the critic who tries to make as inclusive a response as possible to the novel.

For instance, it seems difficult to resist the charge that in *Lady Chatterley* Lawrence has vastly over-simplified, or, depending on our emphasis, over-magnified, the value of sex. Mellors, for instance, gives an account to Connie of his failure with his wife and other women, and the expression of this failure, comprehensive in intention, is in terms simply of sexual 'timing'. That this might have been the result of a failure at other levels of personality, a failure of trust, generosity, patience, seems to be deliberately

The Novel as Prophecy: 'Lady Chatterley's Lover' (1928)

excluded. To judge from *Lady Chatterley*—and as I have said, it is a novel which insists on judgment like this—there can be no contact between people which is not physical, no love that is not sexual. But as one critic has put it, 'a sexual life which has "value" involves a constellation of events, kinds of contribution, confluences of attitudes, moods, personal style and tone, and trying to derive all these from the physiological imposes on it an excessive and eventually destructive burden that leads to the counter-extremism of narrow-gauge faith.'[1] There is in the novel such a literal insistence on the physiological basis of sex that it seems at times as if Lawrence is suggesting that the tragedy of the age would diminish in relation to an improvement in sexual expertise. Whatever truth there is in this can only be discerned when it is recognized as part of a much more complicated mesh of human circumstances than *Lady Chatterley's Lover* reveals.

The same distorting simplicity that attends the presentation of sex in the novel is hardly less present in the portrayal of 'industry'. Of course, there is a sense in which Lawrence's reaction is an admirable one in its recall to values other than business and money, but in 1928 protest, however eloquent, is not enough, if the writer is to be safe from being accused of nostalgia for a golden world. The problem that the modern writer must cope with is how to reconcile an irreversibly machine-based society with the preservation of spiritual and emotional needs. Judged in isolation, the chapter describing Connie's tour of the industrial Midlands is highly effective, but its effect is that of an independent essay on the industrial scene, rather than of an organic episode in the novel. Its note, however powerful, is one of simple rejection. And this rejection is not in any way modified by Mellors's alternatives, which are so little believed in by Lawrence that they are little more than picture postcard scenes of a folksy ruralism:

'The men ought to learn to be naked and handsome, and to sing in a mass and dance the old group dances, and carve the stools they sit on,

[1] R. B. Heilman, 'Nomad, Monads and the Mystique of the Soma', *Sewanee Review*, Winter 1960.

The Novel as Prophecy: 'Lady Chatterley's Lover' (1928)

and embroider their own emblems. Then they wouldn't need money. *And that's the only way to solve the industrial problem*' (my italics). Such deep despair of a cure begins to modify the value of the diagnosis.

Sex in isolation, the pit in isolation, even the word in isolation, mark out the desperation in *Lady Chatterley* for an ultimate position—the revelation of the final good, the final evil. No single man can hope to take a number of words which for centuries have been taboo, and by some kind of fiat restore them to common usage, suitably purged of their traditional connotations. Lawrence's whole purpose in this matter seems very curious, and arguments that he lacked a vocabulary for his purpose are not really convincing. Lawrence can hardly have expected or even desired that Tommy Dukes's example of social discourse would be copied, or that Mellors's private discourse would be envied for its freedom. The whole business seems to have provided an opportunity for a wilful reaction against a falsely-conceived repression. Falsely conceived because Lawrence must have known perfectly well that taboo-words occupy a position *sui generis* in human speech; they are there as expressions of anger or contempt, their actual 'meaning' is virtually nil. And even when the 'meaning' is being more consciously used it is always tone which is dominant. To suggest then that they should be reclaimed because they reflect an undesirable attitude to sex is to be somewhat naïve about their usage; hardly less naïve, however, is the idea that words so highly charged with vulgar connotation can be used in serious conversation, without effectively disrupting it. If the use of these words reveals anything, it is lack of self-control, social insensitivity and verbal bankruptcy, and, if they could be reclaimed, other words would be found to take their place.

Common to all these questions about the adequacy of Lawrence's attitude to sex, to industrialism, to language, is the same fiercely-willed exclusiveness. In the case of sex it is the complexities of human relationship, and particularly the idea of marriage, that is set aside; with industrialism, the whole business of living in a mechanized society—after all Connie's panoramic

The Novel as Prophecy: 'Lady Chatterley's Lover' (1928)

vision of that corrupt society was made possible, partly, by watching it from the windows of a car; with language, it is the whole effect on others that Lawrence ignores, whether that relates to the *dramatis personae* or the reader. It all comes down to the impression that in *Lady Chatterley's Lover* he has lost all interest in the novel as an artistic medium which is essentially public and persuasive. Rejecting personality as the basis of human relations, consequently depriving himself of the novelist's usual resources of conversation and conscious responsibility, Lawrence had only to detach himself from a public theory of 'right and wrong' in favour of 'an instinct for life' to make his novel completely self-communing. At the same time it is entirely prescriptive in aim and method. And so we have a situation where the reader has been bound hand and foot by the writer in order to hear of his own salvation. Even more powerfully than *The End of the Affair* and *Thérèse*, *Lady Chatterley's Lover* suggests that an interest in the personal and moral gradations of human beings may be a minimum requirement for the novelist, and that, without that, attempts to give it a public and religious, or public and prophetic status are bound to fail.

Though I have obviously benefited in a general way from reading the considerable number of critical works on Lawrence that have appeared during the last few years, there has been little written in a detailed way on *Lady Chatterley's Lover*, and the only specific debt I would like to acknowledge is to Eliseo Vivas, *D. H. Lawrence: The Failure and the Triumph of Art*, Evanston, 1960, and to the review of that book by R. B. Heilman, *Sewanee Review*, Winter 1960.

9

The Moral and the Story

[i]

The history of novel criticism reveals, for all its complexity, a basic concern with two things—the moral and the story. The first suggests the novelist's relationship with society, the second his relationship with his art. If we were to seek labels to distinguish conveniently between these two, we could say that the first raises questions of convention, the second of technique. And it is these two terms which I want to use as scaffolding for the discussion that follows.

Discussion of technique has now become developed to the point where it is virtually synonymous with criticism of the novel itself. Here the analytic methods developed by modern critics have felt thoroughly at home. With the large shadow of Henry James's Prefaces in the background we have seen developed in recent years a body of critical work which has considerably sharpened our insight into the way in which a novelist orders and makes effective his narrative material; certain mobilizing centres of interest have become firmly established—unity and coherence, point of view and the time-factor—and undoubtedly they have deepened our understanding of fiction and increased our ability to talk about novels. In these circumstances it is not surprising to find that large claims have been made for technique. Thus we find Mark Schorer, in a famous essay,[1] writing, 'tech-

[1] 'Technique as Discovery', *Forms of Modern Fiction*, ed. W. V. O'Connor.

The Moral and the Story

nique is achieved content—*the only means* a writer has of discovering, exploring, developing his subject, of conveying its meaning and finally of evaluating it' (my italics). We see there how a valuable way of discussing fiction has come to be considered the only way; 'technique' has become a critical term for the novel in which all others have been subsumed.

The consequences of this position, which is central to post-Jamesian criticism of the novel, are far-reaching. It helps to account, for instance, for the curious fact that whereas we speak of 'change' in poetry and drama, in the novel we speak of 'development'. Technique brings with it, inevitably, the idea of progress. While we are willing to concede set-back and failure, we feel at heart confident that the 'twentieth-century novel' is a better kind of novel than the 'nineteenth', and if we look back at the 'eighteenth' we feel for the most part that we are in the presence of primitives. There may be a sense in which this perspective is valid, but what I am concerned with here is not to judge its validity, but to indicate its oddity. Whatever we feel about Restoration tragedy or eighteenth-century pastoral poetry, we do not feel we are saying anything very useful if we think in terms of their being more primitive than modern drama or modern poetry. The history of poetry and drama is, of course, completely different from that of the novel, but, when that has been taken into account, one of the shaping factors in our habitual thinking about the 'development' of the novel is the way in which the concept of technique has dominated criticism. Why technique should have assumed this position belongs itself to the history of the novel, and if we ask why this should be so, then I think we open up a way of looking at the novel which is rather different in emphasis from that suggested by Mr. Schorer.

It is a way which takes us to the second thing which I noted as preoccupying critics of the novel, the function of the moral element in fiction. With one or two notable exceptions the discussion of this question has not been illuminating. Too often it has been thought of in crude didactic terms, and the argument has been conducted to the persistent grinding of axes. What has been lacking is an interest in the moral element in fiction

The Moral and the Story

which will help to show how a novelist's moral sense of his subject, together with how he thinks that sense will be understood by the public, determines the way in which he employs 'technique'. To describe this sense, let us use the term 'convention'.

To secure the meaning of this word more firmly in the context in which I am going to use it, I want to take a number of passages and consider them simply from the point of view of their relationship with 'convention' and with 'technique'. The first is from *Adam Bede*:

> It would be a poor result of all our anguish and our wrestling, if we won nothing but our own selves at the end of it—if we could return to the same blind loves, the same self-confident blame, the same light thoughts of human suffering, the same frivolous gossip over blighted human lives, the same feeble sense of that Unknown towards which we have sent forth irrepressible cries in our loneliness.

The second is from *Tess of the D'Urbervilles*:

> 'Did you say the stars were worlds, Tess?'
> 'Yes.'
> 'All like ours?'
> 'I don't know; but I think so. They sometimes seem to be like the apples on our stubbard tree. Most of them splendid and sound—a few blighted.'
> 'Which do we live on—a splendid one or a blighted one?'
> 'A blighted one.'

The third is from *Madame Bovary*:

> 'I don't hold it against you,' said the doctor.
> Rodolphe remained silent, and the other, his head in his hands, went on in the same dead voice and the resigned accents of an infinite sorrow, 'No, I don't hold it against you—not any longer.'
> He even added the first great thought that he had ever voiced: 'It was the fault of Destiny.'
> Rodolphe who, after all, had been the instrument of the said Destiny, felt that such an attitude, in a man so placed, was good-natured to excess and, on the whole, rather despicable.

The fourth is from *Lady Chatterley's Lover*:

> 'There's a bad time coming. . . . You can't insure against the future, except by really believing in the best bit of you and in the

power beyond it. So I believe in the little flame between us. For me now it's the only thing in the world. I've got no friends, not inward friends. Only you. . . . It's my Pentecost, the forked flame between me and you. The old Pentecost isn't quite right. Me and God is a bit uppish somehow. But the little forked flame between me and you. . . . That's what I abide by and will abide by. . . .'

All these passages are, in their way, representative of the general tone of the novels from which they are taken. And all of them catch, with great clarity, the attitude of the particular novelist towards his readers. In George Eliot's case the situation itself seems to have determined how she will speak. There is no sense here of having to argue a position, but rather of reminding people of what they already know but are in danger of forgetting. The repeated plural possessive pronouns suggest the confidence with which the novelist is relying on a sense of shared values. The situation is analogous to that of a professor giving a lecture, and commanding attention not so much because of what he actually says, but because of the position he holds. Clearly this kind of relationship determines *how* you will speak. Convention determines technique; *Adam Bede* is shaped in the way it is largely because of George Eliot's relationship with her readers. That this relationship is by no means always a stimulus to the novelist is suggested by the Hardy passage. Here is someone for whom the situation is still determining how he will speak, but whereas George Eliot was able to accept it and refine it, Hardy can only become irritated by it. And he can deal with the irritation only in terms of philosophical protest, not in revising his whole way of speaking. But often this very dislocation drives Hardy to an imaginative intensity which compels attention.

With Flaubert we feel the situation to be totally different. Reading the passage we are not aware of anyone being addressed at all, a certain scene is just 'taking place'. This is no longer the novelist as teacher, but the novelist as impresario. Inevitably, our attitude towards him changes also. If there is no teacher, there is no one to be taught either. We are no longer interested in what is said, but in what is done; performance is all. Consequently, our attention is turned away from convention towards technique;

The Moral and the Story

as one diminishes in significance, the other increases. Flaubert's relationship with the reader is established not through a community of moral feeling, but through the spell his art can weave. And consequently it is now that people begin to talk about 'the art of the novel', though what they mean is the art of the spellbinder.

In Lawrence we have work which, of set purpose, is anti-art. As in George Eliot and Hardy, we have very much present the voice of the author, and consequently it would look as if once more convention is to be played up and technique played down. But in fact something rather more complicated happens. And it happens because of the changed moral and cultural conditions that separate our age from the Victorian. This is caught immediately in the assertions they make. In George Eliot we have the broad, inclusive self-accusations, 'if *we* could return to the same blind loves, the same self-confident blame . . . the same feeble sense of that Unknown'; in Lawrence, we have personal assertion, '*I* believe in the little flame. . . . It's *my* Pentecost . . . that's what *I* abide by.' The difference between these two is not one of egoism, it is the difference between moral concurrence and religious assertion. The modern novelist has to create the means by which he will speak, he has no moral situation which will determine it for him. And part of the means by which he does this is to compound his art out of his own personality and convictions, in a way that a nineteenth-century novelist was spared. Of course, all novelists have personalities and their work is the expression of them, but the older novelists were not required to use them in the way that the modern novelist is. His way is that of an actor who is required to use his personality in the building-up of a part. Because the modern novelist has to create the means by which he will speak, critical attention is more profitably drawn to 'technique'—which only exists as a personal accomplishment—than to convention. Lawrence has first to create for us 'the little forked flame' before it possesses the value his novel demands. For the Victorian novelist technique is created out of convention, for the modern novelist, convention out of technique. For the former the problem was to keep an audience, for the latter it is to find one. But this is a generalized sketch which can perhaps be given more substance and shading in the discussion that follows.

[ii]

The danger to a novelist writing in a society with which he holds a great sense of common feeling is that perception will become muffled by platitude and intention will short-circuit creation. And so we find in the pages of mid-Victorian journalism a steady and persistent attack on didacticism and a consequent anxiety to make clear the rights of the artist. This has nothing to do with promulgating 'Art for Art's sake'; rather the reverse. It springs from an increasing awareness that the moral drive of the novel is effective only if the autonomy of the genre is respected, and if it is not confused with a sermon in disguise. The novelists and their critics are not denigrating morality, they are asking for better conditions in which to promote it. Inevitably, however, this brings with it a much more serious and complex view of the novel than, generally speaking, had tended to prevail throughout the eighteenth and early nineteenth centuries, when, not unfairly, the nature of the novel could be described in Richardson's words: 'Instruction, Madam, is the pill; amusement is the gilding.'

Probably the most important single influence on the changing attitudes towards the novel in the mid-nineteenth century was George Eliot, both by precept and practice. From 1852-57 she was the leading novel critic for the influential *Westminster Review* and during that time she was able to build up something like an aesthetic of the novel. She never lost the opportunity of attacking the didactic novel. Reviewing Kingsley's *Westward Ho!*, for instance, she remarks: 'No doubt the villain is to be hated and the hero loved, but we ought to see that sufficiently in the figures of them. We don't want a man with a wand going about a gallery and haranguing us. Art is art and tells its own story.' And when she herself turned to the writing of novels, and in 1859 published *Adam Bede*, her practice was seen by the majority

The Moral and the Story

of critics as matching her precept and giving new stature to the novel. We find a critic in the *North British Review* writing: 'When she has finished her work, she leaves it to tell its own story, pronouncing no verdict, passing no sentence, neither acquitting, nor condemning.' The critic, of course, feels free to talk in these apparently Flaubertian terms because of his confidence that George Eliot has established such moral support from the reader in her fiction that a moralizing gloss is superfluous. The note of mutual moral respect between reader and writer is sounded in Walter Bagehot's review of *Adam Bede* where he remarks: 'It was a quaint idea of the last generation to suppose that the moral tendency of a tale lay, not in discriminating good and evil, but in the zeal which induced the novelist to provide, before the end of the third volume, for plucking up and burning the tares.' These views were not, of course, all-pervasive and there could be found plenty of mid-Victorian critics who shared Mr. Podsnap's criterion of artistic excellence, that it should not bring a blush into the cheek of the young person, and who would have been pleased to endorse Trollope's boast that 'no girl has risen from my pages less modest than she was before'. But, broadly speaking, both Victorian novelist and critic were confident enough in their shared assumptions to resent the self-consciousness about them which didacticism brought with it. The good teacher, they felt, has no need to talk about the value of education.

Henry James, however, writing twenty years later, though having no doubt about the moral nature of the novel, was beginning to be worried about the intrusive presence of the teacher—that authoritative voice, that gesturing hand. Reviewing *Middlemarch* in 1873 he wrote: 'It sets a limit we think to the development of the old-fashioned English novel.... If we write novels so, how shall we write History?' It is a remark which casts light on the fiction both of George Eliot and of James himself. Presumably, what James intends by 'History' is the public character of *Middlemarch*, the element which George Eliot recognizes in her sub-title—'A Study of Provincial Life'. In objecting to the panoramic, typical, parts of *Middlemarch*, James

The Moral and the Story

is objecting to her discursive writing, to the writing where she reveals most obviously her open relationship with the reader. The two factors should be taken together. And James is in no doubt that this is a weakness. 'The great minds', he writes, 'have the defects of their qualities and as George Eliot's mind is pre-eminently contemplative and analytic, nothing is more natural than that her manner should be discursive and expansive.' In other words, James feels that George Eliot is too present in her fiction, and, by implication, the reader is also. Now it is just here that we catch one of those vital shifts in relation between author and reader, between the 'fictional world' and the 'real world', determined by personal temperament and the climate of opinion, that in fact alter the way in which fiction is written. Perhaps we can illustrate this by taking a passage from *Adam Bede* and setting beside it one from *The Awkward Age*.

In both passages the novelist is concerned to describe embarrassment. They both deal with a situation in which a young man visiting an intimate friend is forced by a sense of embarrassment to act a part he hardly intends. In *Adam Bede* we find Arthur Donnithorne visiting the Rector, hoping to pluck up enough courage to be able to discuss his feelings for Hetty:

> 'Hallo, Arthur, that's a good fellow! You're just in time,' said Mr. Irwine as Arthur paused and stepped in over the low window-sill. . . . Arthur was anxious not to imply that he came with any special purpose. He had no sooner found himself in Mr. Irwine's presence than the confidence, which he had thought quite easy before, suddenly appeared the most difficult thing in the world to him. . . . Irwine really suspected that Arthur wanted to tell him something and thought of smoothing the way for him. . . . But he was mistaken. Arthur was conscious of colouring and was annoyed at his boyishness. . . . Was there a motive at work under this strange reluctance of Arthur's which had a sort of backstairs influence, not admitted to himself? Our mental business is carried on in much the same way as the business of the State: a great deal of hard work is done by agents who are not acknowledged.

It is precisely these 'agents who are not acknowledged' that James is anxious to convey to the reader, not by referring to them, but by creating them; the reader must experience them for

The Moral and the Story

himself. Everything, as on a stage, must be performed. Vanderbank arrives for the last time to visit Nanda, a visit in which he must make it clear to her that he has now no intention of marrying her, and in which at the same time he is to reveal unconsciously to her the depth of his egoism:

> Vanderbank had not been in the room ten seconds before he showed that he had arrived to be kind. . . . The first thing the young man said was that he was tremendously glad she had written. 'I think it was most particularly nice of you. . . . The only thing that upset me a little . . . was your saying that, before writing it, you had so hesitated and waited. I hope very much you know, that you'll never do anything of that kind again. If you've ever the slightest desire to see me—for no matter what reason, if there's ever the smallest thing of any sort that I can do for you, I promise you I shan't easily forgive you if you stand on ceremony. It seems to me that when people have known each other as long as you and I, there's one comfort at least they may treat themselves. I mean, of course . . . that of being easy, and frank, and natural.'

Both situations centre on embarrassment and the emotion is a useful one for comparing the passages. By definition it implies a tension, a clash between appearance and reality, and in the two passages the clash takes opposite forms. In George Eliot it runs to nervous silence, in James to loquaciousness. But it is not this which marks the difference between the passages, it is the attitude of their respective authors, an attitude which cannot be adequately discussed at all in terms of technique. If it could be, then the difference is between the more and the less convincing, James making us feel what George Eliot can only tell us about. But this would be to miss the point of the *Adam Bede* passage, and to fail to see that its aim is totally different from that of the piece from *The Awkward Age*.

The movement of the first passage is calculatedly away from Arthur Donnithorne towards a consideration of 'embarrassment'. What we are being invited to consider is man in certain circumstances, rather than this particular man in these particular circumstances. But, equally clearly, George Eliot is not trying to promote a psychological or philosophical meditation as such, and consequently she stops her general reflections short, where an essayist might have gone on to develop them, so that we can note the wider context without becoming argumentatively involved with it. If the generalizations were more precisely formulated and developed, then the novel would harden into the tract. George Eliot's control was by no means always perfect and there are numerous occasions where her intrusive comment gets between us and the incident she describes. This is either because she is trying to reset our instinctive response to the incident or character (' "This Rector of Broxton is little better than a pagan!" I hear one of my readers exclaim,' but of course, she *doesn't*, as the reader has hardly been introduced to the Rector of Broxton), or because she overdevelops her reflections until the motivating incident has dwindled into an illustrative detail. But whenever her failures come they are due to her temporarily losing control of the convention, not because the convention itself is inadequate. The reader is distracted in the same way as he would be by a man banging the table for attention when he already commands it; it is precisely because he wants to hear what is being said that the gesture becomes irritating.

When we turn to the James passage we see it is organized in the opposite way. Here the whole drift is towards the particular, the immediate, the individual. What James is concerned to do is not to make us contemplate an aspect of human feeling but to make us participate in the creation of an individual consciousness, so that at the end of the novel we have come to understand more perceptively not a certain kind of man, but this man—Vanderbank. Consequently, it is because we have come to 'know' him that we can see through this display of solicitude and judge it for the empty thing it is. One of the features of James's intense dramatization is that he will present the same kind of conversation again and again, so that as we grow into the novel —and this is the kind of response the novel demands—we become increasingly aware of its real meaning. A remark on page one may suggest nobility and wit; the same remark made two hundred pages later might well be the final indictment of a character's scurrility. This way of getting to 'know' a person is clearly an idealized analogue of the way in which we know people in real life. When Vanderbank talks to Nanda of 'having

The Moral and the Story

known each other as long as you and I', the irony drives firmly home our response to his duplicity and self-deception; it cuts out, as surely as George Eliot engages, any general reflection on 'the falsities of friendship'. James, no less than George Eliot, has his problems of balance and direction, and if her false notes lead towards the sermon, his lead towards the psycho-analyst's casebook. The individual becomes of interest only because it is the individual case.

In these passages the author's attitudes differ sharply, regardless of the similarity of subject. George Eliot, confident of her shared feeling with her public, can afford to allow that public to complete the moral meaning of her work. It is the confident discourse of a speaker addressing a familiar audience. Like such a discourse, her novels are shaped for this impressionable context. It would be false to say that they cannot be understood apart from it, but they will certainly be understood inadequately. In other words, the convention of these novels, their public relationship, is an inescapable part of their meaning and value. With James, the case is quite different. Increasingly uncertain about who his public are, he devotes his genius to making the novel entirely complete within itself, dramatizing with unremitting concentration all the work that George Eliot counted on being done by her public relationship, her literary ambience. Everything now is brought within the novel and *done*. 'Form alone takes and holds and preserves, substance . . . there is nothing so deplorable as a work of art with a leak. . . .' We might say that for James the successful novel was that which could speak most clearly its own meaning, and was most free from the author's support and the reader's interpretation. Form and substance have become coterminous and irreducible; the meaning of the novel is the novel itself. Given this attitude to fiction, it is not difficult to see why it is James who has dominated all our thinking about The Art of the Novel, and why when we translate that thinking into critical discussion we must be dominated by the notion of technique. While we may appreciate the fact that the James novel is only one kind of novel, we have yet to appreciate that James's criticism is only one kind of criticism.

The Moral and the Story

What happens when a criticism based on Technique as the criterion of excellence is brought to bear on fiction based on Convention, is well, if crudely, illustrated by an essay on *Middlemarch* by F. G. Steiner.[1] Comparing the novel with *Madame Bovary* Steiner notes 'the total lack of technique on George Eliot's part. . . . By interfering constantly in the narration George Eliot attempts to persuade us of what should be artistically evident. . . . At other times she adds to her omniscience deliberate comments and summaries of events. It should be noted that omniscience is an author's most lazy approach and that personal interference in the action must be compared to what occurs in a Chinese theatre when a manager comes on during the play to change props.' This is what happens when Jamesian perception hardens into dogma about the nature of fiction. We notice first of all, characteristically, the great critical play that is made with the word 'technique', so that it becomes a dominant criterion, covering not only the internal management of the novel but the author's relationship with the reader too. That the author's explicit relationship with her fiction should be an intrinsic part of this kind of novel is totally missed because of the underlying assumptions that are being made, assumptions that can only see such a relationship as an 'interference'. Ironically, the illustration is self-refuting. The manager of the Chinese theatre is a good example of someone who is actually part of the drama in a way not unlike that of the Victorian novelist. I quote this example because it reveals in a particularly blatant manner the distortions of a criticism of fiction based on the primacy of technique. It was a preoccupation which arose very much out of James's own artistic needs, and, however momentous it has been for the subsequent history of fiction, it ought to be seen within this perspective and not treated as part of the Natural Law. The weight of pressure that drove James, however obscurely, to create this insulated kind of novel can be gauged if we turn to a Victorian novelist who felt the problem of a changing relationship with the reader without, like James, having the particular ability to accommodate it.

[1] *Nineteenth Century Fiction*, IX (1955), pp. 270–5.

The Moral and the Story

There was mutual literary antipathy between Hardy and James, and in describing it, as we have said earlier, we are describing the differences between the Victorian and the modern novel. For James, Hardy was 'a manufacturer of gauche and heavy fictions'; for Hardy, James's subjects were those 'one could be interested in at moments when there was nothing larger to think of'. It is not difficult to see behind these criticisms the preconceptions of 'technique' and 'convention'. For James, with his view of the novel as a self-contained entity, with his contention that a subject is made important or trivial by the attitude of the writer, Hardy's fiction was crude. Too much was left, in Jamesian vocabulary, unrealized. For Hardy, with his view that the importance of a subject lay within the subject and not within the treatment, James was trivial. Too much was being done about too little. What Hardy failed to see was that James was using 'technique' not only to communicate his subject but, more desperately, to make it 'there' at all; whereas for Hardy, because he still felt the sense of a public, his subject was already *there* awaiting treatment. We find Hardy writing, for instance, in an essay on the novel: 'Good fiction may be defined as that kind of imaginative writing which lies nearest to the epic, dramatic or narrative masterpieces of the past. One fact is certain: in fiction there can be no intrinsically new thing at this stage of the world's history. New methods and new plans may arise . . . but the general theme can neither be changed, nor can the relative importance of its various particulars be greatly interfered with.'

When we say that Hardy 'felt the sense of a public' we mean that in comparison with James he did; if the comparison is made with George Eliot then we see that Hardy's sense was one of loss. And it is out of this loss that Hardy's strength and weaknesses proceed. Society was clearly there as a supporting influence for George Eliot, even when she was most critical of it, in a way that it was not for Hardy, and yet his whole mode of novel writing assumed that it was. For instance, the fact that he is able to sub-title *Tess of the D'Urbervilles* 'A Pure Woman', suggests his closeness to the moral world of Dickens and George

The Moral and the Story

Eliot, even though that title is one of defiance and challenge. In prose-fiction his sensibility belonged to a later age than his expression; only in poetry did he really succeed in reconciling them. Consequently we find in his fiction constant evidence of stress and strain; on the one hand, 'fine writing' seen in terms of grandiloquent latinisms and classical allusions, and on the other, 'serious content' seen in terms of metaphysical rumination. Both of these weaknesses seem to emerge from a common anxiety, to find a form adequate to the expression, with Hardy constantly feeling that his form was trivializing what he had to say. Hence the fine writing and the high thinking. But if Hardy never really felt at home in fiction in the way that George Eliot did, because he could no longer feel her public sympathy, or the way that Henry James did, because such preoccupation with technique was alien to him, it is out of this very unease that his striking achievement in fiction arises. And that is the very fullness with which we feel Hardy's own voice and personality. The profound personal involvement of the author is something that we feel stamped on every page of Hardy, we feel the life of the man animating directly the life of the fiction. This is not simply a question of feeling deeply, of being sincere, it is having fiction capable of conveying that feeling, that sincerity. It is significant that Lawrence was such an admirer of Hardy, because he shares with him this same profound involvement. And it is this discovery of a fiction capable of conveying the author's voice and personality, so that we feel it no longer as a guide but as someone actually undergoing the experience with us, that is Hardy's peculiar, and, one might say, fortuitous contribution to a development in the later twentieth-century novel. By a new route we have come back to the presence of the author within the novel, no longer speaking in the tone of the teacher but in the tone of the exile. In other words, we have a yearning for a social relationship which the situation itself seems to preclude.

The modern situation has been shaped largely by reaction to the 'pure novel', the novel which marks the apotheosis of technique. And here the exemplar was not James but Flaubert, and to a lesser extent Zola. To catch the early excitement provoked

The Moral and the Story

by this influence in England, we can turn to an entry made by Arnold Bennett in his Journal in 1898: 'I have been thinking about a history of the English novel in the nineteenth century.... As regards fiction it seems to me that only within the last few years have we absorbed from France that passion for the shapely presentation of truth, that feeling for words as words ... which is so exactly described and defined in Maupassant's introduction to the collected works of Flaubert.' 'Only within the last few years'—Bennett's historical sense is sound, because, if we are inclined to question the 'development' Bennett assumes, there can be no question at all that welcome of the French novel in England was, to put it mildly, hesitant. The history of that welcome, during the closing decades of the nineteenth century, is of a head-on clash between novelists dedicated to the story and a public dedicated to the moral; it was the clash between 'technique' in its most absolute form and 'convention' in its crudest.

The reputations of Flaubert and Zola in England ran a parallel course and might well be considered together. The only difference was that opposition to Zola was much more intense and widespread. Though the bulk of Zola's work was written after Flaubert's was completed they both arrived, so to speak, in England in the 1880's. The first translation of Zola appeared in 1884 and *Madame Bovary*, the first of Flaubert's books to be translated, appeared in 1886. Before this time critical attention had been virtually non-existent, but after it the work of both novelists became a battlefield for the crudest kind of literary warfare. Broadly speaking, the opposition to Flaubert came because he was morally indifferent, the opposition to Zola because he was morally subversive. Tennyson's heavily ironical lines in *Locksley Hall Sixty Years After* reflect the popular feeling:

> Rip your brother's vices open, strip your own foul passions bare;
> Down with Reticence, down with Reverence—forward—naked—
>   let them stare....
> Have we risen from out the beast, then back into the beast again?

If popular opposition was directed towards the subject matter, intellectual opposition was directed towards the philosophical assumptions that lay behind it. Writing for American readers in the 1870's James had written of Flaubert: 'M. Flaubert's theory as a novelist, briefly expressed, is to begin on the outside. Human life, we may imagine him saying, is before all things a spectacle, an occupation and an entertainment for the eyes. What our eyes show us is all that we can be sure of. . . . We only care for what *is*—we know nothing of what ought to be.' This kind of criticism can be found over and over again. In an article on 'The New Naturalism' in the *Fortnightly* in 1885, a writer remarks sardonically: 'M. Zola has supplied the most pregnant illustration known to me in literature that the visible when it rests not upon the spiritual becomes the bestial.' The didactic drive behind these criticisms is obvious enough; both the popular press and the serious critics were united in feeling a moral indifference or contempt in the work of Zola and Flaubert, and the majority would have agreed with Fitzjames Stephen when he observed, in his review of the original publication of *Madame Bovary*, that the basic immorality of the novel lay not in the depiction of incident but 'in the want it presumes in its readers of any moral distinctions at all'. In that confident reference to 'readers' we have the voice of the public for which George Eliot wrote her novels. By the end of the century it was no longer there, as Hardy and James found out in their different ways. The great tide from France had now come in to help to change the appearance both of English prose and poetry. George Moore could claim that parts of *Esther Waters* were 'pure Flaubert' and of *L'Assommoir* that its greatness comes from 'the immense harmonic development of the idea and the fugal treatment of the different scenes . . . and the lordly, river-like roll of the narrative'. The new aestheticism established the autonomy of technique, the moral was routed, and Arnold Bennett recorded his enthusiasm in an entry in his journal.

'Tell Arnold Bennett,' Lawrence writes in 1915, 'that all rules of construction hold good only for novels which are copies of other novels. A book is not a copy of other books, but it has its own construction, and what he calls faults, he being an old imitator, I call characteristics. I shall repeat till I am grey—

The Moral and the Story

when they have as good work to show, they may make their pronouncements *ex cathedra*. Till then, let them learn decent respect.' Lawrence's contention that his work marked a new direction in the novel was amply justified, and from his reaction to his contemporary writers we can see in what his originality consisted. As he looked at their work he saw it falling into two groups, both of which he disliked intensely. There were Wells and Bennett and Galsworthy representing in their social concern the final exhausted phase of the great Victorian tradition. Reviewing Wells's *The World of William Clissold* Lawrence sees it as 'chewed-up newspaper and chewed-up scientific reports' and his criticism of *The Forsyte Saga* is as devastating as it is inimitable. Finding the characters lacking common humanity, he asks: 'Why do we feel so instinctively that they are inferiors? It is because they seem to us to have lost caste as human beings and to have sunk to the level of the social being. . . . A man may give away all he has to the poor and still reveal himself as a social being, swayed finally and helplessly by the money-sway, and by the social moral, which is inhuman.' From this it might seem reasonable to infer that Lawrence's attack on Wells, Bennett and Galsworthy was essentially like that of Virginia Woolf, when she contended that reality was equated with the observable and that a study of society had become a sociological report. The formula of these novelists, according to Virginia Woolf, was simple: 'Begin by saying that her father kept a shop in Harrogate. Ascertain the rent. Ascertain the wages of shop assistants in 1878. Discover what her mother died of. Describe cancer. Describe calico. Describe. . . .' But while Lawrence's criticism certainly involves this, it by no means stops there. This is suggested by the fact that Lawrence is equally hostile to the novels which described 'the inner flame'—the novels of Proust, Virginia Woolf, and Joyce. If the novels of Wells, Bennett and Galsworthy are framed entirely by society, the novels of the second group are framed entirely by self-consciousness. 'Through thousands and thousands of pages Mr. Joyce and Miss Richardson tear themselves to pieces, strip their smallest emotions to the finest threads, till you feel you are sewed-up inside a wool mattress that is being slowly shaken up and you are turning to wool along with the rest of the wooliness.' This is where the development of technique had led to, a fine ability to treat more and more of less and less.

For Lawrence, if the novel is to have a future it will need to cut below the social categories of the first group of novelists, and the trivializing cult of self-consciousness of the second. As Lawrence surveys the novel of his time he seems to stand at the confluence of two streams which have gradually dwindled into a trickle. One descends from Dickens and George Eliot and Hardy, and the other from Flaubert, and, more circuitously, from James. The current of one carries down the faded remnants of a socially-orientated novel now hardening into a social tract; the current of the other, the faded remnants of a novel of highly personal art now disintegrating into a frivolous aestheticism. What Lawrence saw with increasing clarity was that the only way in which these currents might be revivified was to merge them, and to try and write a novel in which philosophy and fiction should come together: 'They used to be one, right from the days of myth. Then they went and parted, like a nagging married couple. . . . So the novel went sloppy, and philosophy went abstract-dry.' When James criticized *Middlemarch*—'if we write novels so, how shall we write History?'—he was wishing to excise for his purpose the very element which Lawrence, for his, was anxious to restore. In the terminology of this chapter we could say we have moved over the last century from a time when technique served convention, through to a time when technique created convention, and finally to a time when technique needed the support of convention if the public status of the novel was to be preserved.

To put it in this way might suggest that, from the point of view this chapter describes, the wheel has come full circle and Lawrence's conception of the novel is a return to George Eliot's. This would be wrong. While it is true to say that Lawrence sought in the novel for a public relationship, the relationship he sought was not, like George Eliot's, based on social and moral agreement, but on faith. And it is this which differen-

The Moral and the Story

tiates their respective conventions; the one is created by a person who knows her community and is accepted by them, the other by a person who longs for a community but cannot find it. His life becomes a pilgrimage, and at the last he finds himself appealing not to a community but to believers. The fictional drive now becomes essentially a religious one, and a new kind of response from the reader is required by this new kind of English novel. The novel has now become, as Lawrence says, 'the book of life'. Previously we have had the novelist as teacher where the story pointed the moral, then the novelist as disappearing artist where the story *was* the moral, and now we have the novelist with whom prophecy transcends both the story and the moral. What happens when the novel becomes 'the book of life' is suggested by a number of reflections which arise out of reading two novels which at first sight appear to contradict every position held by the other—Lawrence's *Lady Chatterley's Lover* and Greene's *The End of the Affair*.

One of the first things we notice when we look at the work of Lawrence and Greene is the peculiarly sharp sense with which 'life' is conveyed—'life' as something distinct from the actual circumstances of living. And the fact that what they have to tell us about life is radically different does not modify this impression. In both cases the essential nature of life is revealed most fully in the sexual act, it is here that man escapes the confines of his personality. In sex, Lawrence writes, 'man comes to the limits of himself and becomes aware of something beyond him . . . aware of that which surpasses him.' Bendrix, in *The End of the Affair*, reflects, 'we might use the terms of prayer, meditation, contemplation to explain the intensity of the love we feel for a woman. . . . The act of love itself has been described as the little death. . . .' These are the moments when, for both writers, the veil lifts and we see into the heart of things. What we see with Lawrence is the glory, with Greene, the horror. To experience these moments of insight is the beginning of human wisdom, though one affords us a glimpse of a world of infinite possibility, and the other a world irretrievably fallen.

If we look with our ordinary sight we can find only a world

of 'death'. In Lawrence, this death is most fully embodied in the modern industrial world of material acquisition and ugliness; in Greene, in the false happiness which is possible in 'the sinless, graceless, empty chromium world'.

For both writers the kingdom of life and the kingdom of death are savagely juxtaposed in their fictional worlds. No-man's-land does not exist. Lawrence travels restlessly from country to country hoping to find a solution, but the only victories he has are local and fade into disillusion. Greene travels too, to remind himself continually that the world is a battlefield, and that to dream of peace is a victory for the enemy. These travels are really pilgrimages and their object to discover God. Eliot once wrote of Lawrence, in words that could be applied equally to Greene: 'He wanted a religion which would be real, not a world of church congresses and religious newspapers, not even a world in which religion could be *believed*, but a world in which religion would be something deeper than belief, in which life would be a kind of religious behaviourism....' It is the endless search for this that drives both writers in their various ways towards the exotic and the strange. 'I had no permanent feeling of religion,' Lawrence writes, 'until I came to New Mexico and penetrated into the old human-race experience there.... The Red Indian ... is religious in perhaps the oldest sense and deepest of the word.' In *The Power and the Glory* we find this: 'At sunset on the second day they came out on to a wide plateau covered with short grass: an odd grove of crosses stood up blackly against the sky.... No priest could have been concerned in the strange rough group; it was the work of the Indians.... It was like a short cut to the dark and magical heart of the faith —to the night when the graves opened and the dead walked.' When they come to translate this outlook into the language of fiction, both Lawrence and Greene seem to be exploring not so much the relationship between man and man as the relationship between man and God. And this has direct consequences both for their attitude to the behaviour of their characters, and for the response they demand of their readers.

In his essay on Hardy Lawrence is critical of the tragedy that

The Moral and the Story

befalls his characters: 'Necessarily painful it was, but they were not at war with God, only with Society. Yet they were all cowed by the mere judgment of man upon them, and all the while by their own souls they were right.' The remark is more illuminating for Lawrence's fiction than for Hardy's. Here we have a fiction which deals with a conflict between men only in the sense that a character is at war with God. The bar of judgment now becomes 'the soul of man', not the judgment of other men. Whatever consequences this may have in life, in fiction, which is a public communication about man in society, it means the excision of what we would generally understand as moral criteria as a means of evaluating behaviour. In Lawrence this is replaced and undercut by his concept of the 'life-mode' and the 'death-mode'; in Greene, by grace and sin. In both cases, the motive is to establish a more comprehensive set of criteria, a finer judgment.

The consequences of this for the writing of fiction are striking. Where 'the mere judgment of man' was at issue, there was the intrinsic element of the provisional, however profound the analysis. But now that man is to be revealed not in his relationship with society but in his relationship with God, he must be known not as we know other people, by observation and inference, but *as he really is*. Flaubert's dictum, 'The artist must be in his work as God is in his creation', becomes now not an artistic prescription, but a desperate literalism. Because characters are known 'as they really are' there can, in the fictional world of Lawrence and Greene, never be, without a contradiction of terms, an exchange or modification of attitude. These characters are not seen so much as seen through. Lawrence looking at Mellors and Clifford remarks: 'The two males were as hostile as fire and water. They mutually exterminated one another.' Opposition of this kind can only exist below the level of personality; our usual moral categories cannot deal with it. It is one further stage to argue from the inadequacy of these categories to the positive deception of the social and observable. Thus what we call love may only be egotistic indulgence, we might be more honest in hate. Bendrix, we remember, was 'a good hater' and Connie 'for the first time . . . had consciously and definitely hated Clifford . . . it was strange how free and full of life it made her feel.' The difficulty about this writing and the whole attitude behind it is that the reader can have no key to it other than that provided by the author's creation. And in their various ways Lawrence and Greene seem to say that there can be no key, that the ordering of life depends ultimately not on a consensus of public moral agreement but on faith; and it is this kind of response that their fiction seeks to elicit. And indeed we find people reacting to Lawrence and Greene with an intensity of admiration or disgust which suggests very much that their work does present this fundamental challenge to a personal conception of life. They have, however circuitously, achieved a public relationship which the novelists of 'technique' set aside. Looking at the change he tried to accomplish in the novel Lawrence wrote: 'The public will scream and say it is a sacrilege: because, of course, when you've been jammed for a long time in a tight corner, and you get really used to its stuffiness and tightness, till you find it sufficiently cosy; then, of course, you're horrified when you see a new glaring hole in what was your cosy wall.' This seems a salutary place to bring this chapter to a conclusion, as it suitably intimidates us from indulging in the seductive pleasures of literary legislation.

In the course of this chapter, by way of a terminology of technique and convention, I have attempted to describe a number of situations in the history of the novel during the last century in which the moral and the story have been set in very different relationships, and to indicate reasons why this should be so. At this point it is essential to resist the temptation to go 'to a more removed ground' and theorize there about the novelist and society; essential, because a chapter which has been concerned to bring together a number of novelists in order to look at their inter-relationships, and to draw attention to the importance of 'convention' for novel criticism, may suddenly find itself becoming an elegy on the decline and death of the unified reading public. And this myth of decline is a highly misleading

The Moral and the Story

one. If we wish to say that George Eliot owes her distinction largely to the sense of community she felt with her society, then we must also say that Lawrence owes his to the reverse. Homogeneity between author and public is as likely to make for inertia and platitude as fragmentation for challenge and self-discovery. Out of all the literary situations described in this chapter novels of interest and varying achievement have emerged, and the primary business of the literary critic must be to try to understand and make clear the specific nature of these novels; he must abstain from drilling them into general formations of his own devising. What conclusions there are about the moral and the story lie in the particular analyses of this or that novel, and the present chapter can only be an attempt to complement these by taking the whole subject and looking at it from a dominantly historical point of view. To think in terms of anything nearer to a summarizing pattern than this would be illusion; and that, perhaps, is the moral that *we* should draw from this particular story.

Index

Arnold, Matthew, 146, 224

Balzac, *César Birotteau*, 67
Bennett, Arnold, 263–5
Blake, 224
Bourget, Paul, 111

Cobbett, William, 127, 224
Crabbe, George, 126

D'Annunzio, 180
Dickens, 113, 224, 261, 266
Dostoevsky, *Crime and Punishment*, 203–4

Eliade, M., 239
Eliot, George, 99, 125–6, 146, 190, 261–2, 266–7, 271
  Adam Bede, 13–32, 120, 123–6, 251–9
  Daniel Deronda, 30
  Felix Holt, 31
  Middlemarch, 13, 30–2, 255, 260, 266
  Scenes from Clerical Life, 14
Eliot, T. S., 219, 238, 268

Flaubert, Gustave, 99, 120, 124, 262–4, 266, 269
  on Zola, 63, 74
  Bouvard et Pécuchet, 59
  Dictionnaire des Idées Reçues, 36
  Éducation Sentimentale, L', 60
  Madame Bovary, 33–62, 63, 66–7, 72, 97, 110–12, 251–3, 263–4

Salammbô, 59
Tentation de Saint Antoine, La, 35, 52
Forster, E. M., 152, 185

Galsworthy, 265
Goncourt, Edmond and Jules, 64, 97, 114
  Germinie Lacerteux, 64, 66, 97
Greene, Graham, 185–91, 267–70
  on James, 154, 184
  on Mauriac, 185
  Brighton Rock, 194, 214
  End of the Affair, The, 191–208, 213–16, 236–8, 248, 267–8
  Heart of the Matter, The, 214
  Lawless Roads, The, 201
  Living Room, The, 189–90
  Man Within, The, 187, 214
  Power and the Glory, The, 190, 194, 204, 214–15

Hammond, J. and B., *Village Labourer, The*, 16
Hardy, Barbara, 28
Hardy, Thomas, 16, 99, 261–2, 266, 268–9
  on James, 151–3, 261
  Candour in English Fiction, 132–3
  Dorsetshire Labourer, The, 128
  Far from the Madding Crowd, 125, 127
  Jude the Obscure, 123, 125
  Mayor of Casterbridge, The, 127

Index

Return of the Native, The, 127
Tess of the D'Urbervilles, 24–5, 104, 123–50, 151, 179–83, 193–4, 251–3, 261–2
Woodlanders, The, 131
Heilman, R., 246, 248 n.

James, Henry, 31, 126, 146, 150, 249, 260
  on George Eliot, 13, 32, 255–6, 266
  on Flaubert, 178, 264
  on Hardy, 123, 179–83, 261
  on Zola, 93–4, 96, 178–9
  Awkward Age, The, 151–84, 256–9
  Portrait of a Lady, The, 180
  Wings of a Dove, The, 180
Johnson, Lionel, 137
Joyce, James, 265

Kettle, A., 136, 139

Lawrence, D. H., 32, 264–71
  on George Eliot, 32
  on Flaubert, 62
  on Hardy, 268–9
  Apocalypse, 238, 241
  A Propos of Lady Chatterley, 241, 244
  Kangaroo, 234, 241
  Lady Chatterley's Lover, 217–48, 251–3, 267–70
  Plumed Serpent, The, 234, 241
  Rainbow, The, 227, 233, 235
  Sons and Lovers, 232–3, 235
  Virgin and the Gypsy, The, 241, 244
  Women in Love, 232–3, 235, 241
Leavis, F. R., 13, 154, 227
Lubbock, Percy, 152–3

Mauriac, François, 185–91
  on Flaubert, 61–2
  on Greene, 190–1
  Dieu et Mammon, 201 n.
  Fin de la Nuit, La, 208

Fleuve de Feu, Le, 215
Pharisienne, La, 186, 202
Thérèse Desqueyroux, 207–16, 236–8, 248
Moore, George, 264
  on George Eliot, 27, 99, 120–1
  on Flaubert, 98
  on Hardy, 99, 120
  on Zola, 98, 112, 264
  Esther Waters, 98–122, 264
  Modern Lover, A, 98
  Mummer's Wife, A, 120
Morris, William, 224
Muir, Edwin, 233
Murry, J. Middleton, 232

Newman, John Henry, 216

Porter, Katherine A., 230–1
Pritchett, V. S., 26, 28–9
Proust, 265

Ruskin, 224

Sartre, Jean-Paul, 195, 208–9, 212–13
Schorer, M., 249–50
Spilka, M., 230–1
Steiner, F. G., 260

Taine, Hippolyte, 64
Tennyson, 263
Turnell, M., 215

Vivas, E., 248 n.

Weber, C., 129
Wells, H. G., 265
Wilde, Oscar, 99, 110–11, 113–18
  Ideal Husband, An, 116
  Lady Windermere's Fan, 116
  Woman of No Importance, A, 116–17
Wilson, Edmund, 152
Winter's Tale, The, 26, 241
Woolf, Virginia, 185, 265

Index

Wordsworth, 15, 126

Zola, Emile, 98, 110–12, 120, 124, 262–4
   the *Rougon-Macquart* series, 63–4, 67
   Assommoir, L', 63–97, 101, 108–9, 110–12, 120, 264
   Bête Humaine, La, 97
   Germinal, 65, 120
   Madeleine Férat, 64
   Nana, 72, 96
   Oeuvre, L', 95
   Thérèse Raquin, 64